(The Underground) Railroad
in African American Literature

AFRICAN AMERICAN LITERATURE AND CULTURE

Expanding and Exploding the Boundaries

Carlyle V. Thompson
General Editor

Vol. 6

PETER LANG
New York • Washington, D.C./Baltimore • Bern
Frankfurt am Main • Berlin • Brussels • Vienna • Oxford

DARCY A. ZABEL

The (Underground) Railroad
in African American Literature

PETER LANG
New York • Washington, D.C./Baltimore • Bern
Frankfurt am Main • Berlin • Brussels • Vienna • Oxford

Library of Congress Cataloging-in-Publication Data
Zabel, Darcy A.
The (Underground) Railroad in African American literature / Darcy A. Zabel.
p. cm. — (African American literature and culture; v. 6)
Includes bibliographical references.
1. American literature—African American authors—History and criticism.
2. American literature—20th century—History and criticism.
3. African Americans—Intellectual life—20th century.
4. Railroad stories—History and criticism. 5. African Americans in literature.
6. Railroad travel in literature. 7. Symbolism in literature.
8. Railroads in literature. 9. Underground railroad. I. Title. II. Series.
PS153.N5Z33   810.9'356—dc22   2003025255
ISBN 0-8204-6816-9
ISSN 1528-3887

Bibliographic information published by **Die Deutsche Bibliothek.**
Die Deutsche Bibliothek lists this publication in the "Deutsche
Nationalbibliografie"; detailed bibliographic data is available
on the Internet at http://dnb.ddb.de/.

Cover design by Lisa Barfield
Cover image, *Black Thunder*, by Robert West, reprinted by permission

The paper in this book meets the guidelines for permanence and durability
of the Committee on Production Guidelines for Book Longevity
of the Council of Library Resources.

© 2004 Peter Lang Publishing, Inc., New York
275 Seventh Avenue, 28th Floor, New York, NY 10001
www.peterlangusa.com

All rights reserved.
Reprint or reproduction, even partially, in all forms such as microfilm,
xerography, microfiche, microcard, and offset strictly prohibited.

Printed in the United States of America

✢ TABLE OF CONTENTS

ACKNOWLEDGMENTS vii

INTRODUCTION 1
The Train as Symbol in African American Literature

CHAPTER ONE 9
The Impact of the Railroad on African American Life

CHAPTER TWO 33
Flying Trains and the "Tubman Tradition"

CHAPTER THREE 75
Black Supermen and the "John Henry Tradition"

CHAPTER FOUR 121
Riders of the Train: Passage, Passing, and the Great Migration

CHAPTER FIVE 155
"Two Trains Running": Making Choices

CHAPTER SIX 181
Around the Corner and Down the Track

NOTES 199

WORKS CITED 217

☦ ACKNOWLEDGMENTS

The cover art for this volume, "Black Thunder," was created by award-winning master artist Robert West, himself the grandson of a Pullman porter, and depicts the merger of two railroads that were never meant to work in tandem. An Atlantic coastline locomotive pulls the Silver Meteor, a railroading "sacrilege" that results in a stunning and vibrant thunderstorm illustrating that "the Gods of railroading are angry."

I would like to thank Dr. John Yoder and the Friends University community for the awarding of the Friends University research grant. I would also like to thank Dr. Carlyle Van Thompson, Dr. Veronica Makowsky, and Dr. Heidi Burns for their comments and suggestions on several drafts of the manuscript.

Additionally, I owe a debt of gratitude to my friends Carolyn Schmidt and Deirdre King Hainsworth for convincing me that the emergency trips to *La Galette* really were a necessary part of the writing process and to Tammy Sharmer for the long-distance pep talks.

Without the love and assistance of Corey Zabel, who, to quote Toni Morrison's Paul D. in *Beloved*, is the "friend of my mind" who "gathers me, the pieces I am ... and gives them back to me in all the right order," this project never would have reached completion.

Finally, this volume is lovingly dedicated to Florence, Alfred, Sharon and Jerry Litzerman; and to Quin McLamore, my son. He is the real writer in the family.

✿ INTRODUCTION

The Train as Symbol in African American Literature

Since the 1964 publication of Leo Marx's now classic *The Machine in the Garden: Technology and the Pastoral Ideal in America*, the train has become a well-known and well-studied cultural and literary symbol for those interested in representations of the paradoxical nature of America's image of itself. Marx's study shows how the incorporation of the train, a symbol of man's power to create power, into an already existing metaphoric paradigm, the image of America as God's new Garden of Eden, gave rise to a conflicted sense of American identity and purpose.[1] In his study, Marx does not consider whether or not the train, that symbol of the "power to create power," is race specific and, in fact, focuses his analysis on "the European mind" (3). Focusing as he does on the white male canonical writers of the American Renaissance, Marx argues that "machine imagery serves to convey both an inward and historical contradiction" (346). Ignoring women writers and writers of color, Marx divides all American writers up into two groups: those for whom the train was a symbol of a "threat to some cherished ideal of high civilization or art or craftsmanship" (347), and those for whom the train is man's contribution to the progress of nature and natural law, with Nature "adopting" the train "into her vital circles, and the gliding train of cars she loves like her own" (241). His argument about the train as symbol is compelling, but does that symbol mean the same thing for all American writers? Alternatively, is there something distinctive about the way in which twentieth-century African American writers use the train as a literary symbol?

Robert Hayden's haunting poem "Runagate Runagate," for example, suggests that the origins of the African American social, political, legal, psychological, and spiritual rebellion can be found in both the stories black men and women tell, and in the bodies and blood of those women, who are, to use Dorothy Sterling's term, the "black foremothers" of "the promise" (xv). Women such as Harriet Tubman, a main character in the poem, are both the mothers and the midwives assisting at the birth of such rebellion, a rebellion against greed and hate masked as a philology-backed philosophy of white supremacy that demonized all those of African descent.

In the poem, Hayden's Harriet Tubman invites her "children" to ride the train, and the train is portrayed as a vehicle that can rise above the confines of human history, a force that takes its own line, and creates its own track as it journeys through the uncharted "swamp and savanna," traveling through Plato's "caves of the wish" on "a sabre track," composed of sword edges. On another level, the poem, as did the song "Git on Board," discussed in depth in chapter two, is also both warning and inviting readers not to get side tracked by fear and instead to board the right train, so to speak, the train toward ultimate freedom, not just for the individual rider, but for one's as yet unborn children.

Hayden's poem insists on both the renegade nature of the runaways, the "runagates," and also on the incredible spiritual transformation that occurred in the runagate's heart once they were no longer content with finding "mercy" and instead, completed the journey to "Hallelujah," whether that meant a life of freedom in Canada or the freedom of death. In addition, the train, the "ghost-story train," represents the tales told to inspire such "runagate" feelings, becomes the word made flesh in the body of Harriet Tubman, who in 1863 alone brought over 750 slaves to freedom.[2] However, Hayden's poem does not fit into Marx's paradigm unless a violence, similar to that visited upon all those who did not fit the innkeeper's bed in the Greek story of Procrustes, is done to the text. When travelers along the road to Athens stopped at his inn, if they were too short for his beds, they were stretched, and if too tall, their legs were cut off at the appropriate length. The travelers all died, of course, and Procrustes, the innkeeper, took their belongings, thus bringing to light a story that emphasizes the painful cost of conformity. Hayden's poem, like the travelers in the tale of Procrustes, can only be made to fit into Marx's paradigm if violence is done to the text.

Other images of the train in African American literature can be made to fit, however, and one certainly sees ways to apply Marx's reading of the train as a literary symbol of man's power to create power and to change the world in the works of twentieth-century African American writers. Take, for example, the 1903 story by W. E. B. Du Bois, "Of the Coming of John." In this story, the older people have been sadly oppressed by the whites in the town and long for an improved quality of life for the next generation. John is to be the leader of that next generation, and it is hoped that he will, like John the Baptist, be the herald of things to come even greater than he himself. There is a promise of change and of progress in the noisy departure of the train as John heads north to college. For the African American community depicted in Du Bois's story, the lonely train whistle and the labored chugging of the engine up and down the tracks symbolized hope, "When John comes" (257). Marx's reading of the symbol would work here.

What complicates matters, though, is that the story does not end here. When John finally comes back, the train no longer symbolizes promise to him. The train station still seems glamorous and the very point of possibility for the black community who come to meet his train. For John, however, the train station now seems "dingy," "gaudy," "dirty," "dilapidated," "sordid," and "narrow" (254–55). The train, once the vehicle that carried John into "a better world," is now a reminder of the limitations a black man faces, and John cannot stop "thinking of the Jim Crow car" so that the old promise of the train, symbolized by the train whistle, for him is now riddled with hypocrisy (254). The lonesome train whistle still has the power to make his heart and soul ache for the promised freedom of the North, but the train itself is not, in this case, a symbol of progress, man-made or otherwise. It is the vehicle that brings him back to the South, and to his eventual destruction.

As the story draws to a close, John kills a white man for insulting his sister, and he realizes he must leave before word of his deed gets out. He tells his mother that "he cannot live here longer" and that he will go North, but instead of hopping a train and heading North, John heads "towards the sea, whence rose the strange melody, away from the dark shadows where lay the noise of horses galloping, galloping on" and with his eyes closed, he softly begins to sing the "Song of the bride—Freudig geführt, ziehet dahin" (262–63).[3] It is possible to read John's march to the sea as a suicide, or as an ill-fated symbolic attempt to walk across the sea to Europe, a place where John's college education has taught him there is less prejudice, or Du Bois could be having John follow in the footsteps of the "flying Africans" who jumped from the sides of the slave ships during the middle passage and into the sea to escape a life of slavery in America.[4] Perhaps he is simply seeking to terminate his American identity via death. He heads toward his death with joy in his heart, pulled there by an invisible engine that we, as readers, cannot see.

A storm bursts around John as he turns toward the sea, and "the world whistled in his ears" (263). This is where the story ends. The whistle of the world has drowned out the whistle of the train, and John finds refuge in the sea. The Jim Crow car breaks the promise of progress symbolized by the train and alters the meaning of the symbol beyond just taking a positive or negative response to progress. In this story, the train becomes a symbol of the broken promise of the American Dream and a symbol that reveals the conflicted nature of the America of the times indicative of what Du Bois calls the two worlds within American culture (43). In this story the train symbolizes both the promise and the lie.

Thus, while this story, unlike Hayden's poem, can be made to fit into the paradigm established by Leo Marx, there is obviously so much more to be learned by the study of what the train means and how it functions as a literary symbol in the works of twentieth-century African American writers when not examined through a predetermined lens. Without fresh vision, one runs the risk of looking at American literature, in Du Bois's words, "half-consciously" (248), looking only for details that seem familiar or fit into already established literary traditions, a practice Robert Stepto faults as being patronizing, confusing, and ultimately a practice that diminishes the work in question (787). Studying a work by a black writer only because it can be made to seem a missing or an overlooked example of a tradition or practice already deemed canonical, is, Stepto asserts, nothing more than "social science fiction" (787).

What is necessary is an exploratory study of the uses of the train as a literary symbol in the works of twentieth-century African American writers, a study that does not assume that African American texts will simply fit into Marx's paradigm, or that these texts which use the train as a literary symbol do so in a way that must necessarily be in direct conflict with the white authors previously studied, a perspective which would, again, be showcasing an already studied canon and merely pointing out how black writers have done things differently.

This study contributes to the growing list of what Robert Stepto calls intrinsic studies, and, instead of merely adding to or building upon the work of Leo Marx, jumps track and heads off in a direction of its own. African American writers of the twentieth century use the train as a symbol of the dangerous and yet necessary journeys toward a deeper understanding of what power the self is capable of exerting and achieving. When there is a train in the text, instead of being an object symbolizing progress to which an author has either a positive or a negative response, the train most often symbolizes an interstice in time and space that transcends chronological history. There is a touch of the divine, of the eternal, of the spiritual made manifest in the physical world but not confined to it or by it. The train is both a liminal space, a physiological and psychological threshold, and also a symbol of the spiritual and physical choices black men and women select from as they make an inward journey toward a redefinition of self, a self that is sometimes portrayed as the engine, but most often expressed as ghostly, otherworldly with the vantage point being that of a rider whose perspective comes from that of the angel seat.

The angel seat was an observation point for the conductors and trainmen who watched the train ahead of them. From here, they could notice obstacles, derailed cars, hot boxes, shifted loads, and other dangers that threatened the progress of the train that the train engineer could not see. This angel seat was always located in the chariot or caboose of the train. While the engine was always the first car to come into the station, the angel seat, as reflected by the conflating of train imagery and the use of spirituals during the days of the Underground Railroad, was the best seat of all.

In African American literature, the symbol of the train, from the steel black and blue of the engine, all the way to the angel seat of the caboose, gets its power from the riders' refusal to be "railroaded" into accepting a fate that is not of their own choosing. The train transcends its tracks, and those that ride "Aunt Harriet's Underground Railroad in the Sky" with John Henry and the others are "flying among the stars" (Ringgold 1). Alternatively, as Carlyle Van Thompson explains, the symbol of the train "expands and explodes the boundaries of the traditional discourse with the train as a metaphor for Black people's sojourn into subjectivity" as they "challenged the philosophy of white supremacy" and rejected its insistence on controlling the metaphors of success in the social, political, economic, legal, psychological, and spiritual arenas of power ("Letter" August 19, 2003).

Chapter one of this book explains why the train became the chosen symbol. The train as symbol is not an unconsciously inherited characteristic of twentieth-century African American fiction. Instead, twentieth-century African American writers have self-consciously chosen to use the train as a symbol because of the importance of the train in American history, the popular and scholarly interest in the Underground Railroad, the need for legendary black heroes and heroines that can be met by an examination of train folklore, and the metaphoric possibilities associated with trains, tracks, and the modern underground.

Chapters two and three focus specifically on the different uses of the train and legendary railroad people as literary symbols. Chapter two discusses how the Underground Railroad is used as a literary symbol in both stories and the spirituals, and how its most famous conductor, Harriet Tubman, is used to articulate the costs of freedom. One of the costs of freedom, associated with Harriet Tubman, is motherhood. Tubman becomes mother to a nation of "motherless children," but she was physically never able to have a child of her own, and as a surrogate mother, she also threatens her children with death if they give up on the pursuit of freedom. Chapter three focuses on the legend of John Henry and the struggle to control the depictions of black manhood associated with him, a struggle with both physical and fiscal costs at stake as the fight to control the representation of John Henry coincides with the expansion of the railroad and white fears about black men replacing white men as railroad workers.

As will become clear after reading chapters two and three, in order to dispel the myth of the black man or woman as a foolish child or "black brute" in texts by twentieth-century African American writers, both Harriet Tubman and John Henry are presented as mechanized in some aspects, taking on the positive traits associated with the railroad, but it is interesting to note that the Tubman texts focus on her life and her success, while in many of the John Henry texts, it seems as if it is impossible for a black man to be a man and still live. The psychological consequences of this concept are explored in the works of contemporary African American male writers, concluding with an examination of Colson Whitehead's 2001 novel, *John Henry Days*, a novel that, as John Updike laments in his review of the text, may or may not end with the death of the John Henry character.[5] Gender is thus an issue in examining the use of the railroad as a literary symbol in both of these chapters.

Chapter four focuses on texts written or set during the Great Migration and how the lessons learned from train travel may at first seem contradictory. Although all the train journeys provide the stimulus for an inward journey and a changed understanding of one's place in the world, the lessons one learns as a passenger, a worker, and a stowaway are quite different. In the passenger texts, such as Ralph Ellison's "Boy on a Train," the lesson learned on the train is largely negative because of the rider's confinement to the Jim Crow car and the laws of segregation. The train promises freedom through mobility, but the Jim Crow car reinforces a sense of limitation. In the stories about train workers, such as James McPherson's "A Solo Song: For Doc," the trains are an educational space where young men learn about the ways of the world from older, more experienced men, and the Jim Crow cars are never mentioned. These lessons are positive and yet, there is a sense that as a worker, one is always at the beck, call, and whim of the white people's world, and that no matter how far one travels by train, there really is no place in America where a black man can find himself and discover who and what he really is. He is socially, politically, and economically disenfranchised, and yet, by recognizing the importance of belonging to a brotherhood of men, he is empowered. These types of texts emphasize the emotional and intellectual importance of the A. Philip Randolph Brotherhood of Sleeping Car Porters and Maids, a union for black Pullman railroad car attendants. The Brotherhood eventually forced the Pullman Company, one of the most powerful businesses in the country, to negotiate a contract with them, thus becoming the first union controlled by and for black workers.[6] The third and final group of riders considered in chapter four are the stowaways. With the exception of those who betray the race by traveling away from home as part of an attempt to pass for white and to cross over the color line, the stowaway texts, reminiscent of the "Runagate" motif, are positive, and train travel becomes symbolic of the successful journey toward self-awareness and self-discovery.

Chapter five looks at texts that use trains to symbolize a choice between activities or perspectives that are life enhancing or death inducing, accelerating toward destruction as in Amiri Baraka's *Dutchman* or the possibility of a now enlightened, now empowered return to one's point of origin, such as in August Wilson's *Two Trains Running*, a point where one stops running and in a sense, goes home, back to the South, back to God, back to a previous way of experiencing life that was cast off, perhaps, prematurely, an internal and external journey Houston Baker calls "the journey back."

This study concludes with a discussion of Albert Murray's *Train Whistle Guitar* as it includes references to all the topics touched on in chapters one through five. What runs through all five chapters, as is seen in the final Murray section, is a sense of the train as a symbol that articulates the personal costs of freedom. The self must be redefined as the result of an inward journey symbolized not just by riding the train, but by becoming like the train. Though potentially troubling, the individual often becomes "like a train, a bad express train" (Murray 8), a train that can "whistle secret signals" (Murray 9), signals that promise change in churches, schools, businesses, "all this and more" ("Coming of John," Du Bois 247). The train and train people of Hayden's poem and others keep on "movering, movering" throughout the pages of African American literature. The continued popularity of the train and associated train people as symbols in twentieth-century African American literature attest to both the staying power of the symbol and to the importance of what the symbol of the train and the angel seat represent as the blue-black (underground) railroad transcends all tracks and flies among the stars.

✥ CHAPTER ONE

Impact of the Railroad on African American Life

> Thy train of cars behind, obedient, merrily following,
> Through gale or calm, now swift, now slack, yet steadily careering;
> Type of the modern—emblem of motion and power—pulse of the continent.
>
> *(Walt Whitman, "To a Locomotive in Winter")*

> Our house was close to a set of railroad tracks, and trains passed by on a frequent basis. I can remember being awakened out of sleep by the horrendous sound of the locomotive's horn and thinking that I had died and was being resurrected after hearing the sound of the trumpet. These teachings were ingrained in my young mind through a combination of oral teachings and the reading of a set of children's books known as the Bible Story.
>
> *(Kenneth L. Jenkins, The True Story of How a Christian Preacher Embraced Islam)*

In *The Fictive and the Imaginary*, Wolfgang Iser explains the human need for symbols. Some symbols, he says, contain "inherited schemata" which "reproduce affective attitudes, memories, knowledge, mental and perceptual dispositions," but that in literature, there is also always the aim "to symbolize the absent, the unavailable, the ungraspable that they may become accessible" (254). Some symbols are readymade. By being born into a certain time and place, members of a particular discourse community "inherit" those symbols, know what they mean, and instead of creating meaning, in Iser's words, members of that discourse community "imitate" the work of the original creators (255).

Nineteenth-century Americans, for example, were told in speeches and advertising done by politicians and railroad financiers that the train was a symbol of progress, and so in the works of Nathaniel Hawthorne, Henry David Thoreau, and Walt Whitman, whether or not they liked the direction that progress was taking, the train was always, to use Whitman's words from the poem "To a Locomotive in Winter" a "type of the modern" and "an emblem of motion and power" (2153). Thus, according to Iser's theory, while Whitman here appears to be "thinking symbolically," his response to the train is actually a conditioned or taught response to a cultural symbol that members of a community are told has meaning, and through repetition of the message that the train is progress, generation after generation attaches the same meaning to the cultural artifact and the interpretation of what the artifact "means" becomes so clearly associated with the symbol that the association becomes automatic (255). Interesting, too, is Whitman's insistence, in line eleven of the poem, that the train cars are "obedient" and "merrily" follow directions when compared with the far more active and independent representations of the train in works by African American writers to be discussed in chapters two through six.[1]

In Walt Whitman's time and place, Marx explains in one of his later essays, "The Railroad in the Landscape: An Iconological Reading of a Theme in American Art," written after making his original argument in *The Machine in the Garden*, from the first appearance of the train in 1830, "it soon became obvious that this method of transportation was to have far-reaching economic and social consequences" and "the press kept up the excitement with stories about every imaginable aspect of the new technology and practitioners of the popular arts contributed songs and pictures, poems and fictions to the hubbub" (184). These things worked to support, Marx says, a very particular ideology, much of which in the nineteenth century was done "quite deliberately and with a manifestly ideological purpose" (184). African American writers had little interest in reproducing this "very particular ideology" of incorporation of the train into the service of an American Dream that favored land-owners and the wealthy as identified by Marx (184).

However, in literature, Iser argues, writers can, if they so choose, create meaning instead of merely reproducing an artifact of culture. A writer can add additional meaning to a symbol, and by doing so, create several layers of meaning condensed into one symbol. Works by literary scholars who study writers who write from the margins instead of the mainstream of American culture, specifically scholars such as Roger Abrahams (1963), Claudia Mitchell-Kernan (1971), and Henry Louis Gates Jr.(1988), have provided examples in their studies of language usage in black communities, which lend support to Iser's theory about the power of writers to create new meaning for existing symbols in their discussion of the literary act of "signifying." As Theodore Mason Jr.(1997) explains, "the rhetoric of signifying aims at the formation of community rather than at the expression of dominance" and in the act of "copying central elements" of a dominant culture, writers who signify are also "revising those in some significant way" often criticizing "the white literary or cultural source by setting it within the context of African American expressive culture" (665). It is this act of willed creation that makes a literary symbol in African American literature more than just a side effect of the mainstream culture. Alternatively, as Gates explains in his essay "Criticism in the Jungle," the act of writing and self-willed creations makes "a profound definition and defense of the critical self: in an act of self-defense, the writer asserts the integrity of the self" (2).

Literary symbols thus occur when a cultural symbol is interpreted by an artist or writer in a way that reveals the artist's or writer's own response to the dominant ideology associated with the image, and according to W.J.T. Mitchell, such symbols become more than a mere artifact of culture when they become literary or artistic symbol (17–23 and 241–46). Literary or artistic symbols are "a sensitive index of ideology," in a way that artifacts of culture are not because a literary symbol is not only a record of the experience of a nation's history, but also a record of individual responses to the representations and discourse surrounding that history (Miller 2). Nevertheless, these literary symbols themselves can become part of what Iser termed the "inherited schemata" of a culture or subgroup within a community when they are then repeated or modified by writers from that community who are responding to the literary symbol in works of their own (254).

The repeated use of a particular version of a literary symbol, then, within a subgroup or particular discourse community indicates that while there is a need for individual literary and artistic expression that is often met by the creation of new symbols, or to use Gates's terms, the "extended signifyin(g)," there is also a powerful need to feel connected to an inherited tradition of meaning (2). Thus, in terms of twentieth-century African American uses of the train as a literary symbol, some of that use is "inherited" from previous African American uses of the train as a nineteenth-century literary and cultural symbol that may at first have been, to use Iser's terms, "imitative" of mainstream culture, but much of the train's twentieth-century use by African American writers is the result of a consciously made decision to use the image of the train as both a vehicle for revisiting America's history of racism, and as a symbol of the incredible, tenacious, unstoppable, ongoing push for a different definition of self, a formation of an identity other than the one provided by mainstream American culture (255). The repeated use of the train as a symbol in twentieth-century African American literature provides a sense of continuity and of a self-reflective tradition that becomes more and more tangible with each repeated use of the train as a symbol. In effect, the repeated use of the train as a symbol in twentieth-century African American literature is part of a self-created inheritance.

This understanding of the function of the train as a literary symbol fits into current critical approaches to the study and production of African American literature. Many twentieth-century African American writers view their fiction as an important part of what Maggie Sale calls "the process of creating African American history" ("Historical Novel" 359). By creating fictions that seek to retell a "silenced story," African American writers present imagined histories of the "lives of everyday, often enslaved people, whose lives had not been recorded because they had not been deemed worthy by writers of history" (358). Valerie Smith refers to these fictions as "retrospective fictions" and explains how these fictions allow African American writers to "reclaim" history, to "reinterpret" the meanings formerly attached to aspects of American history and culture, and "to liberate the literary ancestors by representing what had previously been deemed unspeakable" (458). In this way, the literary symbol of the train is used to represent, reclaim, reinterpret, and in effect, practice a bit of revisionist history by creating and then presenting different perspectives on historical events, possible historical events, and the events in the lives of both everyday and legendary people associated with the railroad.

It thus becomes imperative to understand the African American experience of the history of the railroad because it is that history that twentieth-century African American writers are inspired by or to which they are responding. As James Baldwin suggests, "the past is all that makes the present coherent" (Baldwin, *Notes* 4). An understanding of America's railroading history will help to explain why the train is such an American icon and also to see why particular aspects of railroad history are specific to the African American experience. It is these aspects of difference discussed here in chapter one that fire the imagination of twentieth-century African American writers and cause them to use the literary symbol of the train in a way that goes beyond the boundaries of the paradigm established by Leo Marx through his study of canonical American texts. A detailed analysis of the train as a literary symbol in the works of twentieth-century African American writers will thus be discussed in depth in chapters two through five.

The Impact of the Railroad on African American Life
Pre-Civil War

When the first American-built locomotive made its debut in August of 1830, it fired the imagination of inventors, industrialists, and inventors across the nation; and, by the end of that same year, railroad mania had begun. By 1831, thirteen railways were chartered by the New York legislature, the Pennsylvania legislature had ordered the building of a railway from Philadelphia to the Erie Canal, and by 1835 there were more than 200 railroad lines under construction. According to Albert McCready and Lawrence Sagle's *Railroads in the Days of Steam*, by 1860 over a billion dollars had been invested in American railroad development (25).

Recent scholarship by Sarah H. Gordon reveals that there were marked regional differences in response to this railroad mania. In her 1997 study of the railroad, *A Passage to Union: How the Railroads Transformed American Life, 1829–1929*, Gordon shows that despite the rhetoric of the railroad barons which articulated a commitment to national unity, promising that the railroads would bring the nation together, the railroads flourished and evolved as local lines serving local interests. The South rejected Northern railroad owners' attempts at owning and operating railroads in the South and made it as difficult for them as possible. Southern states passed laws making it illegal for "any railroad corporation to control track in more than one state, since this would diminish the power of the state" (5). The federal government, however, overruled these Southern state laws and insisted that railroad building was part of America's destiny. As Gordon notes, "the economic promise of railroading had brought about fundamental changes in state laws, all of which reduced the authority of the states to control and regulate business and speeded national development" (17).

The South continued to insist that any attempts at federal control of the railroad violated states' rights and saw the railroads as symbolic of the federal government's desire, intention, and power to interfere in state and local politics. Many historians now believe that it was the billion dollars invested in the railroads more than any true concerns about the moral sins of slavery that "contributed directly to the outbreak of the Civil War in 1861" (Gordon 6). As Paul Johnson notes in *A History of the American People* (1997), there were "huge differences of interest over railroad strategy" and "the railroad interests of the Northeast and the Northwest came into alignment in the 1850s" which "the South saw as a plot" (434). The linking of the Northeast and Northwest by rail connected the two areas of the country financially, which, Johnson asserts, was what finished the South. Jefferson Davis bitterly complained that "the North, while accusing the South of exploiting the blacks, exploited the whole South systematically and without mercy" in order to, in Davis's own words, "promote the industry of the North-East states, at the expense of the people of the South" (Johnson 434). Thus, the train, which many Northerners or Federalists viewed as a symbol of progress, was for white Southerners, symbolic of the Union's determination to assault the Southern, agrarian, plantation way of life.

Given the dislike of many Southerners for the new railroads and what railroads represented in terms of the loss of states' rights, it is no wonder that the term for the secret conveyance of African Americans from the South to the North was nicknamed, by a white proslavery Southerner, the Underground Railroad.[2] The name was quickly adopted by the abolitionists to describe their activities, and the train became symbolic of abolitionists' work in the South to promote emancipation. An 1844 abolitionist song depicts emancipation as the engine that will change America's history:

> Ho! the Car Emancipation Rides majestic thro' our nation,
> Bearing on its Train, the Story, Liberty! a Nation's Glory.
> Roll it along, Roll it along, Roll it along, thro' the Nation Freedom's Car,
> Emancipation.
> ("Long Steel Rail," 1844 abolitionist song qtd. in Gordon 133)

Emancipation is the locomotive or lead car that pulls a train in its wake that will change how the story of America is told, and that new story will be about liberty and freedom for all, a condition that will bring the nation glory. According to the sentiments expressed in the song, without emancipation, one cannot truly talk about America as a place of freedom, thus "Freedom's Car" and the "Car Emancipation" are one and the same. Listeners are asked to help "roll it along," the "it" referring to this concept and passage of emancipation, but there is also the suggestion that because emancipation is like a train, and trains were already at this time viewed as an unstoppable force, making their way into the landscape whether desired or not, emancipation, like the train, would roll on through the nation whether the South liked it or not. As Frederick Douglass once said, "Where the locomotive go, the train must follow" (qtd. in Cottman 9). To Northerners, the railroad was a symbol of motion, power, progress, and money, or as James Alan McPherson puts it, "the central symbol of the expanding industrial economy" (8). This symbol was adopted by abolitionists to describe their cause. However, what did the train symbolize to African Americans of this same period?

Researchers interested in the African American response to the cultural symbol of the train often examine African American attitudes about the use of the train as symbol as indicated by slave song lyrics with train symbolism, such as "Little Black Train Is a Comin'" which tells listeners to get their "house in ordah" as the train to heaven is coming; "Git Yo Ticket," a song about a train bound for Glory; "When the Train Comes Along," a song urging listeners to meet the singer at the station; "Git on Board, Little Chillen," about the sound of the gospel train's wheels rumbling through the land; and many more. There are no dates indicating when these songs were first sung and no recorded history about how the train came to be incorporated as a symbol into these songs, but according to oral tradition, these were slave gospel songs.[3] While apparently simple, as Richard Wright asserts, these songs, even when composed of the simplest of words, are full of many layers of meaning:

> meanings which enabled us to speak of revolt in the actual presence of the Lords of the Land without their being aware! Our secret language extended our understanding of what slavery meant and gave us the freedom to speak to our brothers in captivity; we polished our new words, caressed them, gave them new shape and color, a new order and tempo, until, although they were the words of the Lords of the Land, they became *our* words, *our* language. (Wright, *12 Million Black Voices*, qtd. in Sundquist 27)

Eric Sundquist, too, suggests that many seemingly simple slave gospels or sermons were in fact a "syncretic blend of Christian and African beliefs" used by black slave ministers which "combined spirituality and ideology," a practice which made religious forms into "instruments of revolution"(60–61). In the songs listed above, on the surface, the train is simply a metaphor for a spiritual state. However, once one understands the history of the African American experience of the railroad, a very different understanding of what the train symbolizes in such songs and why the train was picked at all emerges.

In his train history, *Railroads: Trains and Train People in American Culture*, James Alan McPherson, an African American writer and historian, speculates that because of slavery, for African Americans of the time, the train had a separate symbolic meaning and discusses the part music may have played not only in representing this difference, but also in creating this difference. McPherson explains that one of the marketing problems early railroads faced was "the fear aroused in people and animals by the smoke-puffing iron contraption" (5). To eliminate this fear, in 1831 the West Point train line affixed a barrier car between the engine and the cars where white passengers sat. The barrier car was a flatbed car piled high with bales of cotton and "Negro" musicians (5). These musicians were ordered to ignore the flying ash and to play in such a way as to make the sounds of the train seem festive instead of frightening. The musicians were so successful that it became common to hire flatbed cars of black musicians on other lines as well, whenever a train was involved in a public festive occasion.

To these slave musicians and other African Americans, McPherson speculates, the train "might have spoken new possibilities" and their placement up front near the powerful engine might have suggested an affinity with the engine's source of strength that the white passengers lacked (6). McPherson writes:

> To them the machine might have been loud and frightening, but its whistle and its wheels promised movement. And since a commitment to freedom and movement was the basic promise of democracy, it was probable that such people would view the locomotive as a challenge to the integrative powers of their imaginations. It demanded assimilation as a symbol of culture. The problem presented by such a demand was essentially aesthetic: the image of the locomotive had to be rearranged into patterns of experience invested with beauty and meaningful application. (6)

Before the Civil War, African Americans, slave or free, owned little or no capital and were not hired by the railroads except as slaves rented from their masters, so to them the train could not, at this time, function as a symbol of economic progress and power unless it was of progress and power denied. They also did not, McPherson suggests, "view the locomotive as the envoy of commercial powers which threatened the peace of a budding agricultural utopia" because they were denied land ownership (9). Most African Americans of the time, McPherson speculates, "accepted the locomotive as a meaningful symbol" of "progress," but also saw in it the possibility of something more, something not yet articulated in African American culture (9). The train symbolized economic power, but more importantly, it symbolized the possibility of rebelling against or making unexpected, unorthodox, unapproved uses of that power, and served as a symbol of the power to oppose power through creative usurpation of power's own symbols.

With the passage of the Fugitive Slave Law in September of 1850, abolitionists were in need of a new symbol, one that promised power. Trains became that symbol, largely because of railroad politics. On August 16, 1851, against the wishes of Southern politicians, the first international railroad linking the United States with Canada opened, and "rolling stock of foreign ownership was permitted free entry into Canada or the United States" (McPherson 23). Trains carrying cargo into Canada were no longer stopped or the cargo held up for border searches. Since the passage of the Fugitive Slave Law, Canada had become the only safe terminus for escaping slaves, and the creation of a railroad that did not need to stop at the U.S.-Canadian border fired the imagination. Though travelers on foot or wagon might be detained at the border, the trains rolled on through.

Harriet Tubman, who will be discussed in greater length in chapter two of this study, in fact, rode on just such a train, as part of the final leg of many of her trips to Canada. The most famous of these journeys, her November 1856 run to Canada, is told in almost all the biographies of Tubman, beginning with the uses of her biography in abolitionists' records and continuing through today. The month and year were etched in Tubman's mind because it was the first time she had led an escape party with a price upon her head ($12,000), and upon that of one of her passengers, Josiah Bailey ($1,500). According to M. W. Taylor, Tubman led the group from Delaware to the heavily guarded Wilmington Bridge, where Quaker abolitionist Thomas Garrett arranged to pick the group up and placed them in the bed of a wagon filled with bricks. The escaping fugitives lay flat under the stash of bricks piled on top of them. From Garrett's now famous shoe shop with its secret chamber hidden behind a wall of stock, Tubman led the group to a station or safe house in Philadelphia, and from there, to another station in New York. From New York, they journeyed the rest of the way by train. Taylor writes,

> The rest of the trip north was easier. Much of the Underground Railroad's route through New York state involved real trains; Tubman and her charges traveled in a baggage car, watched over by a sympathetic trainman. . . . When the train approached Niagara Falls, the conductor took the group into a coach so they could see Canada on the other side of the bridge. Even there, they were still in danger. Until the train reached the center of the bridge, any slave catcher could legally arrest them and drag them all back into slavery. But the train moved steadily across the great iron bridge. When it reached the center, Tubman gave Bailey a shake and shouted, "Joe, you're in Queen Victoria's dominions! You're a free man!" Bailey used his voice for the first time in days. . . . "There's only one more journey for me now, and that's to heaven." (57–59)

In her typical practical fashion, according to the legend, Tubman replied, "You might have looked at the Falls first and gone to Heaven afterwards" (Taylor 59).

In addition to these trains, the Underground Railroad made use of other steam railroads as well. According to research collected by Siebert, there were agents of the Underground Railroad employed by the Dayton and Cincinnati Railroad, the Newark Railroad, the New Albany and Chicago Railroad, the Michigan Central Railroad, the Chicago, Burlington and Quincy Railroad, the Chicago and Rock Island Railroad, the Illinois Central Railroad, the Reading Railroad, the Pennsylvania Railroad, the Northern Central to Elmira Railroad, and the New York Central Railroad (Siebert 80). Men such as Horace White, who was a director of the New York Central Railroad, used their positions of authority with "surface" railroad as part of their commitment to helping the Underground Railroad. According to White's widow, periodically there would be a knocking on their bedroom window in the night, and Mr. White "always wrote off the passes and handed them out, asking no questions" (qtd. in Siebert 80).

After the passage of the Fugitive Slave Law, however, it was no longer sufficient simply to escape the South and instead, Canada became the final terminus of the Underground Railroad. Moreover, because of an international rolling stock agreement linking Canadian rails with U.S. rails, so that the trains did not need to stop at the border and could instead continue passage from major station to major station, the train became an actual and symbolic tool of deliverance. The image of Canada as the new Promised Land and the train as the vehicle that could carry one there that appears in works by twentieth-century African American writers most likely comes from this combination of historic events.

The Impact of the Railroad on African American Life
The Civil War

The next big moment in railroad history, from the point of view of the African American experience of the railroad and why the train continued its evolution from an artifact of culture into a full-fledged literary symbol of particular power and importance in African American literature, was the Civil War. As David Nasaw notes, the Civil War was a war that "pitted army against army, industry against industry, and railroad against railroad" (15). Trains were used for the transport of supplies and also for massive troop movements. In a single venture, the Federal War Department sent 30,000 men by train to Chattanooga to crush the Confederate opposition.[4] The train came to be seen as a major weapon in the Union army arsenal.

Also important for understanding the attitude African Americans had toward trains during the Civil War is the fact that the military trains used in the South to crush Southern opposition were primarily confiscated Southern trains. In effect, these Southern trains were being turned against the South. Confederate soldiers and civilians took to blowing up and destroying their own railroads in a desperate attempt to keep the Northern invaders out, but they were largely unsuccessful (Stover 60–61). The train thus became a symbol akin to a snake in the garden for Southern whites, and, for Southern blacks, a symbol of the outside world rushing in, and with this, as Gordon notes, "the slaves saw the potential for freedom" (127).

The railroad thus brought soldiers who could be seen by white Southerners as destroyers and by enslaved African Americans as saviors, although many of these "saviors" had very negative attitudes about African Americans in general and slaves in particular. In the early part of the war, slaves were considered contraband of war and became the property of Union army officials. General Butler, during his occupation of Fort Monroe in Virginia, viewed slaves as his contraband of war and put them to work as such (Franklin and Moss 199). After the federal government outlawed the use of slave labor as part of the war effort, these slaves were still not freed. Instead, they were placed in "contraband camps" and held there (Franklin and Moss 201). So while the trains were viewed as the bringers of the Northern troops, troops that would defeat the Southern Confederacy and forever change the Southern way of life, once that change started occurring it was not as pretty as the abolitionist songs had depicted. Instead of finding themselves as passengers on a train bound for glory, many African Americans found themselves uncertain about whether or not they were truly free. The trains had brought these Northerners into the South. Perhaps the way to freedom was still to be found by catching a ride on a train traveling out of the South. This is an idea that occurs again and again in twentieth-century African American fiction, particularly works written or set before the 1960s and 1970s.

The Impact of the Railroad on African American Life
Post–Civil War

Following the Civil War, the railroads in the North were a thriving business, and some newly emancipated African Americans sought to cash in on this reality as well. One of the very first independent black enterprises was the 1865 Chesapeake and Marine Railway and Dry Dock Company (Franklin and Moss 236). For the next five years, the black-owned and black-operated Chesapeake and Marine Railway thrived until forced out of business by Northern industrialists eager to do business in the South with white Southerners and willing to sacrifice fledging black enterprises in order to secure favorable deals. As Franklin and Moss explain,

> The industrialists of the North, who had come to control the Republican party, wanted a satisfactory settlement of the Southern problem in order to hasten the exploitation of Southern resources and to capture Southern markets. When the Radical Reconstruction program served their purposes, they cooperated, as in the period when they sought favorable consideration from the Southern legislatures; but when the program failed to bring peace and order, thereby postponing prosperity, they helped to restore home rule to the South. (245)

African Americans in the South who tried to become involved in the $100 million railroad rebuilding enterprise found themselves frustrated by the Black Codes, Jim Crow laws, and the ruthlessness of Northern entrepreneurs. As Leon Litwack notes in *Trouble in Mind: Black Southerners in the Age of Jim Crow*, the "problem lay not in the willingness of blacks to work" but in "the betrayal of their expectations, in the failure to reap rewards" (115). As in the pre–Civil War period, it was clear to all that the train symbolized change and great economic possibilities, but again, the African American access to this possibility was restricted and then, as now, trickle-down economics is a story believed by those at the top, not at the bottom.

So if the train did not symbolize money or a meaningful change in society's infrastructure, what did it symbolize for African Americans during Reconstruction? Why not simply discard the train as a useful symbol of culture or for African American literature? Despite the limited access to wealth during Reconstruction, it was during this time that many blacks first began working on the railroad as laborers, though quite often the labor was forced. The Jim Crow laws and Black Codes made it possible to arrest young Southern black men for minor infractions of the law (such as poaching or loitering), and each year, during the 1870s and 1880s, tens of thousands of black men were sentenced to five or more years of hard labor. Prison labor made a small fortune for the Southern states that employed it, and under the convict leasing system, Northern-financed railroad builders could purchase "months or years of the lives of prisoners (almost exclusively black), paying a commission to the state" (Litwack 271). Work as part of a railroad prison gang had a reputation for being deadly, and only the strongest, toughest, meanest, "baddest" men survived. Those who did became legendary "bad" men and were able to market their experience in unexpected ways.

A typical example of the life of a black convict leased to a railroad company, such as the New Orleans Northeastern Railroad, would be as follows:

> Convicts were chained in knee-deep pools of muck. The men's thirst drove them to drink the water in which they were compelled to deposit their excrements. No wonder doctors and health officials were sometimes as occupied with signing death certificates as with treating prisoners, most of the victims suffering from exhaustion, malaria, frostbite, pneumonia, consumption, sunstroke, edema, chronic diarrhea, dysentery, scurvy, gunshot wounds, wounds miscellaneous, and shackle poisoning (caused by the chains and leg irons biting into bare flesh). In many instances the cause of death was listed as "not stated." The convicts who tried to escape were whipped till the blood ran down their legs, and some had a metal spur riveted to their feet. (Litwack 272)

Those who survived became men of legends and the forerunner of the John Henry stories, legends, and work ballads that have their root in this period in African American railroad history. The legends of John Henry will be discussed in greater detail in chapter three, but they have their origins here, in this time period, because horrible as the work was, it solidified the notion that railroad building was man's work, and the train became a symbol of manhood, even for those who were not free to live like men.

Concurrently, outside the South, as Litwack notes,

> The railroad and streetcar became early arenas of confrontation, precisely because in no other area of public life (except the polling place) did blacks and whites come together on such equal footing. "In their homes and in ordinary employment," one observer noted, "they meet as master and servant, but in the street cars they touch as free citizens, each paying for the right to ride, the white not in a place of command, the Negro without obligation of servitude. Street car relationships are, therefore, symbolic of the new conditions." (231)

As Edward Ayers observes, despite segregation in terms of schools, orphanages, hospitals, theaters, hotels, and restaurants, "travel was a different story, for members of both races had no choice but to use the same railroads" (93). As a result, in the New South of the 1880s and 1890s, the railroads became "contested terrain" because of the Northern railroad policy of having only two classes of travel (93). First-class travel was for women and men who did not use tobacco, and second-class travel was for everyone else. Both cars were mixed, and black passengers who bought first-class tickets from railroads eager to take money for first-class fares sued the railroads and railroad employees when acts of white violence compelled them to leave the first-class cars. As Ayers notes in *Southern Crossing: A History of the American South, 1877–1906,* because of the Northern–controlled court's insistence on the railroads' right to do business in a way that was economically sound, "blacks actually won several of these cases, even in Southern courts" (97). Often, just the threat of legal action was enough to compel railroad employees to permit black first-class ticket holders to remain in the first-class cars despite the protests of white passengers.[5]

In 1889, however, the tide began to turn when the Interstate Commerce Commission ruled that "equity of accommodations" was what was required, not that black passengers and white passengers be allowed to "take any car or any seat that may please his fancy" (qtd. in Ayers 98). In effect the ruling of this federal commission legally sanctioned segregation. While some hoped that the rule would protect black riders from violence and insult and that the railroads would comply by running two first-class cars on every trip, others were furious at this turn of events and the railroads became a test case for the new "separate but equal" laws.

The most famous of these railroad racial incidents is that of Homer Plessy, an 1896 case, which fueled the imaginations of both black and white writers at the end of the nineteenth century and the start of the twentieth century and resulted in a plethora of stories and novels with significant train car sections. Plessy, legally black but visually white, boarded and sat in a "whites only" section of the train, rode the train for several stops, and then indicated to the conductor that he was legally black. The conductor then ordered him out of the white section as the presence of a black man in a "whites only" car would disturb or disgust the white passengers. Plessy refused and was dragged from the train.

His case, which went all the way to the Supreme Court, highlighted the fictionalized nature of racial definition based on custom or tradition in a country in which the races sexually mixed but did not socially mix.[6] Fictionalized accounts of such incidents are used quite frequently in the works of twentieth-century African American writers as liminal moments for the main characters, such as in the works of Toni Morrison and Ralph Ellison, which will be discussed in chapter four.

The Impact of the Railroad on African American Life
Money and Migration

At the turn of the new century, George Pullman's luxury cars were marketed as affordable to the white middle class, and for these Americans, the train became a symbol of a luxurious time long past. Black porters, waiters, cooks, Red Caps, and shoe-shine boys were at the beck and call of all first-class passengers. White passengers who could afford the luxury of riding such trains were able to indulge in the fantasy, once more, of being served by their own personal staff of willing black servants. While the dining car waiters were, in train slang, called "the traveling slaves," Pullman conductors were nicknamed "high society bosses" (Gould 1–2). The African Americans who worked on the trains were paid well to maintain the white fantasy of willing servants, and these train workers' wages were higher than those of factory workers, laborers, or farmhands. The white desire for the fantasy of white supremacy, in essence, financed the entrance of many African American workers from paid work-hand to financially secure independent home-owner, and the irony was not lost on the black men who "served" as porters.

Nat Love, for example, the famous black cowboy, gave up his life as a cowboy and trick-shooter to become a railroad porter because of money. His 1908 autobiography celebrates both occupations as adventurous, but he asserts that it was his job as a railroad porter that afforded him the financial ability to bring his beloved Mexican girlfriend to America, marry her, own and decorate a nice house with an attached garden, and achieve his American dream. Thus, while the train was the vehicle of a nostalgic memory of times past for white train riders, who longed to experience the luxurious days of plantation living, and was a symbol of that luxury, the paychecks provided by the railroad often enabled African American men and their wives to achieve their personal American dreams. While white riders of the time were looking backward, black train workers were looking forward, and the train did not symbolize the same reality for both groups, in literature or in life.

By this time, the train had also become a symbol of the railroads' power to change the hands of time. Before the Civil War, America had seventy different time zones. After the Civil War, this number had been reduced to fifty, but the railroad companies still found it difficult to establish national train schedules when each region had its own time zone, time being based on the time of the sun's setting and rising. Without government permission or sanction, in October 1883 the railroad companies simply agreed to adopt what they called national railroad standard time to begin on the first of the very next month. Although the federal government refused officially to adopt national railroad standard time until 1918, from its instigation in 1883 until today, national railroad standard time zones established to simplify national railroad time scheduling have prevailed and "railroad time" has replaced "God's time" (Gordon 251). The railroads had demonstrated their power to change the hands of time.

The impact of this power on the American consciousness is difficult to catalog because it involves speculation about how such a change in fact would alter abstract notions of time, God's law, man's power, and tradition. Southern farming communities resisted the change in time more than did Northern urban or industrial areas. The federal sanctioning of railroad time coincided with a Southern labor crisis caused by World War I and made possible by train transport.

As World War I cut the supply of European labor for Northern factories, Northern industrialists turned to the South to find new laborers. White Southerners, no matter how economically disadvantaged, saw little advantage in moving North, preferring their social position in the South as poor whites to any sort of Northern relocation. Northern industrialists' recruitment specialists discovered that southern African Americans were far more likely to relocate to the North and so concentrated their recruitment efforts on them. According to statistics cited by Arna Bontemps and Jack Conroy in their 1945 study of black migrations, *Anyplace But Here*, Northern recruitment efforts resulted in the exodus by train of tens of thousands of black men from the South, thus crippling the Southern farming system (Bontemps and Conroy 159). As the trains sped North, they took with them thousands and thousands of young black men.

According to an article by Joseph Zucker in the December 1998 issue of *RailNews*, the average train ticket from New Orleans to Chicago, in 1917, was twenty dollars (50). Northern labor recruiters would offer tickets to the North on special "Exodus" trains for a mere six dollars, the name "Exodus" referring to the biblical Exodus of Jewish slaves from Egypt. The trains were called Exodus trains, referring to the second book of Moses, the book of Exodus. This portion of the Bible begins with the enslavement of the Jews in Egypt, the life of Moses, the plagues visited upon the Egyptians until they agreed to let the Jewish slaves go, the Jewish passage from the land of Egypt after four hundred and thirty years of slavery which is the exodus, and the Pharaoh's armed pursuit of the Jews as they are leaving so that they must run for the freedom they were just legally granted. During the Exodus, the Jews were given the Ten Commandments, the dietary laws in the new land, the laws governing health, and a host of other new rules for how they must behave now that they were free men. The condition of slavery had made many of them less than men in the eyes of Moses and the elders, and these laws and rules helped shape a code of conduct necessary for success during the journey and beyond. The book of Exodus ends with the journey still in progress, and the people wondering if the journey and the search for a new land will last as long as did their four-hundred-and-thirty-year enslavement.

Similarly, the Exodus trains heralded the start of a journey into the unknown, rather than a final destination, and just as the Jews were chased in hopes of bringing them back under Pharaoh's rule, so, too, did Southern lawmakers seek to stem the tide of black migration with new laws designed to restrict the mobility of black citizens. Even discussing northern migration in the years following World War I became a jail-term offense for Southern blacks under the category of "inciting to riot in the city, county, and throughout the state" (qtd. in Bontemps and Conroy 159). Zucker recounts how the "police dragged blacks from trains," and whites sidetracked cars for days in order to prevent a loss to the Southern labor force (51). Despite such laws, the exodus continued, the most famous of which, the Great Northern Drive of May 15, 1917, funded by Northern recruiters, was advertised only in black papers such as *The Defender*. Northern agents hired multiple cargo trains in order to transport all the black workers who wanted to go North, and these riders of the train chalked on the sides of their train cars slogans such as "Bound for the Promised Land" or "Bound to the Land of Hope" (Bontemps and Conroy 163).

While Northern industrialists were luring black workers North with low-price fares to board these Exodus trains, the South suffered a horrible boll weevil insect migration from Mexico and Texas that devastated the fields, and an unprecedented number of storms and floods in 1915 and 1916 finished off the remaining crops. These catastrophes mirrored the plague events of the biblical Exodus story and seemed to confirm the damnation of the South. Exodus from the land of slavery to the hope of a new life in the North seemed divinely intended. This thought, perhaps, helps to explain the uses of the train as a herald of judgment day in Kenneth L. Jenkins/Abdullah Muhammad al-Faruque's Islamic conversion narrative (cited as part of the epigraphs for this chapter), and the judgment day sermons that appear in Zora Neale Hurston's *Jonah's Gourd Vine* or Leon Forrest's *There Is a Tree More Ancient Than Eden*, discussed in depth later in chapters two and three.

In response to what white Southerners saw as a new form of Northern aggression and the rebellion of their once "content" black workforce, the Jim Crow laws were augmented to include a ban on northern migration, a practice similar to the tactics used today by dictators in Third-World countries. The African American Chicago-based newspaper, *The Defender*, however, continued to carry many advertisements for work in northern factories, and in Georgia it became illegal to read any section of that paper out loud (Bontemps and Conroy 159). It became necessary to speak in code about northern migration and once again, as in the days of the Underground Railroad, various spirituals and traditional folk songs were used to convey, metaphorically, the comings and goings of the Exodus trains.[7] To let people know that the most recent Exodus train had left but that another would come in the weeks to follow, those in the know would sing: "Never seen the like since I been born; the people keep a-coming, and the train's done gone."

Despite attempts to stem the tide of migration, thousands continued to ride the trains headed North. To circumvent the Southern Jim Crow laws banning "Negro migration," in the 1920s, the Northern work agents would hire freight trains, stock the trains with empty crates and boxes, and have the trains leave the depot as if loaded with freight. Reminiscent of the technique once used by Henry Box Brown,[8] who shipped himself North in a train freight box, once the trains had left the station, allegedly full of freight, these trains would then stop several miles outside of town where a hundred or so waiting African Americans were hiding in the woods, dump the boxes, and the passengers would then board the trains (Bontemps and Conroy 158–70). For many, these clandestine departures called to mind the old tales of the Underground Railroad, and some of the same gospel songs were used to indicate anticipated travel. When it became illegal openly to discuss migration North, the same sorts of double-talk disguised as religious rhetoric and gospel became necessary to convey information, just as in the days of slavery.

The secrecy necessary to leave the South, even in the twentieth century, continued to make many African Americans feel that they were still little better off than the slaves in the Bible. However, those who had boarded the trains headed North had great faith that once in the North, they would be able to create new lives for themselves that were rich in opportunity and financial reward. Jazz musician Louis Armstrong, for example, was part of this northern exodus and arrived in Chicago in 1922 as a passenger on one of these trains, having shared the long journey with thousands of other black men and women looking for new lives in order to reinvent themselves in new cities of opportunity (Zucker 51). As Zucker concludes,

> In the long and exciting history of the railroad, the story of its role in the Great Migration north, while not well known and not often told, is one as exciting as the many told of white immigrants who arrived here on the great ships that crossed the Atlantic. (51)

As in all good stories, there were double-crossing villains and noble knights. Because the Northern labor agents were paid to round up workers, their advice, once these workers reached the Northern cities, could not always be trusted to provide good information about where to seek lodgings or meals. Northern agents would send workers to company-run locations, and soon the new traveler would be in debt to the company. The only guides who could be trusted were the black men who worked on the trains. Pullman porters, according to Kurt Bell's feature story in the September, 1998 issue of *Milepost*, like the old conductors of the Underground Railroad, "became the intelligence network for the Great Migration" instructing the black community still in the South "what safe routes to take to minimize trouble, what towns along the way to avoid," and brought to the South copies of black Northern newspapers considered seditious by nervous Southern whites (12). From their position on board the train's angel seat, as revealed in Murray's *Train Whistle Guitar*, these noble trainmen became the heroes of many African American songs. As the migrations continued, African American musicians increased the incorporation of railroad sounds, such as the sounds of the train's whistle or its wheels, into their music. In the summer of 1916 alone, the Pennsylvania and Erie railroads estimate that they carried "12,000 Negroes into Pennsylvania" (Risher 38).

These mass leave-takings by train account for the steady presence of the train as a symbolic feature of the African American music of the time. African American music about trains was music about freedom through mobility, but with the awareness that mobility required a certain kind of strength. According to Gordon, the railroad was central to African American music of the 1920s because

> the rolling bass passages of guitar and piano in blues, ragtime, and boogie-woogie recalled the rumble and rhythm of a train. In the high long wails of

> voices and instruments, the musicians mimicked the long wail of the train whistle, which could be heard for miles [. . .]These people had their lives strung out along the railroad line and stopped in a different town each night. They quite literally must have passed in the night. (310–11)

Once the trains arrived in the cities, the promise of the train was retained in the music of the people. For example, according to the Behring Center at the Smithsonian National Museum of American history, Duke Ellington moved from Washington, DC, to New York in 1923, and "by November 1924, Duke made his publishing and recording debut with 'Choo Choo (I Got to Hurry Home)' released on the Blue-Disc label" (para 2). Ellington's more famous train song, "Take the 'A' Train," was the result of another young man's journey. Written for Duke Ellington by Billy Strayhorn, "Take the 'A' Train," was composed while Strayhorn was on a train from Pittsburgh to New York on his way to interview for a job with Ellington, and the song was written "using the travel instructions Ellington's office had given him to get to the band's venue" (BBC News Special 1999). Repeated in story and song, again and again, the train became more than just the setting for adventure; it had become a symbol of "all possibilities" for those with, as Albert Murray would later say in his novel about the 1920s and 1930s, *Train Whistle Guitar*, "nerves as strong as rawhide" and the speed of "a bad express train" on its way, one more time (6–8).

The Impact of the Railroad on African American Life
From Fact to Fiction

In many ways, only in music and literature did the promise of the railroads survive. By the end of the 1920s, the number of lynchings had increased, and white unions had succeeded in limiting the employment of African American locomotive firemen, flagmen, conductors, and yard-men, while white supremacy groups worked with unions to "renew their efforts to eliminate Negro employees" (Risher 38). As Charles Houston notes in his "Outline of Some Railway Labor Problems Affecting Negro Train, Engine, and Yard Service Employees," by 1920 the General Grievance Committee for the Brotherhood of Railroad Trainmen had "negotiated an agreement reducing the employment of Negro trainmen from 33% to 30%" and prohibited the "future hiring of Negroes in train, engine or yard service, but not including train porters" (9–10).

The 1930s saw attempts in states such as Texas to have the African American train porters removed and to make all railroad work white man's work (Houston 10). As Philip S. Foner and Ronald L. Lewis have shown, the Brotherhood of Railroad Trainmen had always maintained a "demand for black exclusion," but it was not until the 1930s that they were able to accomplish this goal (102). The 1940s saw attempts by men such as African American activist A. Philip Randolph, president of the Brotherhood of Sleeping Car Porters, to curtail these changes and to use recent setbacks as an opportunity for political change so that for a brief moment, the railroads became a hotbed of black political activism. In 1941, for example, Randolph organized a march on Washington, DC, and called for 100,000 black men to march to the Capitol (Franklin and Moss 436).

By the 1940s, these successes had, however, caused the railroad to cease to be a contested part of the changing American political and economic landscape, and other arenas for activism opened up in the 1950s. The railroad itself was no longer the center of power or contention. The train, however, remained an important symbol in African American music throughout the civil rights movement. Similarly, in the 1960s and 1970s, African American literature using significant train symbolism flourished. Although the train had ceased to be an actual factor in the lives of African American people, it had become an important symbol in African American literature and music. "In song, story and even in popular religion," Gordon argues, "the idea of taking the railroad to a better way of life became entwined with the American dream of self-betterment" (348).

For African American writers of the twentieth century, however, the train symbolizes more than just a hope for progress or self-improvement. The history of the Underground Railroad, the commitment of Harriet Tubman, the strength of John Henry, the experiences of riding the train North as a passenger, a porter, a stowaway, the sense of again being driven underground in the modern world, all these facets of African American history add to the power of the train as a literary symbol. To ignore such history is to ignore much of the inspiration and self-exploration at the core of so much twentieth-century African American literature. For African American writers of the twentieth century, the train remains a symbol of the journey toward a redefinition of self, and the importance of the journey is a lesson rooted in the past, which must be retained for the future, but which can only be reclaimed through the power of fiction.

✢ CHAPTER TWO

Flying Trains and the "Tubman Tradition"

Each one who heard the stories, each one who told all of them, or only parts of them, would feel stronger because of her existence. Pride in her would linger on in the teller of the story as well as the listener. Their faith in a living God would be strengthened; their faith in themselves would be renewed.... They said she was so strong she could pick up a grown man, sling him over her shoulder and walk with him for miles, that she talked with God, every day, just like Moses. They said that there was some strange power in her so that no one could die when she was with them.
(*Ann Petry*, Harriet Tubman: Conductor on the Underground Railroad)

The black Madonna called Moses with a man's shoes, laceless upon her feet, her mother rage and coming glory, the feverish perspiration raining down exhausted into her huge river-pouting mouth, stealing away from her woolly-headed scalp down down down into her glowing... as if to issue forth yet another starving life into an unclean world—bruised-blood breasts, like a moody restless river, terrible and beloved.
(*Leon Forrest*, There Is a Tree More Ancient Than Eden)

Sometimes the train is a farmer's wagon. Sometimes it is a hearse covered with flowers.... You missed this train, Cassie. But you can follow.
(*Faith Ringgold*, Aunt Harriet's Underground Railroad in the Sky)

Perhaps the clearest example of how the train has operated as a literary symbol is its use in twentieth-century poems and fiction about the Underground Railroad and its most famous conductor, Harriet Tubman. For twentieth-century African American artists, musicians, and writers looking back at the nineteenth century, the Underground Railroad seems a clear symbol of, in the words of twentieth-century black rap artist KRS ONE, a "lost" people's willingness to fight against the status quo when the status quo is wrong and of the hazard-ridden journey toward the achievement of freedom and sense of personal identity that can only be accomplished through such a journey.[1] That fight and that pursuit can be driven underground, but, as the symbol of the Underground Railroad promises, it can never be destroyed.

Though it may lie dormant during certain seasons, it will awaken and be born again, often through the machinations of an archetypal mother.

Historically, the Underground Railroad was the name adopted by the network of abolitionists committed to the aid of African Americans traveling North from slavery to freedom, first to the North, and then later to Canada. While it is not known for sure exactly when this network of abolitionists adopted the name, according to William H. Siebert, the name first came into use among slave-hunters (44). Apparently the slave hunters could easily track the movements of escaping slaves as far as southeastern Pennsylvania. Once there, however, because of the Quaker efforts in "harboring and forwarding fugitives," the escapees disappeared without a trace (45). Siebert notes that while no one knows for sure which Southern slave-catcher first coined the expression, many credit it to the owner of escaping slave Tice Daniels. According to the legend, Tice Daniels disappeared right before his master's eyes. When asked what he thought had happened, Daniels's master retorted that "the nigger must have gone off on an underground road" (qtd. in Siebert 45). The Tice Daniels story spread like wildfire, and many black and white Americans became convinced, without any additional proof, that there was, indeed, an Underground Railroad.

Recent scholarship has cast doubt upon the actual effectiveness of the Underground Railroad. Studies such as Larry Gara's *The Liberty Line: The Legend of the Underground Railroad* suggest that the actual number of runaways helped by the Underground Railroad was very small (36).[2] In fact, current scholarship tends to focus more on the "real" life stories of women such as Ellen Craft, a slave woman light enough to pass for white, who, dressed as a man, crossed both the color line and gender line, and purchased, as Florence Freedman puts it "two tickets to Freedom," buying two train tickets from Macon to Philadelphia, from slavery in the South to freedom in the North, one thousand miles away (21). During her own lifetime, however, as Tonya Bolden explains, women such as Ellen Craft were "relegated to the shadows" and thus did not serve an archetypal function (19). For example, in his introduction to the Crafts' narrative, it is William Craft who is credited by William L. Andrews for narrating the tale: "no slave narrator outdid William Craft in denouncing slavery" and focuses on William Craft's startling accusation about the poor class of "whites in the South of trafficking in the persons of free white girls so as to satisfy the lust of slavery for more and more marketable bodies" (17).

As Newman and Gates point out, other slave narratives of the time indirectly continued to emphasize the commercial nature of human bodies by permitting the writer to make money by making themselves "real and visible selves in America's racist society" by putting "a face and a name" onto a narrative (xx). For example, the *Narrative of the Life of Henry Box Brown* is a perfect example of this kind of "self-creation autobiography" (xx). However, in doing so, Frederick Douglass laments, Brown draws too much attention to himself and "the manner of his escape" and argues that if Brown had not, "we might have had a thousand Box Browns per annum" (as cited in Newman's introduction, xx). In comparison, in an 1868 letter to Harriet Tubman, Douglass applauded Tubman's service to their people, and thanked her for having "labored in a private way" without "the applause of the crowd," noting that her work was "witnessed" only by "the midnight sky and the silent stars" and the "trembling, scarred, and foot-sore bondmen and women" Tubman guided from slavery to freedom (Douglass as cited in Taylor 105). Thus, while Brown was not a good "father" or "brother" to those seeking freedom, Tubman was sister, mother, Moses, angel—all this and more.

Harriet Tubman's more magical and mythical stature made it possible for slaves to dream dreams of freedom, and that divine intervention in the form of a motherly-looking woman could come into their lives at any time. Thus, while current historical studies have shifted their emphasis away from the Underground Railroad, fictionalized accounts of the Underground Railroad and stories about its most famous conductor, Harriet Tubman, still abound in the fiction and poetry of African American writers; Harriet Tubman, unlike Ellen Craft who was overshadowed by a man, or like Henry Box Brown, who seemed more interested in himself, symbolizes the power of the individual to change the course, or in this case, the tracks of history.

For African American writers of the twentieth century, Tubman's appeal, and the appeal of the Underground Railroad, is that both take on an almost supernatural power. Tubman is the archetypal mother, both an avenging spirit and a guardian angel, who can, like the stories of the Underground Railroad itself, appear and disappear at will. Unlike in the stories of Henry Box Brown[3] or Harriet Jacobs, which focus on metaphors and symbols of containment, in the fiction and poetry about Harriet Tubman, quite often the Underground Railroad is often depicted as a *flying* train, and Harriet Tubman is both machine-like in her efficiency and as an "othermother" (a term coined by Stanlie James referring to fictive kin who take over mothering responsibilities and serve as role models for children who are not their own); but Tubman is an "othermother" whose love will kill before it will allow her "children" to remain enslaved.[4] The repeated use of the literary symbol of the flying train, when used in conjunction with the Tubman figure, is an element unique to twentieth-century African American fiction. Presented as both a midwife in terms of her part in aiding a sort of personal rebirth and a mother in terms of her love, she is also presented as someone who can and will kill the children she loves if they do not learn the lessons she teaches.

Though Harriet Tubman is an important archetypal figure, her power in twentieth-century African American fiction comes from her association with the Underground Railroad and the literary symbol of the flying train. As Peter Bruck observes, flying is a common topos in African American folklore and is often used "to convey the notion of escape, freedom, and ultimately, of the at the time socially unattainable" (296–97). In their *Book of Negro Folklore,* Hughes and Bontemps retell the story, allegedly passed down from the days of slavery, in which some Africans are forced into slavery and carried to an island far from their homes by ship. One day, a new captive, an African, is brought to the island to work with the others. He does not speak the white man's language. In brief, what happens is that each time the overseer unfairly beats a person, beats that person so badly it seems as if the person will die, the native African stretches out his arms, speaks to the fallen one, the fallen one repeats his words, and the fallen one leaps into the air "and was gone like a bird, flying over field and wood" (63). Eventually, the overseer realizes what is going on and takes up a fence post with which to beat the native African to death. The native African speaks aloud to "all the Negroes in the field, the new Negroes and the old Negroes. And as he spoke to them they all remembered what they had forgotten, and recalled the power which had once been theirs" (64). At this point, the whole field of slaves rises into the air, one at a time, and, according to the story, flies back to Africa.

Gay Wilentz's research suggests that the flying done by many of the African slaves was a metaphor for suicide. She writes, "Slavers' reports during the height of the slave trade indicated the need for nets to cover the bows of ships because so many slaves committed suicide by jumping overboard" (22). In some versions of the flying African stories, they walk on water until out of sight, and then fly home, which perhaps suggests, that they drown their physical bodies, so that their souls might fly home (29).

Twentieth-century uses of flying trains, however, are slightly different from the flying Africans discussed by Langston Hughes and Arna Bontemps. As Gay Wilentz explains, in twentieth-century African American literature, flying functions as a "collective symbol of resistance by a specific group within a socio-historic context. In this case, flight transcends a particular state of being" (21). Toni Morrison, for example, uses the flying motif in her 1977 *Song of Solomon*.[5] In the twentieth-century flying *train* stories, however, anything resembling suicide is not celebrated, and Africa is not the final destination. Life, not death, is advocated. Instead of flying home on a spiritual or symbolic level, the flying train stories promise to transport the body safely as well, as it is the magic train, not the people that does the flying. The train is often a ghost train or a train flying through the sky toward heaven, but the heaven is not Africa. The only part of the rider that must "die" is his or her old sense of self or self-identity.

This is what separates the flying train stories from the flying African stories. The train is the vehicle that will carry the traveler from the known to the unknown, and to board, one must leave behind one's family, friends, and old identity—who one was—and join with a new group of people whose only connection is their shared commitment to freedom at any cost. At the journey's end there is the promise, and with it, the threat, that the train rider will become a new man or woman, although to do so may mean *leaving* the country of one's birth and heading to Canada, instead of a *return* to an Africa that many had never seen and could not call home. Although freedom is desired, there is still an element of alienation and loss that feels like dying so that the rider might be born again. In these flying train stories, Harriet Tubman's function is thus that of the midwife or the deus ex machina, the human hand of God that guides questing travelers to the train and turns them into riders of the train.

Part of Tubman's appeal in her own time, and which inspires the twentieth-century African American writers who are interested in using her as a character in their stories, was Tubman's own insistence on her connection to the divine. Jean Humez notes that it was Tubman's belief that all her actions were guided by "direct unmediated contact with the divine—both through spontaneous gifts of prophetic foresight and through miraculous protection in response to prayer" that brought her into favor with "other nineteenth-century African American visionaries" (173). As Judith Nies, Otey Scruggs, and Ann Petry all assert, Harriet Tubman was viewed as magical in her own time as well as in twentieth-century African American imaginative literature. Nies calls Tubman a "messenger to the future," who gave life and vitality to "lifeless symbols" (xi–xvi). Scruggs argues that Tubman gave "birth" to a whole tradition of rebellion, a "Tubman Tradition," an "American Epic" to rival that of the "westward moving pioneers" (113). According to Scruggs, Tubman demonstrated that, although something was illegal (escape), it did not mean it was impossible (freedom in Canada). The repetition of her successes filled with hope those who remained behind in captivity, and "each one who heard the stories, each one who told all of them, or only parts of them, would feel stronger because of her existence," (Petry, 129). Stories about her circulated, and each teller embellished on the tale. As Petry explains,

> the slaves said she could see in the dark like a mule, that she could smell danger down the wind like a fox, that she could move through thick underbrush without making a sound, like a field mouse .... she was so strong she could pick up a grown man, sling him over her shoulder and walk with him for miles, that she talked with God, every day, just like Moses .... there was some strange power in her so that no one could die when she was with them. She enveloped the sick and the dying with her strength, sending it from her body to theirs, sustaining them. (129–30)

As with the Underground Railroad, the propaganda surrounding Tubman's activities and powers was, perhaps, even more valuable than her actual achievements for when slaves escaped from the South and headed North, they headed North into the unknown and into obscurity. Going North meant changing one's name, giving up one's family, community, climate, work, in short, one's entire conception of self and whole experience of life. The mental ordeal was, for many, as excruciating as the physical ordeal. Tubman was the model of successful transformation. Though described again and again in every biography as almost machine-like in her efficiency and drivenness, she is the humanizing element of the Underground Railroad. Tubman is, as Albert Murray has argued, an archetype of achievement: "You don't have a better prototype for the self-created American than Harriet Tubman, Frederick Douglass, or Louis Armstrong" (Murray qtd. in Louis Edwards 48).

Faith Ringgold and *Aunt Harriet's Underground Railroad in the Sky*

The use of Harriet Tubman as an archetype and the train as a literary symbol is perhaps clearest in fiction written for children because in children's fiction, the authors usually explain the symbols in a way junior readers can understand. In this respect, the study of children's literature serves as an excellent introduction into the adult fiction that uses the same two icons: the Underground Railroad and Harriet Tubman. While the adult fiction asks the adult reader to follow the writer's train of thought and decode the symbols through inductive reasoning, in the children's fiction, the authors are much more straightforward about what twentieth-century readers can "get" from the fictional uses of the Underground Railroad and Harriet Tubman. As Maria Nikolajeva explains in "Children's Literature as Cultural Code: A Semiotic Approach to History" (1995), children's literature is often very descriptive, and in its description the adult reader can discern the presence of a double code: a children's code and an adult code (39). There is a message for children, but also for the parents of children.

For example, Faith Ringgold's children's book, *Aunt Harriet's Underground Railroad in the Sky* (1992), is not simply another story about the Underground Railroad or a fictionalized biography of Harriet Tubman. As in much of her work, Ringgold uses history in service of her present audiences' needs and, as Dan Cameron notes, uses historic moments that "almost certainly never took place" in order to "supplant a known history with an unsuspected version" and "to provide a psychic guidebook dedicated to the survival of future generations" (11). When adults read Ringgold's book to their children, they do so presumably because they, like Ringgold, believe that there is a need for stories about heroic black women, whether the stories are historically accurate or not. Children read such works of fantasy and because of how the stories are written, combining fact and fantasy in a way that invites children to view themselves as participants in history. They are also invited to "draw their own conclusions, and accept the notion that there can be more than one truth" (Nikolajeva 44). As adult readers read the texts, they begin to see parallels in the real world and "the boundaries between reality and the magic world are dissolved" for the adult reader as well (Nikolajeva 44). Thus, according to Nikolajeva, "the children's code and the adult code change throughout history, converging, diverging, and overlapping at various points" because of "extraliterary phenomena" which are both caused by and causing a "general shift in the typology in culture" (39–43). In other words, children's literature not only shows what adult readers value, it also shows what adult readers wish was true and what they want their children to value and to believe, what Angelita Reyes calls "emotional truth" (77). Children's literature illustrates that what is made up is often more important than what is true, and that a particular perspective on history can be just as important as the facts of what actually happened.

In the specific case of Faith Ringgold's text, in order to understand how Ringgold has used history and imagined history in service of the present, and what she is doing with the literary symbol of the train, for both her adult and young adult readers, it is necessary to know a brief biography of Harriet Tubman and her actual involvement as a conductor for the Underground Railroad. Most biographies of Harriet Tubman are based on the authorized Bradford "autobiographies" of Tubman, which were written at the end of Tubman's lifetime in hopes of providing enough money to maintain Tubman's physical comforts when she was no longer able to care for herself.[6] Dorothy Sterling's biography of Harriet Tubman provides the most compelling narration of Tubman's early life, while M. W. Taylor's biography of Tubman provides the best organized time-line of verifiable adult life-time events. While the biographies vary in terms of what they highlight, they agree on the key events of Tubman's history.

First, biographers find it worth noting that Tubman's parents were full-blooded Ashantis, and part of her mystique is connected to that and the fact that Tubman's bloodline was not diluted by the presence of any white slaver.[7] According to Sterling, the Ashantis were well known among the other African people as fierce warriors. Her mother was a mystic, and her father was a woodsman on a lumber plantation. It is assumed by her biographers that it is from her father that she learned how to read the signs of nature, and from her mother that she gained a sense of personal spiritual authority.

A pivotal event in American history that occurred during Tubman's early life was Nat Turner's revolt in Virginia's Southampton County. Turner, whose father had escaped from slavery and disappeared into the anonymity of the North, escaped from slavery when he was twenty-five (Jordan, Greenblatt, and Bowes 300).[8] Instead of following his father's example, after a month of living in the Virginia woods, Turner voluntarily returned to slavery. He later said that while in the woods, God spoke to him and told him that it was his job to organize a group of slaves in a fight for their freedom (Jordan, Greenblatt, and Bowes 300). For six years after his vision, Turner lived as a slave and secretly preached his gospel of revolt. Although characterized by some as a product of religious dementia, others saw Turner as a Christian warrior and viewed Turner as a "weapon of God" (Sundquist 59).

On February 12, 1831, there was a partial eclipse of the sun, an event which Turner told his followers was a sign from God that it was time to act (Jordan, Greenblatt, and Bowes 300). Six months later, Turner and an army of sixty slaves burned five plantation homes to the ground, killing fifty-five whites before they were captured and later executed. Though unsuccessful, Turner's uprising caused white slave owners to impose new restrictions on their slaves that forbade the congregating of slaves in groups of larger than five and made it illegal for slaves to read, even their Bibles. Dorothy Sterling suggests that this event may have been a pivotal one for Tubman because instead of teaching Tubman that black rebellion was doomed to failure, it taught Tubman that the whites could be made to be afraid.

Tubman was familiar with the story of Nat Turner and also with the story of Tice Daniels, the Kentucky slave whose master allegedly first gave its name to the abolitionist network, blaming them for the disappearance of his "property."[9] In fact, Tubman's own spiritual awakening occurred because of her belief in the Tice Daniels story. While Tubman was working as a field hand on a plantation, she witnessed a slave make a break for freedom. As the overseer ran off in pursuit of the runaway, Tubman followed. She told her biographer, Bradford, that she followed in order to see if the stories about Tice Daniels and the secret underground railroad that would open up when the runaway reached the magic terminus were true. As the runaway, the overseer, and Tubman all converged on a crossroads store, the overseer noticed Tubman for the first time and ordered her to block the door so he could corner the runaway. Instead, Tubman positioned her body in such a way that the runaway could slip by and the overseer could not. Angered, the overseer picked up a two-pound weight and struck her in the forehead. Knocked unconscious, her skull crushed in, she slipped into a coma for six months, deaf and mute to the world around her.

According to what Tubman told Bradford, during her six-month "sleep," Tubman was visited by God, chosen for a special mission, and given the gift of prophecy and sight. Her dreams revealed a host of black men and women, dressed in white, flying among the clouds over a rushing waterfall. That, Tubman knew, was the place she had to go and bring others. Where the weight had crushed her forward, Tubman had a deep, permanent, disfiguring crease in her forehead. She was plagued by sudden, violent headaches. Often, she simply lost consciousness as a result of the pain and slipped back into what looked like deep, sudden, unexpected sleeps. These could occur while she was standing, doing housework such as sweeping, or talking.

What these sleeps sound like is narcolepsy. The American Medical Association describes narcolepsy as a sleep disorder, one that some doctors believe to be an inherited condition while others believe it to be the product of an intense physical trauma to the brain. Narcolepsy usually produces vivid hallucinations in place of actual sleep and can also result in cataplexy, which mimics paralysis but without a loss of consciousness. While today Tubman, no doubt, would have been diagnosed with narcolepsy, in her own time, Tubman and the other slaves viewed her near-death experience and her repeated deathlike sleeps full of religious visions as proof that she was truly touched by God.

Her owner, obviously, had a different opinion and told her that the next time a slave trader came through, he was selling her. According to the Bradford biography, Tubman blurted out something like a prayer that God would see fit to kill her master before he would let her be sold down river. Unexpectedly, her master died. Instantly, Tubman became respected in the slave quarters as the woman who had the ear of God and whose prayers could kill. In the wake of her new status, Tubman married a freedman, one she hoped would work to buy her freedom. Because of her "illness," her price was very low.

Her husband, however, did not want to buy her freedom. He quickly moved into her slave quarters and settled down to a life of dependency. For the next five years they lived together unhappily. Tubman could not seem to become pregnant, and John showed no interest in buying her freedom. In 1849, word came through the grapevine that Tubman and her three brothers were to be sold. Instead of allowing that to happen, the four of them made a pact to escape. According to Bradford, less than one hour from the plantation, her brothers panicked. Though Tubman refused to return, the three brothers dragged her back. Two days later, she escaped on her own. She celebrated her thirtieth birthday alone, but free, in Pennsylvania.

What separates Tubman's story from all the other slave narratives is that instead of disappearing quietly into freedom, as did the majority of fugitives, Tubman joined a select group of primarily male former slaves who rejected the safety of obscurity and went back again and again to the South in order to bring others out to freedom.[10] What she told the other members of the Philadelphia Vigilance Committee was that many slaves lacked the courage to escape because they thought that to do so meant they would never see their loved ones again. Her first three trips back to Maryland were to bring out family members. Her fourth was to contact her husband and bring him to where she now lived. He, however, had married a young slave girl, and had no interest in leaving the comforts of being a freeman married to a slave wife (Sterling 86). Heartbroken but resolved, she returned North with a small group of slaves who wanted to be free.

According to Sterling's biography of Tubman, music served as the medium of communication, and the song about the heavenly chariot was the song Tubman chose to signify the arrival and departure of the Underground Railroad. Tubman would sing:

> When that old chariot comes
> I'm going to leave you.
> I'm bound for the promised land.
> Friends, I'm going to leave you.
> When that old chariot comes,
> Who's going with me? (Sterling 87)

The correct response, to the song was, of course, "When that old chariot comes, I'm going with you" (Sterling 87). Tubman gathered up those who were ready to go, and became, Petry says, "the Moses of her people" (130).

Periodically, on some of her escapes, Taylor reports, Tubman would have "visions." She would go into one of her trance-like sleeps and awake with a change of plan in mind as a result of something she had seen in her vision. In these trying situations, sometimes a runaway would grow rebellious, thinking that perhaps he or she had trusted his or her life to a mad woman. Suspicious, they would start to look for ways to break free on their own, or would ask to be returned to their plantation where they would throw themselves on the mercy of their owner. Tubman did not permit this, for she feared they would reveal the names of the stationmasters. For these times, she had a gun and a brief speech ready. Pointing the gun at the head of the disgruntled traveler, she would say, "Go on with us or die." Every biography of Tubman has a version of this story in it, beginning with the first Bradford biography.

The trip to St. Catherine's, Canada, took a little over a month. Twice a year as a conductor on the Underground Railroad, Tubman made the "run" from Maryland to Canada, now that the Fugitive Slave Law had made the United States an unfriendly place for any escaped slaves. By the mid-1850s, the reward for her capture was up to forty times the average selling price of a full-grown, able-bodied male.

Her heroics continued into the Civil War. Colonel Thomas Wentworth Higginson, Colonel Robert Shaw, and Colonel James Montgomery all used Tubman at one time or another as a scout. In 1863 she worked with Colonel James Montgomery, a man who had fought at the side of John Brown in Kansas and served as his scout behind Confederate lines (Taylor 86). That same year, General David Hunter set Tubman on a mission to take several gunboats up the Combahee River to collect the torpedoes placed there by the Confederate armies. Tubman and the men with her also carried away 756 contraband slaves, many of whom would later be organized by General Rufus Saxfoot into contraband regiments (Taylor 88–91). In addition to her wartime work as a scout, Tubman served as a military nurse and was part of Colonel Robert Gould Shaw's famous 54th Massachusetts base camp, which housed a black infantry regiment led by the 26-year old white Shaw (Taylor 89–90).

After the war, Tubman settled in Auburn, New York, where she struggled to establish a home for indigent African American soldiers and aged African Americans, people who despite the outcome of the Civil War were still not treated with the respect and dignity she felt they had earned. She believed that America had failed to keep the promises made to African American freedom fighters during the Civil War. She also petitioned the United States government for a pension on the basis of her three years of military service. Despite supporting letters from Brigadier-General Rufus Saxton, Colonel James Montgomery, J. K. Barnes, the 1865 Surgeon General, and Senator William H. Seward, the United States government refused her request because, according to their records, women did not serve in a military capacity (Sterling 184–87). They did, however, increase her widow's pension to twenty dollars a month (Sterling 172). She used the money for her home, which she named the John Brown Home, in honor of her former friend, a white abolitionist who believed that slavery's end could only come by blood, and who wanted to put guns into the hands of black men and women and, instead of talking about freedom, fight for freedom side by side.

There is brief mention of a kidnapping story involving Tubman that is not usually mentioned in the children's biographies but is standard in the biographies of Tubman written for adult audiences. As previously stated, Tubman was never able to conceive children. At one point, she became so obsessed with her inability to have a child of her own that in 1855 she abducted her brother's daughter Margaret

(Taylor 67). Unable to continue her freedom journeys with a nine-year-old child to care for, Tubman placed the girl in the care of Frances Seward, the wife of U.S. Senator William H. Seward. Frances Seward raised the little girl. The girl was afraid, but she so loved her Aunt Harriet that she recalls both wanting and not wanting to return to her parents. According to Margaret's daughter, Frances Seward raised Margaret "to speak properly, to read, write, sew, do housework, and act as a lady" (qtd. in Taylor 68). Margaret's daughter believed that Harriet Tubman had stolen the little girl because Tubman saw in her the person "she herself might have been if slavery had been less cruel" (qtd. in Taylor 67). Tubman took the girl from her birth parents, from Tubman's own brother, in order to ensure that the girl would be raised in freedom and protected by the authority and power of a U.S. senator and the former governor of New York. Tubman chose the girl's surrogate parents wisely, for in 1861, Seward became the United States Secretary of State. For Tubman, the loss of the girl's birth parents was a small price to pay for the new life possible for the girl in the Sewards' home. Though the decision should not have been Tubman's to make, it is in keeping with her personality that once she had decided that her plan was best for the girl that it became the only plan possible. Like a train, to which Tubman often compared herself, once on track, there was no turning back.

When she was too old to care for herself or the home she had worked so hard to establish, she deeded the John Brown Home over to the African Methodist Episcopal Zion Church, and it was renamed in her honor as the Harriet Tubman Home. She spent the last years of her life there, dying on March 10, 1913, at the age of 93. At her death, it is said that she asked her friends to join her in a song of prayer, "Swing Low, Sweet Chariot" (Sterling 177). In summing up the impact of her life, Otey Scruggs concludes:

> Harriet Tubman's nearly century-long life consistently personified the quest for human dignity that has been so basic to the national self-image ... At the same time she was growing up in slavery, the defenders of the "peculiar institution" were perfecting the myth of the childlike, improvident Negro who required constant supervision.... She set out to demolish that myth. The result was the rise of a counter-myth: the Harriet Tubman legend. She became transformed into Moses, Joan of Arc, and John Henry—all rolled into one dark body. (120–21)

Alternatively, as Nies says, Harriet Tubman became more than a hero; she became the lens through which people in the twentieth century could look back to the past and make sense of the past, the present, and the future. Her life and history make "personal coherence" possible by giving people a sense that "they are not acting alone, that they were part of a tradition of struggle, and that their acts were not isolated," a necessary perspective as "Tradition provides connections, and connections give courage" (xv).

This is the same point that author Faith Ringgold makes in her children's story about Harriet Tubman and the Underground Railroad, and explains why Ringgold and others use pieces of Tubman's biography in their fictional stories. Ringgold's *Aunt Harriet's Underground Railroad in the Sky* (1992) is set in 1949, just before the celebration of the hundredth anniversary of the Underground Railroad with two children, BeBe and Cassie, "flying among the stars" (1).

While flying among the stars, the two children come across "an old ramshackled train in the sky" (1). A tiny, almost child-sized woman in a train conductor's outfit, Harriet Tubman, invites them to board the train. By understanding the past, she promises them, they will better understand why they are where they are now, and where they must go in the future. The boy, Bebe, readily jumps on board, but the girl, Cassie, is afraid of what she perceives to be a threatening message written in clouds on the side of the train, "GO FREE NORTH OR DIE!" (4). Terrified of both the message and the train, Cassie orders her brother off the train, demanding that they return home this instant to their Mommy and Daddy. However, the train flies away with her brother still on board.

Here BeBe is representative of the "flying Africans," what Langston Hughes called "the People who could fly," and who would "fly anyplace to get away from Jim Crow," flying "over the South only long enough to spread [their] tail feathers and show [their] contempt" (qtd. in Bruck 299). Cassie is more like Milkman Dead in Toni Morrison's novel, *Song of Solomon*, because she is, at first, afraid to fly, and because of her fear, falls out of the sky. She lands back on earth and back in time, and a voice in her head introduces itself as Harriet Tubman:

> I am Harriet Tubman. People call me Aunt Harriet because I take care of them .... Every one hundred years that old train will follow the same route I traveled on the Underground Railroad so that we will never forget the cost of freedom. Sometimes the train is a farmer's wagon. Sometimes it is a hearse covered with flowers—inside a live slave hides in a coffin. You missed this train, Cassie. But you can follow. (11)

The figure of Harriet Tubman is introduced here as a gentle guide figure for those, like Cassie, who are afraid of the past, who wish to ignore recognizing the price one's ancestors paid for freedom, and who must be nurtured into taking any sort of journey toward freedom. Harriet Tubman's voice offers comfort, even as it speaks of coffins.

Cassie lacks faith in the flying train that her brother so readily boarded and therefore cannot understand what the train symbolizes until she experiences, firsthand, what historic event the train commemorates. The train frightens her and is for her an empty symbol until she experiences the actual blood, sweat, and effort, the "cost" or "price" of the journey to freedom. She cannot make the trip until the Underground Railroad becomes humanized for her in the person of Harriet Tubman. Tubman's voice becomes Cassie's gentle guide.

This belief that some people need actually to experience something firsthand in order to garner understanding is a consistent theme in Ringgold's work. In her stories, people must often slip in and out of the past, in and out of geographic locations without border constraints, and in and out of racial identities in order to learn important lessons firsthand. Her Web site asks people to comment, for example, on what they think it would be like, one morning, to wake up black in America, or, for black Web site visitors, to wake up white. In a speech at Sweet Briar College in Virginia, Ringgold explained that for the most part, she thinks that people, both black and white, purposely forget history in order to avoid thinking about certain issues and cautions, "Forgetting is as difficult for some people as remembering is for others"(*http://gos.sbc.edu/r/ringgold.html*). The character Cassie is representative of a type of person Ringgold believes must "rendezvous" with the past. For the Underground Railroad to mean anything to Cassie and for the train in the sky to generate the appropriate feelings of pride in the strength and determination of her people, respect for the sacrifices of those made in the past, and faith in herself rooted in an understanding of her place in the narrative of an understanding of her place in the narrative of African American history, Cassie must make the journey on foot.

While BeBe and the others will cross into Canada by flying over Niagara Falls in the cloud-covered train, Cassie's journey involves learning to read the secret maps encoded in the freedom quilts that hung outside abolitionist supporters' homes, being chased by a slave catcher through a swamp, and hiding in a cemetery until a "railroad agent disguised as a gravedigger" brings her "a ticket for the railroad" (16). The ticket turns out to be a faux pass indicating that her name is Cassie Lightfoot, a Native American last name, and that she was free-born in New York. She then takes a steam car to a shoemaker's home (most likely a reference to Quaker Thomas Garrett), and from there is delivered to a funeral parlor, put into a coffin, and then driven across the bridge into Canada.[11]

Midway across the bridge, Cassie bursts from the coffin, the same coffin that once terrified her but that is now symbolic of her rebirth because she understands exactly what the Underground Railroad was, what it was like for the escaping slaves, and how much the travelers had to want to reach Canada in order to be willing to undergo the hardships and isolation of the journey. As she emerges from the coffin, she finds herself flying parallel to the ramshackle-train-in-the-sky. Beneath them, Niagara Falls "looked like a giant tea party with a billion cups of steaming hot tea being poured to a resounding applause," and the steam from the falls carries her to the place in the clouds where the Underground Railroad has stopped to let its passengers out (20). The tea party references echo other children's stories about the Boston Tea Party and America's own struggles to be free. Ringgold suggests here that this is the African American equivalent of the famous Boston Tea Party. Ringgold's use of this imagery reinforces not only the idea of freedom, but of the right of the African American people to refuse to be slaves, to refuse to stay in a country that allows them no political representation, and lends validation to the actions of those involved with the Underground Railroad.

As the two children are reunited on a cloud under the watchful eye of Harriet Tubman and all the other passengers from the train in the sky, Ringgold has BeBe explain Harriet Tubman's message to his sister, and thus, to the reader. As Cassie begs her brother never to leave her again, he paraphrases what the historic Harriet Tubman told her husband, brothers, mother, and father, and adds a bit of his own new awareness about the importance of history:

> I love you, Cassie, but I had to go. Freedom is more important than just staying together, and what's more, I got to ride on the Underground Railroad with Harriet Tubman. Now I know what our great-great-grandparents survived when they were children. (24)

This is the lesson of the text: that freedom is more important than staying with one's family or original community. There is a sense, in the text, that a love for one's family or original community could hold one hostage, but that a community of like spirits waits if one is bold enough to ride the flying train and pay the price of the ticket for freedom. The price is not in dollars; it comes straight from the human heart. To be free, BeBe is willing to leave his biological sister behind. On the train, he meets a new sister, Freedom, and a new family of choice who share the journey. Auntie Harriet will be his surrogate mother and his new sister, Freedom, is the one that he will nurture and love in place of his biological sister, should Cassie fail to materialize on the other side of Niagara Falls. GO FREE OR DIE is the message of the flying train.

Targeted at children ages six to twelve, this message would, perhaps, be as terrifying to them as it was to Cassie were it not for the fictionalized and much-altered figure of Harriet Tubman. Tiny, like a child, and beautiful, she promises to take care of Cassie and nurtures and guides her progress. She also calls herself Auntie, a term, she tells Cassie, which signifies her function as someone who takes care of people. She lets Cassie know that, even though Cassie has been afraid, Harriet Tubman has not given up on her, and by extension, has not given up on any of the readers who have yet to learn to value what the old train in the sky symbolizes. Although the lesson is a difficult one, the guide toward enlightenment is a loving one.

Ringgold, through the figure of Harriet Tubman and the symbol of the train, provides a tradition and a historical justification for leaving one's community in order to be a part of a greater journey toward freedom that will eventually benefit all people. Instead of choosing physical death, as did the flying Africans, those who ride the Underground Railroad in the Sky, or those who learn what it symbolizes, learn that the correct choice is life, difficult as that may be when it requires that one let go of one's birth community, and become one with a new community with a radical tradition of rebellion. This is a message Ringgold sees as one that still has value for today's black children. In the final illustration in the book, Cassie and BeBe are back home in a 1949 gray, crowded city, dodging wash-lines strung out between tenement buildings, with something that looks like the Brooklyn Bridge in the distant background. There is the suggestion that to truly be free and to become all that they can, Cassie and BeBe must not be afraid to leave this city when the time is right. Being true to one's people means being true to the historic tradition of insisting on freedom; it does not mean staying, forever, in the ghetto.

Ringgold's Tubman asks a lot of her "children." Her representation of Tubman seems in keeping with the historic Tubman's demanding and assertive personality except that the story's Tubman is made into a maternal figure as either an aunt or an older, nurturing woman, what Stanlie James calls an "othermother" (44). Ringgold must play fast and loose with the character of the historic Harriet Tubman to transform her into a member of the family or a loving guide in order to lead young readers to embrace the lessons of Harriet Tubman. Because the lessons are so tough and the Underground Railroad so mysterious, Tubman must come across as familiar, knowable, and gentle. In works for children, the train is the vehicle of transcendence and symbolizes a secret journey to freedom undertaken at great cost, while Harriet Tubman, the ideal conductor, is a maternal figure who will instruct and guide children toward the achievement of a freedom they do not fully understand until after they have journeyed with the Underground Railroad. For some, the journey may result in death, and thus the Tubman figure would be the guide to the afterworld. For others, the journey results in new life in the Promised Land of Freedom, and Tubman the heavenly conductor. However, the message in the text is the same: GO FREE OR DIE. Difficult as the message may be, death, children are taught, is preferable to a life not lived with freedom, but unlike in the flying African stories, death is not the first choice vehicle for freedom.

Leon Forrest's *There Is a Tree More Ancient Than Eden*

Leon Forrest's *There Is a Tree More Ancient Than Eden* (1973 first edition, 1988 revised and expanded edition), an adult novel edited by Toni Morrison and published with an introduction by Ralph Ellison, uses similar literary symbols. When asked by an interviewer if he felt there were specific kinds of imagery that had special meaning in black history and culture, Forrest replied that he was "always trying to bring into my work those images or motifs that seemed to have sustained themselves longest in the culture" (qtd. in Cawelti 150). The train is one of those images. Set in the pre–civil rights movement part of the twentieth century, in Forrest's text, the train is used as a symbol of deliverance, but one which carries one away from all that is known, including one's own former identity. In Forrest's *bildungsroman*, Aunt Harriet is both a nurturing character who replaces the boy's dead mother and the figure who demands that the narrator strive for a very specific type of transcendence, even if it kills him. She is as loving as the Harriet Tubman in the children's books, but she is also more deadly. As Dayle Delancey points out in her article on mothers in the work of Toni Morrison who kill their children, motherlove can be a killer, and the "leitmotif of motherlove as killer" is very much ignored by most scholars because it both "denies and affirms the popular perceptions of motherlove" (15). As Morrison herself says in *Beloved*, "unless carefree, motherlove was a killer" (132). In Forrest's text, there is always a sense that although the father figure is the one who occasionally swaggers and threatens violence, it is the mother figure, his Aunt Harriet, who would, out of her deep love for him, rescue him from death should the occasion arise, but also, like Eva Peace in Morrison's *Sula*, "deliver him to death in order to save him" if the situation called for such an action (Delancey 16). Nathaniel Turner Witherspoon's Aunt Harriet promises him ultimate freedom, but the narrator is uncertain if the track she has placed him on will kill him. Throughout the text, the narrator wonders if the destiny she claims is his will be worth the price she demands that he pay, or if his father's world as the third cook on a luxury train is the real world, representative of the narrator's true fiscal and physical destiny. The aunt represents one life path, the father the other, and the symbol that dominates the narrator's quest for identity is that of a flying black train with a mystery man at the throttle. As a boy, the narrator can not yet discern whether that train is the gospel train of his Aunt Harriet's sermons, or his father's train, the Old Cannonball Express, on which black men may serve as dining car attendants but may never be served drinks in the first-class cars.

Harriet Tubman, we are told in the character descriptions that make up the first chapter, is Aunt Harriet Breedlove Wordlaw's "antecedent," and Tubman symbolizes "honor" (35). The narrator, Nathaniel Turner Witherspoon, sees his Aunt Harriet as a mystical mother-figure sent from God to replace his own dead mother. Aunt Harriet is a religious, oracular woman whose word is, as her name suggests, law. She makes prophecies about Nathaniel's future as God's mouthpiece, and the boy, Nathaniel, feels compelled to try to live up to her expectations, but as a child and privy to all the normal temptations and experiences of childhood, judges himself as incapable of becoming the spiritual being she demands he be.

Nathaniel also feels pressured to fulfill the dreams of his father, a third cook on a luxury passenger train, who tells the boy that it is up to him to make something of the father's branch of the family tree and that he must do so either in the classroom, in politics, or as an athlete. The father rejects God and all things religious after the death of his wife, respects worldly achievement, and measures his son against this standard. He pushes the boy to be smart, ever on the look out for an opportunity for success that will come from being able to read the signs of the time while, at the very same time, his aunt instructs him to look for heavenly signs. The two worldviews collide in the symbol of the train. The novel tells the story of a boy who must choose. Will Nathaniel Witherspoon be the successful man of the world his father wants him to be, or will he transcend the world of man and work for a higher cause, as his aunt demands? Both want Nathaniel to work for the racial uplift of black people, but they differ in how they think that should be done.

The father, for example, wants his son to read the histories of great men as blueprints for success. For the father, these lives are models to study and then emulate, and success means fame. The boy is allowed to pick from an available list of heroes: movie actors, athletes, scholars, men of history. Aunt Harriet selects a different reading list for Nathaniel, a list of Christian martyrs, which includes his dangerous namesake, the black preacher and warrior, Nat Turner.[12] A religious woman, Christ for her is the ultimate hero, and a hero should fully expect and joyfully enter into death if that is what must be. Influenced by both adults, the child thus reads the life of Lincoln as indicative of the fact that Fame, Freedom, and Death are synonymous.

After reading about Lincoln's life, death, and the famous death processional by train, the boy dreams of a Lincoln who looks like "a runaway mulatto castoff," and who is saying, as Jesus did, "This is my Body this is my Blood," as "the train lifting him above the decomposition streaking him homeward, as it vaulted over the harpooning horizon and back back back Lord" (38). Thus, early on in the novel, the train appears as both a symbol and the vehicle of transcendence as it lifts the mulatto-body of the assassinated Abraham Lincoln above the "decomposition." The decomposition refers to the rotting body of the man that was once Lincoln, but also to the rot of post–Civil War America. As the actual funeral train disappears over the horizon line, a second ethereal, spiritual train vaults above the horizon line, carrying Lincoln to the freedom of heaven. The funeral train continues on one track, toward the capital, with the decomposing body. The real Lincoln, his spirit, is carried back to God via this second, more important train. For the boy, being a hero seems to mean dying, as does the achievement of fame and freedom. Fame, Freedom, and Death seem to ride the same train.

In an interview with Maria K. Mootry, Forrest discussed what he called specific patterns in African American literature present in his work. One of the repeated patterns in African American literature utilized in this text is the use of a young character somehow identified as a "chosen one" who was expected by his community to change the course of history. To do so, this chosen one must, according to Forrest, first deal with his "ancestral past," and his "social, spiritual and metaphysical longings are countered by an awareness of the character's lowly social origins, his demanding flesh, and his human epistemology" (150). As part of the pattern, the character's quest for social equality and freedom is at odds with his physical body's needs and fears, and the character must rise above the physical and become metaphysical, even if that rising or transcendence means death. As Leon Forrest pointed out in a December 1994 interview with John Cawelti and ten of Cawelti's graduate students at the University of

Kentucky, in African American literature and culture, there are historical reasons for associating freedom with death (Cawelti Appendix).

Forrest discusses how the deaths of Abraham Lincoln, Martin Luther King, and Malcolm X impact the ways people think about the "consequences of social responsibility" (Forrest qtd. in Calwelti 290). These life stories seem to teach that the price of social activism for the cause of freedom is death. Moreover, as Aunt Harriet makes clear in the text itself, the story of Christ's crucifixion also teaches would-be saviors to expect alienation and death for their efforts. When asked if he believed that the only freedom to be found was in death, as was the case for so many of the famous men and women in his texts, Forrest replied, "I think I have to have faith that I can do things that these eloquent men couldn't do. I have the benefit of history. I have the benefit of other literatures" (290). Forrest's point here is that unlike the characters in his novels, he has read beyond just American history and American literature, and that through his immersion in other traditions, he is aware of other possibilities, at this point in his own life, he possesses a sense of optimism and hope that his young protagonist Nathaniel Turner Witherspoon does not demonstrate in the first version of the novel. Nathaniel seeks death in the first version. It is not until the very end of the revised version of the novel when the character's skill with words becomes his vehicle of transcendence that death is not necessarily the only avenue for freedom.

In both versions, however, the train is a vehicle of transcendence and is associated with being on-track for a heavenly mission. As a boy, Nathaniel often dreams of trains and often associates those trains with heaven, even though he knows his father is but a third cook in a railway dining car. As the boy takes communion, and his aunt places money in the collection plate, money from his father's railroad paycheck, the boy daydreams of streaking trains, headed home to heaven, and worries that he will not be able to go to heaven because he has had sexual thoughts about women that have resulted in the spilling of his seed. At night, these daydreams become nightmares about ghost trains to heaven.

Even though these nighttime dreams are often nightmares, the train is a positive, though dangerous, object. It is positive because it carries Nathaniel to freedom; it is dangerous because he imagines that the rhythm of the train is in sync with blood pumped from a wounded heart. In the nightmare Nathaniel sees

> the liquid train, milk-white . . . moving like the whispered Word; urging my soul back and down through the century's bead-budded grapevine—its vibration and sparks flying towards me, as if the very splitting rail upon which the pale-hooded ghost train (with a deadhead upon its lips) streaked was a rollicking, electrified, blue-jawed harmonica track—ringing the train down down down the improvised, refashioned, blood-bruised tracks—and behind *that*, the soul of a ringing nine-pound hammer still laying more track in the handing distance. (62–63)

In this passage, the liquid train refers both to the child narrator's spilled seed and the ghost train of heaven. Although during the day the boy worried that his sexual sin would bar him from entering the gates of heaven, in his dream, his seed and the "Word" are linked by the word "like." There is the suggestion that God moves through history by being born into the ebb and flow of history through the seed of man. Though the soul longs for heaven, the Word of God urges the soul back down into history, not to punish man, but because the soul of man is needed, the "soul of a ringing nine-pound hammer" (a John Henry reference) is necessary, as part of "laying more track" for all mankind (62–63). The dream is terrifying; the "rollicking, electrified blue-jawed harmonica track" attests to that, as does the "pale-hooded ghost train" and the "blood-bruised track" (62–63). However, the dream also summarizes some of the contributions of African American culture to the building of America: the blues, jazz, improvisation, soul, strength, and the building of the national railroad that linked east with west and, eventually, north with south.

The description of the train as a milk train also attests to a clever bit of wordplay on the part of the author. Milk trains, in railroad lingo, refer to "a mixed train running to the sticks made every stop to serve the hicks. Its cars would pick up cans of milk and even dresses made of silk" (Lund 196). Milk trains were mixed trains, trains that had some refrigerated cars, some baggage cars, some passenger coaches, some mail cars; instead of carrying one kind of cargo quickly from point A to point B, a milk train carried a little bit of everything. The mixed nature of such trains becomes increasingly important as Nathaniel's dream continues.

FLYING TRAINS AND THE "TUBMAN TRADITION" 57

As the boy tosses and turns in his sleep, he finds himself trying to identify the train in his dream. The ghost train solidifies into a train that looks familiar, and the boy wonders if this ghost train is really only his father's train. As the train gathers speed, however, Nathaniel decides the train in his nightmare cannot possibly be his father's train because "Father's train didn't streak like that—and thinking of Father too, I think of how I heard him say, in an aristocratic Southern gentleman's voice: 'And corn whiskey sold in a fruit jar'" (63). Even though the train is moving too fast to be his father's train, suddenly in his dream Nathaniel sees his father there, as a dining car attendant, selling people drinks. All the people on the train are black and all the boys and men from his neighborhood are there. The train has become a luxury train, but one on which black passengers are served alcohol by his father, still dressed like an attendant, and offered their choice of sleeping berths.

One of the passengers on the train is his mixed-race uncle, Jericho Witherspoon, a legally black man with white skin who had disappeared from the family tree and begun passing for white many years earlier. While seated in a comfortable seat, sipping his drink, a voice that the child narrator identifies as Jesus booms out, "Mister Jericho Witherspoon, you ain't passing up there, are you? You ain't gone back to changing your name and pitching your voice and remaking your face, have you?" (66). The suggestion here is that when it was advantageous to be white, Uncle Witherspoon passed for white. Now that it is clear that only African Americans are welcome on the luxury train to heaven, Uncle Witherspoon wants to be black again. The liquid white seed and the white milkiness of the ghost train are acceptable forms of whiteness, but the whiteness of Uncle Witherspoon's face is not because he has used his whiteness as a mask, and he and all the others who had ever "passed" are kicked off the train by the other passengers at the request of the voice of Jesus.

The boy, still a passenger on the train, becomes frightened. He no longer can see his father since the porters and dining car attendants have all disappeared, and all his relatives who passed for white are gone as well. He begins to wonder, "who am I, and where am I going" and asks himself, "what is my name, and who am I?" (68). As the train approaches a transfer juncture, he wonders if he, too, should get off the train and, instead of changing trains, just stay there on the platform. Into his nightmare now comes the figure of Aunt Harriet Breedlove Wordlaw:

> I'll knock you into Thursday 'fore I'll allow you to become a runner for satan against breedlove; because son I know ain't nobody in this world love you more than me. . . . I got that peculiar duty of protecting you and making certain that you are potentially a prophet—not a wishbone—which means that I have to understand that you can also be dangerous, and if you are not smart—or if I am not wise—you could easily be used against us by the enemy. (70)

In this passage, Forrest's Aunt Harriet is very much a Harriet Tubman figure. Aunt Harriet will kill the boy rather than let him live in bondage, or worse, enslave others with his attitudes or actions. She will not permit him to be like his father or his uncle. Her great love is her justification for the threats of violence against his person, and she sees it as her duty to make sure he is not torn apart by wishful thinking like a wishbone; nor will she allow his power to wither as might be suggested by his last name, Witherspoon. She spreads her love over him, but because she loves him, her word is law and he must obey her or die. She promises him ultimate freedom and salvation, as heaven is the train's terminus, but threatens death before failure, a terrifying message for a child.

In the dream, her love chills him but decides his course of action. As the passengers rush forth from one train to make the transfer for the next, he is in the crush of passengers. Suddenly, his secret childhood playmate, Jamestown, appears. Nathaniel and Jamestown were friends, even though Nathaniel's family did not think Jamestown was "good enough" because he was very dark and sold melons and old clothes from a peddler's wagon in order to make enough money to eat. In the dream, Jamestown is dressed in a cowboy suit, like the historic black cowboy, Nat Love, and appears to be the porter of the new train, shouting for them to give him their tickets, waving a sample ticket in the air. Nathaniel looks "frantically for *that* ticket," but cannot find it. He looks in his pockets,

> To search out for this ticket. . . . Lord, no tickets in my pockets, nor pockets in my wings. Only patches like the trap-door pocket of youth. And I reached around again at the tunic-like dress, like that hospital gown. . . . But sometimes I put my money and my tickets in my shoes . . . but I didn't have any

> shoes on; yes and sometimes I put money in my robe, but Lord I didn't have any robe on. But sometimes I put the show tickets in the felt band of my father's old Dobbs hat . . . but Lord I didn't have any hat on, and I felt—crownless, Lord, even as I felt fatherless, but especially motherless. (71–73)

Here Leon Forrest shows plainly the way in which the train is used as both a symbol of freedom and the way to heaven, but also, at this place in the text, reinforces the idea that freedom can only be found in heaven, thus that freedom requires death. The passengers are in hospital gowns with wings. Hospitals are places people go when they are sick or wounded, and the wings indicated that they, perhaps like Jesus, have died from these social wounds. The passengers got wings at the last train change. They could go no further without transferring trains.

Nathaniel has no robe to go over his hospital-like gown and so he feels naked and exposed. Likewise, his feet are bare, and he seems to have lost his shoes—his sole and his soul. He has committed himself to riding this train, exchanged his secular self for a self with wings, but now he cannot find the ticket he needs to ride the train all the way to heaven. The ticket is not in anything his father ever gave him, and the ticket is not where he keeps his money. Unsure of what to do, he feels motherless, fatherless, and crownless. At this moment, he is certain that Aunt Harriet was wrong, and that Jesus had found out that Nathaniel has not done as Jesus would do, and is thus "crownless," and not a candidate for heaven.

In this passage, Forrest captures the tension associated with expectations of greatness and the fears felt by those about to experience a rebirth. Brave stories about journeys and spiritual rebirths or identity quests are usually written by those who have reached the happy ending. What Forrest is trying to capture here, as did Ringgold, is what it feels like to be on that kind of journey before knowing whether or not the story will have a happy ending. Ringgold and Forrest try to capture the true costs of even the initial decision to make the trip on board the soul train or the Underground Railroad in the sky. The physical journey is mirrored by an inward journey of self-discovery that forces the main characters to question all that has formerly been accepted as the "truth" about their ancestors, their roots, their sense of self, and their plans for the future.

Nathaniel feels isolated by the expectations his family places upon him, as well as alienated by the choices other members of his family have made that, on a cosmic level, forever separate them from him. The various trains separate people: father from son, nephew from uncle, mother from child. There is no family travel pack to heaven, and this idea is symbolic of the way things are in Nathaniel's waking life as well. He will have to make difficult choices about how he will or will not carry on the family name, and whether he will or will not turn to religion as the outward expression of the greatness of God, or instead, do as his father wishes, and become famous in his own right. He longs for the freedom to make these choices for himself, but in freedom, finds loneliness and confusion. He does not know which train to take or whether or not he has the price of the ticket. All he knows for sure is that his little wings are not sufficient to fly him to heaven.

As the final boarding for the heaven-train is completed, and Nathaniel finds himself locked out for lack of a ticket, he begins beating on the window, begging the other passengers to let down their windows and let him fly in. Jamestown continues to guard the door, collecting the boarding tickets. As Jamestown prepares to shut the door, Jesus appears to extend his right hand over Jamestown's body, lifts Nathaniel up into the train through a window, saying "Git Aboard," and places Nathaniel beside him at the throttle (73). As Nathaniel looks closer, he realizes that it is Jamestown's hand upon the throttle, and that Jamestown and Jesus are one. Curious, Nathaniel reaches out to touch the wounds on the body that is at once Jesus and Jamestown, and as he does, "light years broke open like stars," and he awakens to find himself seated in church beside his Aunt Harriet.

At this point in the novel, Forrest chooses to make the connection between the narrator's Aunt Harriet and Harriet Tubman even clearer, by redescribing Aunt Harriet in terms commonly used to describe Harriet Tubman. The purpose of doing so is to lend support to the idea that the aunt will, no matter how much she loves him, kill the child rather than let him live a cowardly life in service of the things that seek to enslave him. Old stories about Harriet Tubman make the same sorts of claims. Allegedly, she carried a gun not for use on slave catchers, though no doubt she would have used it on them if the situation called for it, but to use on the people she was leading to freedom. No one was allowed to turn back, once beginning the journey to freedom with Harriet Tubman by their side. Once that individual had dared to make that first initial step toward freedom, she would not permit them to return to the life of a slave as this compromised the safety of the group and future missions. To begin an escape was to die free, either during the journey itself, or at the end of a new life, often with a new husband or wife, and new family of children, in Canada.

Forrest has Nathaniel Witherspoon describe his Aunt Harriet with the same traits commonly associated with Harriet Tubman, a woman known as the Moses of her people, and famous for her masculine strength, her military mind, her love of children, and yet her own infertility, which caused her to view all children as her children. Forrest writes:

> The black Madonna called Moses with a man's shoes, laceless upon her feet, her mother rage and coming glory, the feverish perspiration raining down exhausted into her huge river-pouting mouth, stealing away from her woolly-headed scalp down down down into her glowing . . . as if to issue forth yet another starving life into an unclean world—bruised-blood breasts, like a moody restless river, terrible and beloved . . . and in the muted distant howl of the bloodhounds her saying: *if I dies 'fore I wake I pray this baby's soul to take.* (84)

The trains associated with his aunt lead to heaven, but at great cost. He cannot find his mother in heaven, and his father and uncle are not permitted to even try to make the journey. All those his father's family has tried to teach him to look down on are those who are closest to Jesus. Beside him, his aunt is transformed into a second Harriet Tubman, a mother figure who will love him fiercely, and who will kill him rather than see him fail. The suggestion here is that at his current age, the aunt does not trust him to pick the right path, and should she die in the night, she prays that God will kill him too. Like Sethe in Toni Morrison's *Beloved*, this Harriet Tubman figure would rather kill her children than let them live, unprotected by the powers of mystical-mother-love, in, as his Aunt Harriet puts it, an "unclean world" (84).

Religion has not made Nathaniel's Aunt Harriet soft. Moreover, as much as he loves her, in his teen years he finds himself turning away from her because her religious faith is so powerful that it seems dangerous. The strength of her love, that she could kill him as an act of love, makes him feel that he would never wish to love that much. Similarly, in his teenage years, he rejects Jamestown's commitment to The Brotherhood, a militant black organization that, though different from his Aunt Harriet's beliefs, mirrors her in intensity. As Nathaniel grows to manhood amidst a minefield of black lynchings and the sordid deaths of his friends both in war and at home, he avoids becoming one of the dead because of his aunt. However, on the eve of her death, he must finally decide what kind of man he is and what "track" he will take. On her deathbed, she tells him, "you got the ticket to get on home now to be a man and behold yourself and lead us forward and remake the world for us in this dungeon" (91). Her deathbed, symbolically, is also a birthing bed, for she is telling Nathaniel that he is now born a man and must make his way without her. He thinks back on his childhood and sees it as one might see the scene from a train window: family members, scam artists, black Muslims, drunks, Uncle Toms, soldiers, jazz musicians, preachers. As in his dream, he must decide whether to make the transfer; which ticket will he pay for? Which train will he ride? It is at this point the two versions of *There Is a Tree More Ancient Than Eden* diverge.

The 1973 edition ends with the narrator's acknowledgment that "the prayers of both could not possibly become realities" (106). By both, the narrator means the desires of his Aunt Harriet and those of his father. The first edition ends with the retelling of the crucifixion of Christ combined with the ramblings of Shakespeare's Hamlet. Following the death of his aunt, the narrator wants to die for the sins of the world, like Christ, and yet, like Hamlet, also avenge the wrongs and indignities suffered by his father, the third cook in the train dining car. He thinks seriously about being born again as "X," motherless, fatherless, and remade new, but ultimately does not see how that would help him or anyone else escape the legacy of slavery. "How could I change my name before I perceived an answer," the narrator speculates, "I couldn't change my name back to that first, not knowing upon which continent did it / I did spring" (154). Looking at his own skin, skin that indicates a mixed bloodline, Nathaniel realizes that his soul is anchored in the side effects of America's particular history. He cannot be born again in the Lord or Islam or anything else because anchored as he is to the side effects of a marginalized history, he has no "face, love, center, flight, duty, honor, freedom, intra-love, juices of body-loins, sex, salvation, redemption, mother, father, eyes eyes eyes, soul soul soul: just that self, which was a crucifying and an arc without true representation" (159). Standing naked before a mirror, he takes a switchblade to himself and guts himself, carving out the place where his womb would be, and crumples to the floor as a result of his own symbolic and yet deadly Caesarian rebirth. In 1973, to Leon Forrest, this seemed the likely culmination of Nathaniel's life journey: a self-administered C-section resulting in death.

The ending of the expanded and revised 1988 edition is much different. In the 1988 edition the narrator survives this attack on himself, and this simply becomes another episode in his journey toward an authentic freedom. According to Kenneth W. Warren, this added-on section of the novel, titled *Transformation*, makes

> the novel itself into an object lesson in thinking beyond catastrophe, a discussion of what to do when "the worst" has come to pass . . . . As regards the novel as a whole, however, the "worst" is nothing less than history itself. And the process of thinking beyond catastrophe might be described as thinking simultaneously both through and against history. (410)

In the second version, instead of dying, at thirty, the same age at which the historic Tubman made her escape, the narrator goes off to college to become a writer. He attends rallies, listens to speeches, and writes them down like a reporter, including one made by an ancient little shriveled woman who had been born a slave, and Nathaniel continues, through writing, to try to fit all his life experiences, and all the people he has ever known into some system of thought that leads to a comprehensible final destination.

The 1988 edition ends with Nathaniel in a bar on the night of the twelfth anniversary of Martin Luther King's death. The people in the bar are of two minds; they cannot decide whether to celebrate King's life and accomplishments or to give into their anger over the unfairness and hate that caused his death. A preacher in the bar captures Nathaniel's predicament when he says to them all, "Thank God Almighty I am free at last, but free to uncover what freedom? Is paradise without politics? What is that Yonder? What unshrouded, unsheathed chariot is that Yonder?" (214).

Kenneth W. Warren reads this as a potentially negative final scene and compares it to the movies Nathaniel used to watch as a ten-year-old boy. Warren uses a movie analogy to explain his reading of the end of the novel. Viewed "cinemagraphically," Warren argues, the final scene of the novel resembles a movie set where

> the scaffolding and set remain intransigently visible as if we had come upon a project abandoned part way through because of tragedy or bankruptcy. One can wander about, looking for clues and guideposts as to the "original" plan, but the best one can do is construct possibilities that remain unverifiable. The feature film was never shot. (418)

While Warren's reading of the ending of the book is interesting, references to movies appear only in the first chapter of the novel, and then only on one page of the novel. Leon Forrest is not James Baldwin, and does not share Baldwin's interest in movies as a metaphor. The guiding metaphor of Forrest's text, more prevalent in the text than even the tree, which appears in the title of the novel to express the ancient roots of the "family" of man, is the train. In this final scene there is no mention of movies. There is, however, a train reference, an "unshrouded, unsheathed chariot" in the distance (214).

The word "chariot," as Lucius Beebe (1938) records in the appendix of railroad terms to his study of trains, *High Iron*, in railroad language means "caboose" (219). The "chariot" of the train is the last car in the train, and yet, this is the most desirable position as it is the furthest from the soot and noise of the engine. Unexpected train-riding dignitaries often rode in the caboose. The caboose or chariot was also called the angel seat. Herbert Lund records that this angel seat "was the domain of the train conductor. . . . from the cupola on top, he could see for miles in all directions and spot fires both on and off the train" (4). In train lingo as in the Bible, the prevailing sentiment is often that the last shall come first; in the case of the train caboose, its position as being last in place is misleading. The engines are considered "leashed," the mechanized animal that pulls the train. The caboose, or as railroad people put it, the "chariot" or the "angel seat," gives one a perspective of one's journey that even the engine lacks.

As the preacher is talking about the "unshrouded, unsheathed, chariot," in Nathaniel's mind he sees a foundling child, reaching out to lift a shroud, a shroud that, one suspects, covers the "chariot," mentioned in the preacher's final words. In Nathaniel's mind, the child is willing to board that chariot and take that ghostly ride. In the words of Frank Herbert in *Dune,* "the sleeper has awakened." Members of a new generation are ready to ride the old train, and take their place in the sweet chariot, the angel seat. The standard interpretation of the old gospel song, "Swing Low, Sweet Chariot," the song Harriet Tubman requested be sung on her deathbed, is not negative. Instead of a negative ending, as Warren suggests, reading the text in light of the train symbolism, the ending of Forrest's expanded edition is hopeful. The lyrics of the song have the "old chariot" bringing the passenger "home." Warren's misreading of the end as negative emphasizes the need for critics to understand not only the history of the African American experience, but also the specialized symbols, such as the train. Instead of trying to fit Forrest's novel into the current vogue for cinematographic studies, the novel needs to be read with an understanding of the powerful symbols in African American literature, and the flying train associated with Harriet Tubman is perhaps one of the most powerful.

In the first version of the text, published only five years after the death of Martin Luther King, it seems that freedom could only be found in death. The narrator could not reconcile the Hamlet-esque promptings of his father's spirit with the demand for freedom through spiritual rebirth insisted upon by his aunt, and guts himself. The train makes its last appearance in his childhood dreams and disappears. In the expanded and revised version of the text, published in 1988, other options remain to be discovered in the mysterious "yonder," final destination unknown, and the train remains a positive symbol, though shrouded in danger and uncertainty. Not only has Forrest's narrator learned to think beyond catastrophe, as Warren suggests, but he has also learned that after the thinking comes action. This is illustrated by the final image of the novel with the foundling child lifting the shroud. As his Aunt Harriet prophesized, he will not be a "runner for Satan." Instead, precisely because his Aunt Harriet taught him how to stand alone while simultaneously standing up for what is best for the collective black community, he will be the motherless, fatherless child that drives train-America into the future.

Robert Hayden's "Runagate Runagate"

Robert Hayden's 1962 poem "Runagate Runagate" also uses the Harriet Tubman figure as a guide and the literary symbol of the train in order to comment on black history and the continued need for remembering black history. What separates this poem from the texts already discussed is that this is a text without children in it, and there is the suggestion that adults, not just children, must learn and know their history. In his poem, Hayden reveals that it is through the remembering and celebration of black history that people can summon the power and commitment necessary to continue the fight to be free. In this haunting poem, Tubman and the train are depicted as supernatural forces that work within history and throughout history, like the Jewish concept of the golem, and that can be called upon again in times of need.[13] Tubman is depicted as being like a train, and once she has begun a journey to freedom, nothing can derail her, not the slave catchers and not the fears of those traveling with her. There is also the suggestion that racial uplift is like this as well. Once begun, there is no turning back.

Hayden's poem begins in the same way as a dramatist might stage the directions for a play. Hayden uses third-person singular, active verbs which situate the reader in the midst of a slave's flight to freedom. A montage of voices makes up the next sections of the poem. There is an excerpt from a wanted poster regarding the rewards available for information leading to the capture and return of two escaped slaves. The voice of a slave catcher interjects here with a warning that all too often, the slaves seem to disappear under ground.

Here Hayden is making use of the previously discussed Tice Daniels legend surrounding the naming of the Underground Railroad. In brief, in 1831, a fugitive slave, Tice Daniels, swam across the Ohio River with his Kentucky master and a posse of slave hunters in pursuit. Siebert writes that once on shore, Daniels's former master could not find him:

> No one had seen him; and after a long . . . search the disappointed slavemaster went into Ripley, and when inquired as to what had become of his slave, said he thought "the nigger must have gone off on an underground road." The story was repeated with a good deal of amusement, and this in-

cident gave the name to the line. First the Underground Road, afterwards Underground Railroad. (45)

The slave catcher's expression "underground road" appears in Hayden's poem. The use of the legend in the poem lends an air of veracity to both the legend and the poem. Legends, Angela Yannicopoulou tells us, work because legends are "collective creations" and thus have a "claim to authority" because of their "factual foundations" (26). Imbedded in the core of the story are historical facts, and because the collective recognizes these facts as true, the "fictitious innovations" resonate with the feeling of veracity as well (26). The legend seems even more real because it is repeated again and again. Whether or not the Tice Daniels story was a fact, or merely a legend, it becomes a component of actual cultural history through repetition and lends authority to Hayden's poem.

The image of darting underground also carries with it a sense of mythology. There is a perception of this place underground as a dark and dangerous place full of mazes and quicksand; dangerous, and yet this Hades is still preferable to living the life of a slave. The "underground road" of Hayden's poem refers to the Underground Railroad, but it is also the world of the dead, where things that are prematurely buried or wrongfully repressed rarely stay laid to rest.[14] In part two of the poem, rising from the ground itself is Harriet Tubman. She is described by Hayden as both a woman "of earth" and "a summoning, a shining" (130). A once ordinary woman, a tiller of the earth, now filled with supernatural powers, Tubman is summoned or called into being and becomes a shining, which means a spirit with a mission to protect or destroy as needed. In Hayden's poem, Harriet Tubman is summoned back up into existence to bring a lost people to freedom. Once summoned into existence, like the golem Jewish mystics summoned from mud or clay and set forth on a righteous mission and were then unable to recall until the mission was complete, Harriet Tubman, once summoned, once a shining, cannot be called off or back.

She will be free and lead her people to freedom, even if they lose faith in the process. The next section of the poem retells one of the most compelling legends about Harriet Tubman. As Hayden makes clear in his poem, although the escaping slaves are afraid of getting caught by the white slavers who will send them home in chains, they are even more afraid of the black woman with the gun who has promised them new life in the free land of Canada, or death, but she will not let them let themselves be taken back in chains or "jay-bird talk," referring to the unpleasant sounds blue-jays make when they sing. The suggestion here is that if captured, the fugitives will "sing" or tell all, but that it will be the unpleasant sound of the fugitives selling out their own people, and she will see them dead before she permits such dangerous tattling (130). She will make men out of the men who have forgotten their manhood, and the women will follow in her footsteps or die, willing or not.

The appeal of this part of Tubman's story, particularly as Hayden presents it, is that Tubman's unusual behavior makes her seem like a divine instrument, truly the hand of God come to correct and to guide a people who are lost, so lost, that they have forgotten themselves, their dreams, their hopes, their intrinsic right to freedom.[15] Hayden captures the voice of Tubman-the-mother-figure as she says, "Hush that now," the voice coming from the very same woman who levels a pistol at their heads. It is this contradiction that makes her seem filled with a spirit or a force larger than herself. She is a mother-figure who so deeply and profoundly loves her children, that she will kill them and free their spirits if she cannot succeed in freeing their bodies.[16] Tubman is the arm or extension of a one-track collective mind, a mind that means to be free. Slowly, the group moves on through the night, single-file, like cars behind an engine, with Tubman in the lead.

This section of the poem is followed by an excerpt from another wanted poster, offering a large reward for Tubman, dead or alive, and cautioning slave catchers that she is both armed and dangerous (130). As Fred Fetrow notes in his article, "Portraits and Personae: Characterization in the Poetry of Robert Hayden," these excerpts "lend authenticity to the portrait" of Tubman and "the epithets and aliases by which Tubman was known characterize her place in history" (51). Fetrow suggests that, although Hayden "admired the selfless sacrifice and heroic deeds" associated with Tubman, Hayden's Tubman "transcended" her "individuality" (51).

The disembodied voice of Harriet Tubman fills the "ghosted air" and calls upon the other "hants" (130–31). These "hants" are most likely very similar to the "haints" Ishmael Reed speaks of in *Mumbo Jumbo*, when he speaks of the whites who refer to all that they do as "destiny" or "progress," to which Reed's narrator replies, "Progress. We call it Haints. Haints of their victims rising from the soil of Africa, South America, Asias..." (qtd. in Snead 64). Hayden's Tubman transcends the ordinary and invites others to do so by repeatedly calling for her listeners to come and ride what she calls her train. Repetition, James Snead argues, is "in some senses, the principle of organization" in black literature and music, revealing, as it does "the thing that is there to be picked up" (68). Repetition becomes, in Snead's words, "a remedy for the failure of memory" which bridges "ruptures" and can "smooth forward" in "the insistently forward motion of time on those occasions when, Snead continues, quoting Tom Stoppard's play about Henry Carr, history, "like a toy train ... jumps the rails and has to be restarted at the point where it goes wild" (74). Again and again, Hayden comes back to Tubman's suggestion that to be a car in the flying freedom train is the greatest glory possible. Slavery is far more dehumanizing than becoming part of an analogy or metaphor in which one is a railroad car coupled with the freedom train. It is better to be a car in this train than a slave.

This train, she tells us, is no ordinary train, and Hayden reinforces that with his use of italics for the entire final stanza of the poem in which he defines the train as an ever-moving *"ghost-story"* train (131, original emphasis). Ghost stories are often terrifying but can also be instructive. Ghosts, according to those who believe in them, do not rest when, like Hamlet's father, they seek revenge or like the main character, Jimmy Bones, played by rap singer-turned-actor Snoop Dogg, and black actress Pam Grier, in Ernest Dickerson's supernatural thriller movie *Bones*, they have unfinished business to attend to before they can be at peace. Harriet Tubman's train is this ghost-story train, and the train will keep running until the need for running is over. However, this running is not a running from; it is a running to. The train runs through the swamps and savannas of Southern history, and over trestles and through "the caves of the wish," referring both to the archetypal notion of the cave as womb and to the Platonic pursuit of the ideal. The name Midnight Special refers to both the color of the engine and its connection to the bewitching hour of midnight. To travel this track requires a special kind of strength to reach the final destination. The first stop is Mercy, where riders experience the sensation of compassion for those who have been in the wrong, and the last stop Hallelujah, the Hebrew word for God-induced-joy that has no direct translation in English and instead requires a phrase such as "praise the Lord." When the ghost-train is no longer needed, when the need for revenge is over, and all the business left undone is complete, Hallelujah awaits for the people who have become the train.

The poem ends with Tubman's call, again, to the reader to come ride her train, and there is no end punctuation. Instead, the poem ends with the word "free" (131). Here, Hayden is suggesting that the Midnight Special, the ghost-story train on the sabre-track, will repeat the journey and continue to ride, each night, until the people who still have need of what Harriet Tubman represents are free. Though this freedom is desired, it is also dangerous because the push for freedom will push the individual into what Fetrow calls a "collective racial or human mass identity" (51).

As Mark Sanders suggests, it is not Harriet Tubman who becomes the key literary symbol of the poem; it is the train. The train as symbol reasserts "perpetual agitation through the historical specificity of the Underground Railroad," and the final line of the poem "condenses and transforms the competing voices into a singular voice and impulse ultimately transcendent of its own immediate circumstances" (638). As in Faith Ringgold's text, in Hayden's poem, loss of individuality, or rather, the loss of individual identity in order to gain a larger sense of the range of the continuum of a shared destiny is, in this case, the price of the ticket.

Nikki Giovanni's "One More Boxcar"

In Nikki Giovanni's poem, "One More Boxcar" (1999), the depersonalization is even more complete. The genderless voice in the poem is that of a fugitive who sees him or herself as "one more boxcar," inching along, totally focused on inching his or her way toward freedom. In this poem, which is dedicated to the Underground Railroad as if it were, itself, a person, one gets a sense that the individual runaways themselves become their own vehicles of escape. Each slave becomes a boxcar, and each boxcar a part of a huge line of individual cars all coupled together by the same desire, and yet all separate, all isolated, moving single-file instead of side by side, in an endless train of people dedicated to finding freedom. Ekaterini Georgoudaki theorizes that Giovanni does this in her poems in order to break free of "the negative stereotypes (domineering matriarch, Amazon, castrator of the black man) which prevailed in the USA from the days of slavery times" (70). Georgoudaki suggests that Giovanni's intention is to raise her reader's "race consciousness, pride, and solidarity, and to enhance their sense of historical continuity" and that to do this, Giovanni must downplay the importance of female gender. A man, too, would thus be able to be "in leading positions in both the biological and the societal black family" and possess a "sense of responsibility, love of freedom, love of family and other virtues" usually associated with strong black women (70).

The slave in the poem, assuming the slave is a woman, must learn this for herself. When she first escapes, she must overcome concrete obstacles as part of the running away process. She accomplishes this objective on her own. When night falls, the runaway keeps hoping that she will be able to spot the lights of the freedom train and hopes that the conductor will stop or that the ground itself will simply open up, and the runaway will find herself safely on board an underground train. When none of these things happen, however, the runaway slave keeps "on inching . . . inching along . . . one more boxcar . . . inching along" (24). Giovanni uses the ellipses here to suggest all the things that are happening to the slave while she is making a run for freedom. They also suggest the head-down, forward-thrusting progress of the slave as the slave pushes on, no matter how difficult or how slow the journey.

The escaping slave herself becomes the above-ground, visible manifestation of the strength and power of the idea at the root of what is called the Underground Railroad. The real Underground Railroad, the poem suggests, was composed of the individuals who never actually boarded a train, received no help, and made the journey alone, inch by inch. History and heroism, Giovanni suggests, is written not in milestones but in inches. The slow, individual creep toward freedom becomes a massive force to be remembered when all the inches are measured up in miles.

Giovanni's historical fiction of the Underground Railroad also reveals an imagined emotional terrain, the immediacy of which can only be experienced by the act of reading her poetry. What she imagines, and asks us to imagine with her, is what it really felt like to be an anonymous part of what is now the most famous and celebrated icon of nineteenth-century African American history, the Underground Railroad. Her suggestion is that the Underground Railroad did not come to the rescue of the anonymous escaping slaves. Instead, they, as did William and Ellen Craft, with their own bodies become their own vehicles of salvation and it is they, not the name, that should be remembered and celebrated.[17]

Giovanni herself was a former undergraduate history major. As Judith Pinkerton Josephson reports, the same year that Dr. Martin Luther King won the Nobel Peace Prize and President Lyndon Johnson signed the Civil Rights Act, Giovanni returned to Fisk University to complete her undergraduate degree with a major in history, and worked as an assistant to Black Arts Movement writer John O. Killens (Josephson 38). In interviews, Giovanni has said that "the role of the writer is very much like that of the historian" (Elder 71). She clarifies that, however, by saying that what the writer does is superior to that of the historian or the philosopher. The historian, she says, "Says 'A is A.' We are not Ayn Rand either. We're sitting there saying, 'I saw this through my eyes'" (71). By this, Giovanni means that the writer, unlike the historian or philosopher, places the reader in the living moment. The reader is invited to experience the event and to become, in this case, "one more boxcar" in the freedom train. This allows the reader to imaginatively feel the fact firsthand. As Arlene Elder puts it, Giovanni "communicates the meaning of some chaotic or historical circumstance" and as a result of reading it, people understand "the meaning of what has happened" and "understand a little bit more about what is going to take place next" (71).

What is troubling about Giovanni's poem, as in Hayden's poem, is the linguistic act of equating people with machines. As Mark Seltzer has pointed out in his essay, "Statistical Persons," there are dangers to "this body-machine complex," and there are strengths (84). When people begin to imagine themselves as machines, no matter how powerful or potent a symbol that machine may be, there is the danger that they may then behave in a way that is inhumane. The danger, identified by Seltzer, is that "automatisms. . . . threaten to erode or undo character and agency" (89). However, Seltzer suggests, there are also positive consequences of equating man with machines. Typical ordi-

FLYING TRAINS AND THE "TUBMAN TRADITION"   73

ordinary persons can "transcend" their ordinariness by becoming the "embodiment and personification" of the power produced by the machine with which they are associated (97).[18] Furthermore, if a person has the choice of being equated with a beast of burden or with the single most important force that reshaped the social and economic life of nineteenth-century America, to be equated with the train seems a logical choice.

The Tubman Tradition and the Train

Despite concerns about the equating of bodies with machines, for twentieth-century African American writers looking back at the nineteenth century for inspiration, the Underground Railroad seems a clear symbol of a people's willingness to fight against the status quo when the status quo is wrong, and the hazard-ridden journey toward the achievement of freedom. That fight and that insistence can be driven underground, but, as the symbol of the Underground Railroad promises, it can never be destroyed. The twentieth-century emphasis on the train's ability to fly is evidence of that.

Twentieth-century African American writers who use the Underground Railroad as a literary symbol also emphasize that while the train itself is filled with like-minded passengers, the decision to begin the journey toward freedom and to board the train is always highly individual. To board, one must be willing to leave behind one's family, friends, and old identity—who one was. At the journey's end there is the promise, and with it, the threat, that the train rider will become a new man or woman. Although freedom is desired, there is still an element of alienation and loss that feels like dying, a necessary death so that the rider might be born again. Harriet Tubman's function is thus that of the midwife or the deus ex machina, the human hand of God that guides questing travelers to the train and turns them into riders of the train, a train bound for glory.

☥ CHAPTER THREE

Black Supermen and the "John Henry Tradition"

> The race which first learns to balance equally the intellectual and the emotional—to use the machines and couple them with a life of true intuition and feeling such as the Easterns know—will produce supermen.
> —*Paul Robeson, quoted in the London Daily Herald, 1935.*

> Every white man I've known has wanted me to join his basketball team, softball league or book discussion group. They invite me on week-long, fly-fishing trips to Montana. One day I might say yes. They think they admire my superb athletic skills and my broad education, but it's nothing more than my color. I am The Black Man the whole world mythologizes and envies.
> —*"Autobiography of a Black Man," (1999) by Raymond Patterson*

> John Henry's life was about power—the individual, raw strength that no system could take from a man— and about weakness—the societal position in which he was thrust. To the thousands of railroad hands, he was an inspiration and an example, a man just like they who worked in a deplorable, unforgiving atmosphere but managed to make his mark.
> — *"The John Henry Steel Driving Man Project: The Man, Facts, Fiction, and Themes," (2002) at the University of North Carolina at Chapel Hill, by Carlene Hempel, Deb Procopio, Dan Shaver, and Beth Novak.*

Perhaps the most famous figure ever to do battle with "the machine" is the legendary John Henry. As Gale Patricia Jackson notes, "John Henry is about the railroad as a symbol: one 'track' of American entrance into a 'free' and industrializing America" (62). Furthermore, despite the attempts of mainstream culture to control the representation of black men in general and John Henry in specific, "John Henry is about the black male contest for human recognition and a truly radical proposal for social reconstruction" (62).

The representation and "ownership" of John Henry has always been hotly contested and continues to be, even though a full century has passed since the day John Henry "took on" the machine. Take for example, the controversy surrounding the United States Postal Service and its 1996 commemoration of John Henry. David La Fleur, the Kansas artist selected to design the John Henry stamp is best known, according the Smithsonian National Postal Museum, as a designer of "posters, billboards, packaging, menus, annual reports, calendars, apparel, CD covers, shopping bags, murals, and greeting cards," which "have been commissioned by an impressive client list that includes Milton Bradley, Federal Express, Starbucks, Heinz, and General Motors" (para. 1). While pleased that a black American was selected to be honored with a stamp, the categorization of John Henry as simply a fictional "folk legend" bothers those who, like Jackson, see John Henry as a historical reality inspiring myth, and not a myth that became a part of history, and certainly not an icon to be packaged by a Kansas designer of shopping bags and menu cards regularly commissioned by Milton Bradley, Starbucks, and Heinz.

In effect, while on the one hand celebrating the legendary John Henry, the stamp also commodifies him while at the same time "marketing" him as a "fantasy figure" right alongside the other fictional characters in the series: Paul Bunyan and his big blue ox Babe, Mighty Casey, a completely fictional creation from the mind of Ernest L. Thayer, a Harvard crony of William Randolph Hearst, who worked for Hearst; and Pecos Bill, a cowboy Hercules who allegedly rode a mountain lion instead of a horse and carried a whip, made out of a live rattlesnake, and single-handedly created Death Valley and Puget Sound in addition to other notable western landscapes. Instead of placing the John Henry stamp alongside portraits of other American heroes, the stamp was released as part of the fantasy four-pack placing John Henry's hammer in the folklore context of a big blue ox, a batter who forever strikes out, and a cowboy who allegedly drained the Rio Grande in the process of watering his own property.[1] The cartoon nature of the other three stamps diminishes the impact of the John Henry stamp. Additionally, even the release location for the stamp turned into a battle for ownership of the legend. Originally, Pittsburgh, a steel town, was picked to be the site of the "John Henry Steel Driving Man" stamp's unveiling, but the people of Talcott, West Virigina, argued that they had better claim to that honor because they were the "home of the John Henry legend."[2] According to Gina Allison, who, with a grant from the National Endowment for the Arts, came to Talcott during the controversy over who would have the honor of the stamp's unveiling to produce "a portrait of the John Henry legend and the remote community that lives in its shadow" for National Public Radio, Talcott was little more than

> a typical southern farming town, with a history of economic difficulty and racial segregation. The railroad used to be the major employer here, but since labor has become increasingly automated over the past few decades, unemployment is high while morale and opportunities are low. There are two Baptist churches, one white and one black. Most black residents now live up the hill in a section of town called "Pie Holler." Racial conflict doesn't tend to be overt but there's little socializing between the races. This is the context from which John Henry emerged, a hero to black and white alike."[3]

Ultimately, Pittsburgh was dropped as a contender for the honor, and in 1996, Talcott, West Virginia, the new home of the now annual summer "John Henry Festival Days" complete with fair midway and railroad museum gift shop, where statuettes of John Henry in various sizes are on sale at various prices—some statuettes going for less than five dollars—collared the right to be the location of the stamp's unveiling.

Published two years after this media event, in his article, "John Henry: Then and Now" (1998), W. Nikola-Lisa examines eight different versions of the John Henry legend, spread over thirty years, versions composed by men and women, black and white, and versions written to accompany children's picture books in order to trace John Henry's transformation in word and pictures from "the personification of the medieval Everyman who struggles against insurmountable odds and wins" as he was portrayed in the 1960s, to John Henry's stature in the 1990s as a race man and a specifically black cultural hero, a "free self-determined man" who "is exercising his political will" and whose story is about "the struggle to save man's soul—the black man's soul—in the face of three centuries of white oppression" (54–55). Concerned with reclaiming John Henry as a hero for the black community, Nikola-Lisa argues that what positions a portrayal of John Henry firmly within the black community is a rejection of the Everyman versus the Machine motif, a story which centers on a nation coming of age, and instead, a recognition that the history of slavery and racism is a significant part of all black male coming-of-age stories such as John Henry's (56).[4] Nikola-Lisa asserts that through a chronological examination of the evolution of the John Henry stories, one can read the story of the African American community's struggle to define black manhood against a backdrop of white racism, and concludes that the battle over John Henry has been won and that John Henry is no longer viewed as a race-neutral Everyman.

However, as the events of the 1996 John Henry stamp's unveiling reveal, unfortunately that is not the case. As scholars from a wide range of disciplines continue to focus on the "problem" of black masculinity, it has become increasingly important to look at the literary portrayal of figures such as John Henry as a way of tracking these changing representations of, to use Du Bois's terms, what it feels like "to be a problem" and how white America attempts to "deal" with the "problem" of black masculinity (43).[5] In this case, the problem is that black manhood is still under assault, even when an organization such as the United States Post Office attempts to be racially sensitive and politically correct. Although John Henry may be a "race man" in twentieth-century texts by African American authors, by placing John Henry alongside fictional characters such as Mighty Casey and Paul Bunyan's blue ox, black masculinity is rendered "safe" for the general public's consumption of black masculinity and the real challenge, identified by Paul Robeson in the opening epigraph for this chapter, which is the race for self-actualization and the application of all one's intellectual, emotional, physical, and spiritual gifts, is rendered negligible.[6] Alternatively, as Raymond Patterson observes in his "Autobiography of a Black Man," black masculinity becomes a commodity that white men want to control through the incorporation of black manhood into "their" already existing schematics of race and manhood. Indirectly, white men become "more masculine" when they associate with the mythological black supermen spoken of by Robeson and Patterson. The conflict between man and machine represented by John Henry is thus a battle between the machinery of a culture that seeks to control and contain representations of black masculinity and that of the natural man himself. No single postage stamp can put that controversy to rest, particularly a stamp that celebrates a particular kind of black masculinity—one in which a dead black man is turned into a cartoon alongside three fictional creations in order to earn America's stamp of approval.

So if it is not John Henry's status as a universally acknowledged "race man," what is it about the man versus the machine conflict that is particularly central to the African American experience? Why keep recycling the John Henry story, adding more and more fictionalized elements to it? What makes John Henry and his work on the railroad so important for black writers? John Henry's appeal is that he was and continues to be representative of a man who even when the dominant society equates him with a machine, an animal, or a commodity, he chooses to achieve a higher spiritual and creative, world-shaping destiny, a destiny symbolized by John Henry's connection to the train. It is John Henry's connection to the train, and not the phallic hammer, that enables him to transcend all labels and limitations. The hammer is only a tool. The man and what he can achieve is represented by the train's passage through the unaccommodating American landscape and on into a future that transforms American culture, an achievement made possible only through repeated acts of sheer strength of character and of will, represented by a black superman who, though not a machine, possesses attributes of the train, and who refuses to be derailed or to get off track, even in the face of almost insurmountable odds, both natural and manmade. As Paul Robeson explained to a London reporter who asked about Robeson's feelings about starring in Roark Bradford's racist version of the John Henry story, "The race which first learns to balance equally the intellectual and the emotional—to use the machines and couple them with a life of true intuition and feeling such as the Easterns know—will produce supermen" (cited in Allen 90). Though Roark Bradford did not understand Robeson's perspective on the character, it is clear that what appealed to Robeson about the part was that even with Bradford's racist script, John Henry is that superman, and it is not just his strength Robeson celebrates—there is a philosophy of life involved as well in John Henry's persistence and insistence.

However, in order to fully comprehend what John Henry symbolized and symbolizes for African American writers and why it is important that he is always connected to the railroad in African American versions of the legend, it is first necessary to examine the earliest published version of the John Henry story, the version published by Roark Bradford, a white man from a former slaving family. In Bradford's version, John Henry was always a cotton-picker with lots of animal sexual magnetism.[7] In fact, in Bradford's telling of the tale, trains and other machines confuse and thus anger the brutish John Henry. John Henry is decidedly not a railroad man in the first published versions of the story. Even in contemporary times, John Henry's connection with the railroad is still hotly contested by some who reject the notion of Henry as a railroad man. Charleston journalist L. T. Anderson, as late as 1979, was still pushing the "Don't Turn John Henry into a Railroad Man," theme, insisting that John Henry "didn't even work for a railroad" (para 1). Quoting his grandfather, who had worked on the tunnel, according to Anderson, "there were a hell of a lot of big darkies" who were working at the time, but that he "knew nothing of a steel driver's race with a steam-powered drill" and that he doubted "that work time would be allowed for that kind of frivolity" (para 4).[8] The linking of John Henry with the railroad instead of cotton or simple construction first occurs in the black oral tradition. When comparing and contrasting the early versions from the black oral tradition and the printed white editions, it becomes very clear that part of what the John Henry story is about is the controversial history of black men working for the railroad coupled with the history of the conflict over representations of black manhood in literature as either a "child" or a "brute" but rarely as a fully actualized adult "man."[9] These two histories converge into one in the uses of John Henry as a character in literature and explain why working for the railroad was such a symbolic and important occupation for black literary versions of the legendary John Henry. Working on the railroad was man's work. If black men could be denied manhood, then they could be denied jobs as well. John Henry was a figure to be reckoned with, and, as such, control of the legend became a matter of representational importance.

Roark Bradford's *John Henry*, the first published novel about John Henry, is in the style of a blackface minstrel show, and in fact, was made into one. Bradford's publicist claims that Bradford's understanding of "Negro Life" is complete because Bradford had grown up on a plantation near the Mississippi River where he was cared for by a black nanny and was able to observe black life closely: "He has seen them at work in the fields, in the levee camps, and on the river. He knows them in their homes, in church, at their picnics, and their funerals,"[book jacket ad copy, 1931]. No mention is made of his World

War I experiences in the army, where he worked alongside black Americans, a situation in which he would have been exposed to, at the very least, stories about the heroism and bravery of black men who, like himself, were serving their country. Instead, it is his childhood experiences of rural black life, and his childhood memory of black men as being pleasure-seeking and foolish, that is considered "real" and representative.

Black manhood, as Bradford presents it, is not pretty. John Henry sleeps with hundreds of women, drinks gin mixed with cocaine, and fights when other men complain about him sleeping with their women, even though the women are often portrayed as sexually promiscuous as well. Roark's John Henry wears dandified clothes, bets all his money on card games or on bragging contests about his own strength and prowess, and lives off his main woman, Julie Ann, until threatened with the chain gang for vagrancy. The projected model of black manhood here is that of a hedonistic, ill-tempered, sensuous, and yet tasteless brute. Julie Ann encourages his lazy behavior, saying that as long as she is able to work, he should not have to because he is the type of man that is so much man he should not need to take orders from anyone. This, too, presents a negative stereotype about black masculine behavior and suggests that black women get what they deserve for encouraging such things. John Henry beats Julie Ann frequently because she cheats on him as much as he cheats on her.

The railroad appears only briefly in Bradford's version of the John Henry story, and it is identified each time as "old Jay Gould's railroad" (71). John Henry does not lay tracks or swing a hammer. In this version, the engineer calls him "boy," and asks him if he thinks he can shovel coal faster than "that nigger named Sam" (70). The whole point of John Henry's shoveling is to get enough coal in the burner for the engineer to do a train whistle trick called "the highball" which is "two longs and a shawt" (71). These are the sorts of childish things that interest Bradford's John Henry. In the end of Bradford's story, John Henry's bragging finally gets him into a cotton-loading contest he cannot win, and he dies. The lesson of Bradford's text is that John Henry's pride and inability to control his baser appetites lead to his doom.

Bradford's text was serialized in magazines before its 1931 book publication, and then, after the novel's publication, produced as a play. It was next bought, rewritten as a minstrel-style musical, and performed in major cities across the nation. In all of these versions of the Bradford text, John Henry was portrayed as a dangerous man who, in the end, gets what he deserves for having lived his life as a womanizing braggart who wasted his talents and his strengths fighting the inevitable for no reason other than stubborn pride and animal desires. Bradford's text has episodes of humor where one can laugh at the big man, John Henry, for thinking he is better than anyone else, and Bradford's John Henry dies repentant, a comic-tragic figure, having learned his lesson about the limitations of pride.

It is, of course, very interesting that Bradford chose to ignore the folk legends of John Henry that make him a railroad man. At the time of his writing, acknowledging these legends would have made white audiences uncomfortable. White audiences of the 1930s greatly preferred to think of John Henry as a great, black brute, hooking cotton and focused entirely on the tawdry pleasures of gin, cocaine, and loose women, dying repentant. This was much more comfortable than any reminders about the black-white conflict about working on the railroad.

Maggie Montesinos Sale argues that while the key ingredient in the definition of American "manhood" has always been "righteous rebellion," or the "willingness to die in the cause of liberty," the rebellions of African American men have instead been viewed by the white majority as brutish (12). In the early John Henry tale penned by Bradford, this is clearly the case. Sale explains that while manhood was once defined by property ownership and one's husbandry of land, in nineteenth-century America race replaced class as the minimum requirement for participation in the social contract of America, thus denying black men their manhood. Sales writes,

> Race figured significantly here because, although economic structures dramatically shifted and re-formed during the early nineteenth century, considerable differences in economic status among the European population remained the norm. Now whiteness rather than property—all along with masculinity—determined one's access to political participation and economic opportunities. In fact, masculinity gained a new visibility and abiding sig-

nificance as the conjoining figure that bridged the shift from class to race. (31–32)

White men, particularly those without property, had a great deal invested in insisting that whiteness was a prerequisite of manhood. Social depictions of black men as childlike, animal, or brutish served to reinforce a white sense of identity and dignity.[10]

In literature, the words *black* and *brute* were commonly allied, and very little print was devoted to the recognition of the fact that one could be both "black" and a "man." In *The Black Image in the White Mind,* for example, George Fredrickson discusses the works of novelists such as William Gilmore Simms, a writer who, in 1837, presented his male black characters as "a cannibal, destined to eat his fellow, or be eaten by him" (52). Pro-abolitionist Northern writers attempted to counter such representations of black masculinity with their own brand of equally racist romanticism, with Harriet Beecher Stowe's "romantic and feminine conception of the Negro character" in the person of Uncle Tom being the most widely remembered by today's reader (Fredrickson 115).

Ironically, the Civil War did little good in changing the depiction of black men in literature, nor did the coming of a new century. As Clare Eby notes, "while historians debate how far back the stereotype goes, the 'beast' exploded in notoriety in the 1890s, a time of massive black disenfranchisement and the rise of legalized Jim Crow" (1). As Edward Ayers, Lee Baker, Martha Hodes, Leon Litwack, Eric Sundquist, Joel Williamson, and many others have also observed, most of the common negative representations of black masculinity came into existence after the Civil War. Some alleged that black men were not truly men because of their animal-like sexual appetites.[11] Others asserted that with their almost deformed, lumbering bodies and great physical strength came a brutish capacity for violence, coupled with great laziness in terms of using that strength for anything resembling hard work.[12] Still others argued that the black man's willingness to accept bribes and to do anything for money except work indicated a lack of moral capability, a prerequisite of humanity and thus manhood.[13] Many pointed to the black man's alleged inability to reason, his animal lust for food and sex, and general lawlessness as proof that no black male was ever really a man in the civilized sense of the word.[14] As Williamson explains, all the traits that had once been "conceived as a rationalization of slavery" when it was said the "childlike improvident Negro would perish" without slavery, were transformed into the characteristics of an immoral beast and now became rationalization for white violence during Reconstruction (240–65).

Additionally, images of the black beast proliferated in magazines, illustrated monthlies, and newspapers throughout the 1890s. The writers and illustrators "often recast the stereotypes that were being perpetuated within the literary genres and grounded them in science or expertise," and "the circulation, authority, and prestige of the magazines lent themselves the appearance of truth. The better the copy, the greater sense of truth and the more convincing the stereotype" (Baker 74). Such negrophobia reached its height in the early part of the twentieth century and resulted in letters to the editor about "the Negro brute" and his "savage nature and murderous instincts of the wild beast" who was, of course, responsible for "the rise of crimes against white womanhood" (qtd. in Baker 277).[15]

The resurgence of interest in blackface minstrel shows at this time provided whites with an opportunity to lampoon the black "beast" and ridicule his body and his virility. Lhamon attributes the popularity of the blackface shows to the public demand for "racist sugar" to feed "the sweet teeth of magazine publics" (153). Eric Lott notes that, although the intent is to burlesque the black man, the minstrel shows reveal a strong white fascination with the physical power and assumed sexuality of black male bodies (Lott, "Love and Theft: The Racial Unconscious" 25). In a later work, *Love and Theft: Blackface Minstrelsy and the American Working Class,* Lott expands on this argument, asserting that minstrel shows often became very popular with whites in areas experiencing struggles between black and white workers competing for the same jobs as these shows indicated that all the black male was truly suited for was dancing, lovemaking, and other activities that would result in downward rather than upward social class mobility (111–12). Despite the efforts of groups like the NAACP and the UNIA to publicize the heroics of black soldiers in World War I, and the efforts of the writers and scholars of the Harlem Renaissance, white America, particularly working-class white America, was not interested in seeing black men as heroes.[16]

Thus, from the end of the Civil War and up through World War I, while the white brotherhoods were not able to keep black men out of railroad service, Bradford and other white writers use their literary and artistic representations to depict black men as too animalistic and too brutish to control or to participate in anything technological. However, despite such cultural and political pressures from white brotherhoods, railroad companies in places as diverse as Pennsylvania and Florida refused to hire inexperienced white workers or to replace experienced black yard foremen, flagmen, brakemen, and baggage men. The railroad companies were profit driven and large enough to ignore local color or race prejudice in their pursuit of the lowest bottom line. The railroad's actions were not based on any sense of social justice, and yet, the result was the same. Black workers who were good at their jobs found their jobs protected because of merit. In places where racial prejudice was a serious consideration, the best that most of the white brotherhoods could attain in the first half of the twentieth century was a promise "not to increase the percentage of colored trainmen" (Houston 6).

As Philip S. Foner and Ronald L. Lewis note in *The Black Worker During the Era of the American Federation of Labor and the Railroad Brotherhoods*, the white supremacist brotherhoods did not succeed in "their efforts to drive blacks from the roads" until the 1940s (72). As late as 1920, blacks still made up 33% of the trainmen positions (Houston 9) which Foner and Lewis speculate meant that approximately 15,000 skilled trainmen jobs were held by African Americans (72). There were higher percentages of skilled jobs available on the railroad for African Americans than in any other industry, a fact that added to the positive feelings about the railroad in the African American community. Foner and Lewis's and Houston's numbers do not even include the number of African American workers working for the railroad as unskilled laborers or who made money, locally, off servicing or supplying the railroad crews. According to Franklin and Moss, during World War I, "approximately 150,000 blacks assisted in the operation of railroads" (342). Now that white men had returned from fighting overseas in World War I, they wanted those jobs back, hence the increased racial tension and contested nature of working for the railroad after World War I. Consequently, white representations of black men became increasingly negative in the imaginative literature of the time. Roark time. Roark Bradford's very popular 1931 version of the John Henry story is thus consistent with this negative depiction of black men. Moreover, it also served to create an image of black men that served a white commercial and political agenda.

In contrast, in African American Sterling Brown's 1932 collection of poetry there are two poems in which John Henry is very much associated with the building of the railroad. He is depicted as a hero with heart and spirit enough for the long haul that is life. In both poems, what is important in life is commitment to the long haul, the long journey, symbolized by the train and the railroad, which John Henry is integral in constructing. John Henry is celebrated for his perseverance and for his pride, the very things Bradford perceived as stubbornness and foolish egocentricism.

In "The Odyssey of Big Boy," John Henry is a minor character, but a very important one nevertheless. An odyssey, of course, is a long wandering journey or a spiritual quest in which the reader metaphorically accompanies a single traveler to far off places and points unknown. Each stop along the way is filled with adventures and experiences that often teach the reader, if not the character, valuable (and often highly visual and symbolic) lessons. As anyone who has been forced to sit through four years of Latin and Classics can tell you, one significant characteristic of odysseys is that they are usually begun unwillingly, and the main character often finds his character tested in unusual and often embarrassing ways. Ulysses does not want to leave his wife in order to travel to Troy to bring back another man's bride and even resorts to trickery, dressing as a mad man and eating sand, to avoid going, but in the end he must. Blown off course, Lemuel Gulliver is, at various points, treated like a child's toy, treated as less intelligent than an animal, and covered in excrement.

Brown's "Odyssey of Big Boy" fits this pattern. Big Boy is blown by the winds of time from one place to another where he performs different tasks, learns what he likes and does not like, will or will not do, makes love, makes mistakes, and learns some more. He learns to persist in what he is doing and to follow through on what he starts. He learns to move forward even when his heart yearns to turn back. In short, he learns the lessons all heroes must learn. By titling his poem the "Odyssey of Big Boy," Brown is placing the life of his narrator, Big Boy, with the lives of other well known heroes, suggesting his life is also worthy of artistic memory. In many ways what odyssey stories reveal, because of the respective protagonist's frequent initial reluctance to begin the odyssey, is that life makes heroes out of ordinary men. Moreover, ordinary men, like Big Boy, can still find a place in heaven with the likes of John Henry.

In the final stanza of the poem, as the narrator, Big Boy, considers his death, he has only one request. He wants good companions for this next journey when he must go from this world to the next. He wants to be headed the same place they are, the good-time place where all hard-working men go for their final reward. He wants to be with other men like John Henry whose lives have also been lived largely in the quest mode, a man who was always moving forward, on to the next railroad building adventure, never turning his back on a challenge or going back "home" to the plantation days of his youth.

The importance of John Henry, the difference between how Sterling Brown represents black manhood via John Henry and how Bradford does, and the connection between the figure of John Henry and the railroad is even clearer in Sterling Brown's other John Henry poem, "Strange Legacies." In this poem about manhood and what men who have nothing concrete to bequeath have left as "property," Brown suggests that racial pride and persistence, a willingness to keep trying even in the face of certain destruction, can be a beautiful inheritance, one worth more than jewels or money. Whereas Bradford's John Henry is a cotton roller who swings a mean cotton hook, in this poem, John Henry is clearly a railroad man. He is a steel driver who swings a heavy hammer as he lays tracks from one part of the country to another. He is also a hero because he gives his best even when he feels his worst, even when his heart is about to burst.

A hero is often defined as somebody who represents what is best and most noble about mankind, a person who makes others proud of being human. That is the appeal of John Henry for Sterling Brown. He is a hero and knowledge of him is part of each African American's heritage; he is part of their legacy, something that can be called upon in times of need. When the narrator of Brown's poem calls upon John Henry to "help us get it" is, perhaps, the most dramatic line of the poem when the whole poem is read aloud. It sounds like both a summoning and a prayer, almost in the same vein as, in Anglican services, the retelling of the Last Supper, followed immediately by a prayer of need or the start of an ancestor summoning in which the spirits of the dead will be called upon to fight current enemies.

The narrative voice in the poem speaks directly to the spirit of John Henry saying that "we," black Americans in the 1930s, need John Henry's spirit of persistence and his strength to keep swinging, even when the heart grows sick and weary. As Michael S. Harper notes in his introduction to Brown's collected poems, "Brown's world is grounded in his perceptual faith in the long haul, and in the spirit which needs no hiding" (xi). By perceptual faith, Harper means Brown's belief that perception is grounded in an understanding that comes from becoming aware through one's senses, an understanding of the felt or lived life. Faith comes from the long journey of living, enduring, waiting, hoping, a sort of loyalty and fidelity to life itself based on the lived feeling of physically being alive, for where there is life, there is hope.

Clearly the John Henry of Bradford's 1931 novel and the John Henry of Brown's 1932 poem bear very little resemblance to each other. On the cover of Bradford's book is a white-lipped, grimacing, pigeon-toed, giant black man, slightly bent over with a vicious looking cotton hook in one hand and a bale of cotton hoisted up on his bent back. While Sterling Brown's John Henry is never physically described, his spirit and heart are, suggesting perhaps that while white writers and audiences were impressed with stories about John Henry's body, black poets and readers were celebrating the man's strength of spirit. In the battle over representation and how the black man should be portrayed in literature, Sterling Brown's 1932 portrayal of the black man's heart is much more positive than that of his white contemporary's 1931 portrait of a black legend, John Henry, and Sterling Brown is insistent on John Henry's connection to railroad building. Though early white writers have attempted to fix the reader's attention on the animal sexuality of black men, and in later minstrel shows, objects like the hammer become a comic phallic extension of black manhood, thus emphasizing the sexual "codpiece" rather than what John Henry and the other men were a part of building, the power of nation-building is denied, reduced to a sexual joke. However, in the texts by African American writers, it is the hammer of creation, not mindless procreation, and the railroad emerges as the black man's "manly" legacy to his America, replacing slavery as the primary legacy.

In the next forty years, John Henry would become a contested figure as his life and death were told, retold, interpreted, and reinterpreted by black and white storytellers and historians alike. Increasingly, the story of John Henry became an instructional story for children. In versions by white authors, John Henry's blackness became indicative of his simplicity, and his death was a lesson about the impossibility of fighting against the tide of technology. Later on, white and black children alike were taught to read into the story a message about the necessity of learning to control technology rather than to fight against it, such as in Ezra Keats's 1960s version of the John Henry story, which suggests that a man must adapt, evolve, and keep pace with the changing times or perish fighting the inevitable.

In the 1970s, African America writers began to self-consciously use the figure of John Henry in connection with the train with increasingly regularity as a way of grounding the legend of John Henry in an occupation known to be man's work and known to be an important part of America's history. Black writers of the 1970s used the John Henry legends to invite the reader to share a response to and perspective about representations of black manhood that are conditioned by a pre-acceptance of what the train symbolizes and means, as for example, in John Oliver Killens's young adult novel, *A Man Ain't Nothin' But a Man* (1975).

According to the dedication, this novel was written to provide his son with a "truer" history of black heroes, in this case, a history that concerns the birth, childhood, life, life work, importance, and death of John Henry. In Killens's novel, working for the railroad symbolizes freedom and manhood. As a boy, each time John Henry sees a train or hears a train whistle, he wants to be a part of that life. The cotton he has been ordered to pick equals slavery. Here Killens is clearly rejecting the Bradford version of the story and insisting on the black folk tradition versions. The train, because of its longtime mystical associations with freedom and the many gospel songs, symbolizes everything the young John Henry desires, and it seems also to offer him a chance to make a man-sized contribution to the country. A contribution to American history, not just freedom, is what this John Henry desires. Here, John Henry assumes what Killens terms, in an earlier essay, "the black man's burden," which, he explains, is "to inject some black blood, some black intelligence, some black humanness, into the pallid mainstream of American life—culturally, socially, psychologically, philosophically" (9–10). This John Henry does not just wish to be left in peace; he, like his creator, John Killens, wishes to change America.[17]

Early in the text, which is set sometime in the late 1880s, the young John Henry looks out over the plantation on which, even though the war between the states has been over for twenty years, he still lives as a tenant wage-slave.

> He stared out across the miles and miles of cotton rolling all the way to the hills and back again. . . . All them years of sweat and muscle he'd put in all that cotton and didn't a goddam inch of it b'long to him. Not to him or his mama or his papa or to any of the hundreds of Black hands that worked in all that white stuff all those years from kin to caint. It was not the first time thoughts like these had gone a-romping through his mind. Black and white thoughts bouncing up against each other. Open warfare. Warm Black souls and snow-white cotton. (8)

Agricultural life, plantation life, even for wages, is equated with slavery and the whiteness of the cotton seems to taunt him. Although the white cotton looks soft and fluffy from a distance, the sharp hooks of the cotton plant regularly cut black hands and make them bleed. Cotton and cotton picking symbolize white corruption, greed, and wage slavery.

In contrast, the black locomotives and their whistles seem to speak to John Henry's soul. The fire of the engines is matched only by the fire in John Henry's "warm black soul." Once he begins working on the railroad, it is almost as if a magical transference occurs, and the fire that animates his "warm black soul" flows out of his body, through his hammer, and into the great stretches of track that are destined to become the lifeblood of the nation. John Henry's life force flows out of his human body and becomes the "blood" pumping through the miles of track that form the arteries and veins of the post–Civil War nation. In a sense, the fire that is in him is the animus, the life-giving energy that gives the railroad life. He has animated the steel with his human life force and made it more than just a railroad. When given a choice between rousting the white man's white cotton and all that this double whiteness represents, and working for the railroad, John Henry, of course, chooses to answer the call of the train whistle and leaves the plantation in search of railroad work.

It is also at this point that the boy becomes a man. When he picks cotton on the plantation, he is a boy and is called boy by the overseer, Mr. Ben. When he leaves the plantation, no one is ever allowed to call him boy or nigger again. His decision to quit the cotton plantation and to search for a job on the railroad is his initiation into manhood. Additionally, doing railroad work is equated with doing the work God wanted man to do. His father, an old railroad man himself, tells John Henry that when a man is working on the railroad, he "[f]elt like a man was supposed to feel. Like the Power and the Glory was flowing all thru me like the Mississippi River. I used to feel mighty close to the good old Master up there in that Heavenly Place" (12). The suggestion here is that working for the railroad as a steel-driving man brings a man closer to God because man, like God, is doing creative work. When a man is doing God's work of creation, man is closer to God. Working on the railroad and freedom are, for Killens's John Henry, one and the same, and they are connected to a purpose couched in almost religious or messianic terms that is even bigger than John Henry's big heart: improving America through racial uplift. John Henry will, in effect, become one with what it is he is building, almost as if the new railroad will grow, seeded by his sweat, and the locomotives will pound down the track in time with the pounding of his heart. John Henry is not in opposition to the train. The perfection of the powerful black locomotives is mirrored by the perfection of John Henry's powerful mind, body, and spirit. John Henry tells his wife that when he is "swinging that hammer and building them railroads" he feels like

> I'm leaving part of me clean across this country. Like a mighty monument. When I'm dead and my soul is laid to rest, I'll still be living on in that Big Bend Tunnel! That's how come the Good Master gived me so much more strength than he gived most other mens. The Good Master always have his purpose. (103)

The train is somehow God's machine, not man's, and it is God's intention, the text suggests, to knit the broken bones of the nation together with railroad tracks. However, first, John Henry must get the white men to hire him, and he must prove his worth and earn a position on the construction team for the greatest railroad project ever in order to achieve something "the whole Black race could be proud of" (111).

Because of the train's historic importance and his target audience (young black men), Killens does not have to work hard to convince his readers of the value of John Henry's work or the validity of his ambition. Because of the way in which the train has been used in African American literature as a symbol of spiritual hope and a vehicle of freedom, when Killens's John Henry chooses to view his work for the railroad as God's work, it is not too much of a stretch for most readers. Killens's John Henry goes one step further, and on the day of his final contest with the steam drill, John Henry prays that God will do with him as God sees fit because today John Henry represents God. Man was made in God's image and if mankind lets machines replace man and destroy the image of God on Earth, then man will get what he deserves. John Henry prays that the crowds of people watching will see the beauty of God's creation in him and value it above the machine designed to replace man. He says, while in prayer,

> I'm trying to show the world that man is your greatest creation. . . . the oniliest thing you ever made on this earth in your own precious image. . . . I'm saying it in the only way you gived me to say it, Lord. With this mighty strong body you gived me. This is why you gived it to me. (166)

His prayers, in a way, come true, but not in the way he expected.

The end of the story is the usual end. John Henry beats the machine, but then his heart bursts as a result of the effort and he dies with his hammer still clenched in his fists. The lesson, for the crowd and for the reader, is the same lesson revealed in John Henry's prayer. His black body is representative of God, made in the image of God, and is representative of the creative brilliance of God. Man, in this case, white men, in their arrogance and pride, like Lucifer, strike at God, through his people, with their own puny, metallic, dirt-spitting, creations. John Henry is so beautiful and the machine so ugly in the way it "clogged and coughed and sputtered and barked like an angry shotgun. And it finally came apart" (171).

In contrast, John Henry has rainbows round his shoulders and his muscles ripple like streams. Man must learn to value God's creations more than their own, and at the end of this contest for their souls, through the death of John Henry, God's chosen representative, God wins because the crowd mourns the death of John Henry with great passion and great pain. No one but the machine operator even notices the fall of the machine. The loss of the great John Henry is palpable, by every person present. There is an aching sense of loss. Killens avoids having his John Henry figure be seen as an Uncle Tom figure, a character known for his spirituality and willingness to sacrifice himself for others, by keeping his novel's focus on the black community and on the representation of black men. John Henry dies while physically and fiscally defending himself and the jobs of other black men. He is not afraid to raise his hands or his voice, and when he strikes his aim is true.

In case John Henry's virility is in any doubt, Killens adds a final scene with Polly Ann and an epilogue. In the final scene, Polly Ann is pregnant, and after John Henry dies, she can feel the kick of their unborn child inside her. She picks up his hammer and "feels a growing strength flow through her body as if it were transferred by John Henry's mighty hammer" (175). The sexual imagery is, perhaps, a bit overdone, but when Polly Ann stands up and looks around at the sea of black faces around her, she "saw John Henry in all of their faces" (174). In the epilogue, Killens asserts that every time a train passes through the tunnel, it sings a tribute to John Henry. Every locomotive "come roaring by, singing there lies a steel-driving man—Great God! Singing, there lies a steel-driving man" (177). John Henry is not a boy, a nigger, or a black brute; he is a real man. The choir of angels that sing his praises is composed of manly train whistles, and the train sings heavenly praises to John Henry's memory. John Henry is in the tracks, in the whistles of the trains, and in the hearts and minds of all the people who saw him that day. Thus, if Killens is successful, every time his reader now sees a train or hears the lonesome whistle of a train, he or she too will think of John Henry, and the story of the man will come rushing back.

Sterling and Killens both use the railroad to comment on specific aspects of black manhood by assigning anthropomorphic attributes to the train that suggest the train mirrors a man's moods and emotions. Both also use John Henry, in particular, as a model for black masculinity. Brown's emphasis is on the validation of black manhood, while Killens's intent is both to validate and to create new models of black masculinity based on fictionalized history. Killens also insists on making racial pride and commitment to racial uplift a qualification of black manhood, something Brown did not. For Killens, being a "race man" is part of the definition of black manhood. For Brown, manhood is an individualistic thing. The difference between the two writers' philosophies is consistent with their different historic contexts. Brown was a product of the Great Depression, and Killens, a product of the period William L. Van Deburg has nicknamed the "Black Camelot," a time in which "the African-American heroic . . . rose to prominence" and "the contemporary black hero served both as a projection of dreams and as a model for emulation" (1–2). Black pride was part of Black Camelot, and it was expected that writers and thinkers of Killens's generation would reinforce that pride. For Brown, black manhood was something to be validated in general, but could only be achieved in the specific.

By the 1990s, the necessary traits of a black male hero had again shifted, and the use of the train as a symbol became even more pronounced. While still valuing traits such as loyalty, racial allegiance, and perseverance, writers in the 1990s also emphasized the need for spirituality and sensitivity as part of true manhood. Terry Small's 1994 *The Legend of John Henry* begins with John Henry still a slave, "when freedom seemed as far away as the end of a railroad track" (1). As soon as he is emancipated, Small's John Henry heads North, where he works for the railroad, "drivin' steel in the days of the Great Expansion," and discovers that "happiness ain't but a twelve-pound hammer ringin in this soul of mine" (1). Small also makes much of John Henry's spirituality, something not common to the commercialized Disney "Everyman" versions of the John Henry myth. In Small's version, John Henry does not want a shaker who "sang to the rhythm of the hammer"; instead, he picks as his shaker, "Ole Titus, he sang to God" (3). Religion, freedom, railroad building, and manhood all coalesce in this story of John Henry.

Small makes the case that what a man does for a job, in this case, John Henry's railroad building, is also his purpose in life. Small's John Henry is emotionally and spiritually committed to building America via railroad expansion. As John Henry builds railroad tracks, he is symbolically building part of himself right into the building of America, a fact that, again, would be recorded for all time in the whistle of the trains. John Henry's soul and spirituality are integrally tied to railroad building. When Josiah Haley announces that his steam drill has come to replace the men, and begins to fire people, Ole Titus's heart bursts. This shaker and singer of gospel songs dies of a broken heart when his connection to the railroad is threatened. Small's John Henry will fight for his right to fulfill his destiny. He refuses to be replaced by a machine, and when all the other workers decide to head North to look for factory work, Small's John Henry takes a stand for staying put and continuing to do the work God planned for him: railroad building all across America. The white man may try to keep silent about the part the black man played in this historic event, but the truth is told by the whistle of the train.

For readers to consider the heroism of Small's John Henry important, what is being fought over must be considered important. Small chooses to make his John Henry take a stand for staying put. In his version, John Henry and the other black men are pushed from one job to the next, over and over again. Even though they are free, there is the suggestion that they are still viewed the same way they were when they were slaves. They are valuable only when there is work to be done. Their value is work-use value, not human value. Their souls are not considered important at all, nor are their hearts or minds. Old Titus's death shows that his commitment to the railroad is more than heartfelt; it is something he feels in the depth of his soul.

After the death of Ole Titus, Small's John Henry is tired of being pushed from one job to the next. His soul needs a home. He tells his new shaker, a child named Lil' Bill, that, "they ain't no man, ain't no machine ever make me leave again"(9). Instead of leaving the South and heading toward the will-o'-the-wisp freedom in the North, as did figures such as Harriet Tubman, Small's John Henry takes a stand for staying put in the South, finding work for himself and Lil' Bill and marrying Ole Titus's daughter, Polly Ann. Together they make a home. This is the third part of Small's definition of manhood. To be a good man, one must be a settled family man. Freedom, requirement number one, and purpose, requirement number two, should not be used as an excuse to avoid requirement number three, family life. Freedom and family life are compatible in Small's definition of true manhood.

One fateful day, however, John Henry's boss tells him that Josiah Haley is back with a new improved steam drill and that the company will no longer need the black work crews. The steam drill plus a white operator can replace a whole black work crew. He tells John Henry that he appreciated all their good work, but "progress come to the rails, and progress don't need you"(14). John Henry's response is very telling. He speaks eloquently of the amount of muscle and sweat and life he has poured into the making of the nation, and now that the nation is made, it no longer wants him. Every ache, every callous, has come from the effort of his soul. The drill operator misses the point entirely and says his drill, "don't need rest, it don't need food, it don't need housin either. Come heat, come cold, the Haley Drill, ain't bothered much by either" (16). What Small wants his readers to feel is that John Henry and the other black men first made the nation agriculturally successful with their labor on the plantations, and then formed the human bridge that made the Great Expansion possible, but that now that the initial work has been done and it is payoff and settle-down time, white America would prefer that these black workers disappear. They were wanted only for their work, not for their human contributions. John Henry insists on trying to get Josiah Haley to acknowledge the importance of having a soul and the contributions of the soul. This is another aspect of true manhood: A man must speak the truth, even when others refuse to hear.

As in the other versions of the John Henry story, John Henry wins, but then he dies as a result of his great effort. What Small's text makes clear, though, is that part of the beauty of John Henry and the thing that makes him better than the machine is that he *can* choose to give his heart to a cause; he can choose to die nobly for something he believes in. A machine can never give a job that level of commitment. As he dies, he can hear the voice of God whispering in his ear and the sound of Ole Titus's shaker song in the background, and he knows he is assured a place in the kingdom of heaven. He is buried at the edge of the railroad track, the monument to his immortal contribution. Then, in the tunnel when the train whistle blows, it says, "John Henry was a steel-drivin man, Lawd, Lawd, John Henry was a steel-drivin man." The train and its whistle represent the true history of this period in America. "Progress come to the rails, and progress don't need you" Josiah Haley told John Henry, but the train itself proves Haley wrong (14). John Henry is in the rails, in the wheels of the locomotive, and in the whistle of the train. John Henry is not a child, a brute, or ill fitted for the future; John Henry, with his better than machine-like efficiency and with his incredible human heart and strength of spirit, is the man who has made progress possible.

In the Julius Lester version of *John Henry* (1994), as in the Killens and Small versions, John Henry is clearly presented as one of God's greatest creations. His birth is described in much the same terms as the birth of Jesus. His birth is humble but attended by the animals. Instead of a distant star marking his birthplace, it is our own sun that beams down upon the new baby, circling him with light, suggesting that the son of God is closer than we think. Instead of a distant sun/son, the son of God is right here, right now. Even a unicorn, from the Arthurian legends, makes an appearance to see the new baby. Lester's John Henry is Christ and King Arthur, a religious savior and the king who would unite a warring nation, all rolled into one.

As in the other versions, John Henry's passage from boyhood into manhood is marked by his decision to leave home and find work with the railroad. Whereas in Killens's version it was John Henry's father who had been a railroad man, in Lester's version, it was the grandfather. John Henry inherits his grandfather's two twenty-pound sledgehammers "with four foot handles made of whale bone" (11). Whaling was once one of the few equal-opportunity occupations for African Americans, and so it is fitting that Lester chooses to make his John Henry potentially the descendent of a great whaling ship sailor. Because there is so little property to inherit and pass down through the generations, one of the significant and often repeated characteristics of the John Henry story is that the manhood is a legacy of sorts, even when chronologically or historically impossible. In Lester's text, part of being a man is having a set of traditions or values to hand down to one's sons. Unlike the Tubman tradition, which suggests the need for walking away from the original community or one's family in order to find a community of like-minded freedom seekers, the 1990s John Henry tradition emphasizes the importance of bloodline family, and of staying put, putting down roots, and becoming the link between God's creation and man's creations.

Throughout the Lester version of the John Henry story, John Henry is surrounded by rainbows. Whereas in most versions of the story rainbow imagery is reserved for the final conflict, there are rainbows all throughout Lester's text. They are forever "draped around him like love" (19). In religious imagery, the rainbow is a sign of God's promise and is his covenant with his people. Its pervasive presence in this text serves to remind readers of John Henry's status as one of those chosen by God for the difficult but important work of remaking the country after the Civil War.

The contest in the Lester text places the machine at one side of the mountain and John Henry on the other in a race to the center of the mountain. As the contest heats up, "there wasn't enough room inside the tunnel for the rainbow, so it wrapped itself around the mountain on the side where John Henry was" (23). He wins the race to the middle of the mountain, walks out of the tunnel into the sunlight, and the rainbow drapes around his shoulders. He smiles, closes his eyes, and dies. The sun sheds a tear. As the people are gathered, mourning John Henry's death, the rainbow whispers, so quietly it feels like a thought, that "Dying ain't important. Everybody does that. What matters is how well you do your living" (28).

A combination of the Jesus myth with our sun, instead of a distant star, as the celestial sign at both his birth and death, signifies, perhaps, John Henry's status as a native son. As a version of the rainbow covenant/Noah's Ark cleansing of the sin-filled world, Julius Lester's version of the John Henry story is the most invested with modified versions of Christian symbolism. In addition, it makes great use of the train as a symbol, for in the end of the text, John Henry's body is placed on a flatbed railroad car so that people all the way from West Virginia to Washington, DC, can cheer, clap, and pay their last respects. In the illustrations accompanying the texts, a black locomotive, looking for all the world like a hearse, is draped with three American flags. The illustration is reminiscent of Whitman's poem about Abraham Lincoln's funeral procession by train, "When Lilacs Last in the Dooryard Bloom'd." Like Lincoln, John Henry is here depicted as a Christ-figure. The story ends with John Henry's body secretly being buried under the White House lawn while the president sleeps. The suggestion here is that a true man is deeply rooted in American politics and becomes part of American history, even when that history is not recorded. The final illustration shows a shooting star with a rainbow trailing after it, passing over the top of an American flag that is fluttering from the roof of the White House. The shooting star is John Henry's spirit as it makes its way to heaven, and the rainbow, both a sign of his strength and, biblically, God's covenant with man which, in this case, because of the flag, seems to intersect with American politics.

In all of these versions of the John Henry legend the suggestion is made again and again that in the construction of America, there are traces of black blood giving it life and sustenance. No machine can ever give that. John Henry refuses to equate black manhood with a robot-like machine or to let the people around him think that not only is a black man not a man, but that he can be replaced by a white man's construct. John Henry's battle against the machine is a rejection of white America's insistence on using up and discarding black men, upon whose backs the nation was built during the agricultural revolution and then again during the railroad-building mania for expansion. Unlike the Harriet Tubman figures discussed in chapter two, the John Henry figure resists dehumanization.

John Henry is, however, firmly associated with the train and what the train symbolizes. The train is not "the machine" against which John Henry battles. The spiritual element is loud and clear in the whistle of the train. After death, the spirit of John Henry, in a sense, rides the rails, and every train pays tribute to him. Associated over time in the black religious community with spiritual liberation, the train is a "soul" train that can rescue and carry the weary traveler home to Jesus. John Henry's association with the train, even after death, elevates him to the status of a saint. There is a sense of reification. John Henry's body may have died, but his spirit lives on in the continued presence of the train and the way in which the musical wail of the train whistle stimulates the imagination and pulls at the heart. John Henry dies of heart failure, but not of a failure of heart, and unlike in the 1920s and 1930s John Henry stories and minstrel shows written by white Americans, he is certainly not a failure in the texts by twentieth-century African American writers.

As a "type" in African American literature, John Henry, according to H. Nigel Thomas, represents "good" black masculinity (43–56). According to Lawrence Levine, John Henry types represent "the moral hard man," a type who achieves fame and fortune without preying upon his own people. John Henry types "defeated white society on its own territory and by its own rules" (421). As Marshall Fishwick notes in his essay, "Uncle Remus vs. John Henry," John Henry's manhood is based on the fact that he does not result to trickster tales or any sort of shucking and jiving (77–85). According to Jerry Bryant, John Henry's popularity as both a figure and as a type or model of manhood was a direct result of African American history:

> Having emerged from a condition in which they were sometimes ranked with animals or treated like retarded children. . . they needed to think of themselves as full human beings who believed in their own manliness. The warrior image provided that model. The warrior's violence asserted one's masculinity as well as one's humanity. (54–55)

Bryant calls John Henry a warrior, a hero, and a martyr in the battle to uphold black male honor and glory in the face of white America's commitment to destroy black manhood.

Chronologically, James Baldwin's 1968 novel *Tell Me How Long the Train's Been Gone,* which begins rather than ends with a heart attack, could have come before the previous discussions about uses of the John Henry legend because it uses a John Henry type rather than actually promising to be the story of John Henry. However, it provides an interesting conclusion to this discussion of typecasting, black masculinity, representations of manhood, the part the train plays as a testing site for manhood, the figure of John Henry as a model for true manhood, and the spiritual costs of the politics of representation. It also suggests that "staying put" can be destructive, that a man must be, as the Tubman tradition suggests, willing to "get on board," but that in the end, to be a real man, a man must also be strong enough to make the journey back to the home and the people of his youth, and to become a leader of his people.

James Baldwin's Leo Proudhammer, in *Tell Me How Long the Train's Been Gone* is, according to folklore scholar H. Nigel Thomas, a "John Henry type" (43). In *From Folklore to Fiction: A Study of Folk Heroes and Rituals in the Black American Novel* (1988), Thomas examines the "transposition" of African American folk heroes from folklore into more "literary" fictions such as stories, poems, and novels. He suggests that these African American folk heroes form archetypes particular to African American fiction, springing as they do from the concrete particulars of African American history. Even when the characters do not exist by name, they are known, recognized, and perceived on the basis of this typecasting.[18] In fact, typecasting is exactly what Leo Proudhammer, a gay black actor and reluctant political activist, is fighting. White America cannot "see" a black man as a possibility for playing the male lead in its Broadway plays, and black America cannot see a black man as manly or as fulfilling the community duties of fatherhood and manhood if he is gay. In this text, the other black male characters do not respect other black men unless those men are politically active race men. Baldwin's agenda is to redefine manhood to include black men, to include a better rounded approach to life that does not insist on every aspect of a black man's life being lived as a political statement, and also to include the possibility of erotic love between men in his redefinition of masculinity.

As Hazel Carby points out in her 1998 study *Race Men*, "ideologies of masculinity always exist in a dialectical relation to other ideologies" (2). In his essay, "Making Ourselves from Scratch," writer, editor, and gay activist Joe Beam says that when one is black and gay in America, it becomes "imperative for . . . survival" that one does not "attend to or believe the images . . . presented of black people or gay people," and that instead, a black gay man must create his own reality and "create images by which I, and other black gay men could follow, could live this life" (262). While some people prefer to, in the words of the modernist poet Ezra Pound, "make it new," others require history and tradition to lend veracity to the images and icons they hold dear.

In *Tell Me How Long the Train's Been Gone*, James Baldwin attempts to meet both needs. Baldwin wrestles with both white stereotyping of black men and with the definitions of manhood based on physical demonstrations of typically "male" behavior that, ironically, would force a gay man to deny the authority of his physical body and to reject its erotic desires as unnatural. Baldwin's other concern in the text is to redefine manhood so that it is something that is part of private life and not just something for public show and consumption. His suggestion is that current definitions of black masculinity are just for show so that one looks like a man when in actuality it is far more important to be in touch with one's true self and actually *be* a man.

Even so, some scholars misread James Baldwin as valuing "inner experience" more than a social experience, suggesting that the author was forever grappling with his "desire for privacy and the necessity of public involvement" (Gibson 116). [19] Donald Gibson concludes that Baldwin's novels, which Gibson sees as highly autobiographical, reveal that "Baldwin has come to see that love, the personal feelings of individuals for each other, is not enough" (117). This is Gibson's explanation for Leo Proudhammer's heartbreak. However, Gibson's reading would only make sense if Leo Proudhammer actually died of a broken heart as did the historic John Henry. Baldwin's Proudhammer lives.

Despite these differences, Leo Proudhammer undeniably is, as Thomas suggests, a John Henry type. The name alone suggests as much. Leo Proudhammer is the spiritual descendent of the great John Henry. Both are committed to hammering away at harmful stereotypes about black men, and to metaphorically improving the social and political landscape of America. The structure of the novel is such that it begins where most stories of John Henry end. This reversal is significant. The typical John Henry story ends with his heart attack, death, and the lesson of his death. Baldwin chooses to begin his story with his main character, Leo Proudhammer, in the midst of a powerful, life-draining heart attack, a heart attack that, like John Henry's, occurs publicly at the height of his fame and glory. The story begins with his recovery from a heart attack because in contrast to the other John Henry stories, in Baldwin's it is Proudhammer's continued life, not his death, which will provide the lesson.

The title of Baldwin's book comes from a stanza in a traditional folk song often sung in association with the Exodus trains, the trains that carried black laborers from agricultural wage slavery in the South to factory work in the North from the turn of the century through World War I. The song alludes to the earlier pre–Civil War era, which associated the train with freedom as in the gospel song, "Git on Board Lil' Children." It also refers to the mass exodus of African Americans, who would show up, sometimes by the thousands, for the hundred or so advertised jobs waiting at the end of the train line. What the song shows is that the needs of the people are great. They keep coming, searching for something better and a place that, to use the title of Arna Bontemps and Jack Conroy's book about the Great Migration, is *Anyplace But Here*. Even though the train has already left the station, and the implication is that the narrator has just missed the train, the needs of the people, and hence their hopes and faith, are so great that they keep coming. The suggestion is that it is great need that creates great faith, and the train is the symbol of what that faith can do: It can carry them to a place beyond the place they are in now.

Baldwin's title, *Tell Me How Long the Train's Been Gone*, is an implied question phrased as an imperative. Trains are synonymous with choices and with possible lives, possible, symbolic journeys, tracks, paths one's life may take. Just as the Exodusters saw the trains and their various stations as possible lives, each station or city signifying a different possibility or choice, so too does Baldwin's narrator, Leo Proudhammer, as he looks back over his life's journey and realizes that the choices he has made have led to other choices and that it has been a long, long time since he, like the train, has been gone. His near-death experience forces him to rest and be still. In this stillness, he reflects upon his life, his choices, and the results, and then compares them to those of his father and his brother. He has, in effect, left them behind. Whereas he, metaphorically, rode the train out of town to parts unknown and reinvented himself, his father and brother kept to the pre-established tracks with the expected results. They have not forgiven him for leaving, even though he has become famous, and he has found it difficult to be proud of them, to respect them for their choices, for staying put.

The novel was originally a short story, "Tell Me How Long the Train's Been Gone," and this short story becomes the pivotal scene in Leo Proudhammer's childhood. In the novel, Leo's older brother Caleb is saddled with the responsibility of watching his younger brother on the weekends. Caleb shrugs off that responsibility so that he can engage in illicit activities. Instead of taking Leo to the movies, as they tell their parents, Leo goes by himself and then waits at a drug store for his brother to take him home.

Leo takes to riding around on the trains while waiting for his brother. He has no money for train fare so he becomes adept at seeming to belong to different adults as they pass through the turnstiles. Just as he used to watch the movies and imagine himself living the different lives of the different white movie stars, he watches the people on the train and imagines what their lives are like. On the weekends, he notes, the black women are "almost as beautiful as movie stars" with "their hair all straightened and curled and the lipstick on their full lips looking purple and make-believe" (26). The white people, by contrast, in real life are not as beautiful as the movie stars and are "less attractive . . . under the ruthless subway lights" where "they were revealed literally, in their true colors. . . a mere steady, unnerving pinkish reddish yellow" (26–27). The train brings him into contact with blacks and whites, and, in the comparison between the two races, in terms of beauty and magnificence, the whites fail to bring satisfaction. This is significant because it is under the lights of the Saturday night trains that Leo Proudhammer sees and believes that black is truly beautiful, and sees that black people are as interesting to watch and as endlessly imaginatively evocative as any white face on a movie screen.

On one particular night, while riding the train, dreaming of lives not his own, Leo loses track of where he is going and finds himself on a train with no other black riders. All the other black people had gotten off the train, and he, in his dream-state, had kept riding, playing the movie reel of all his imaginings in his head. He panics and rushes off the train, into the station, unable to tell if he is uptown or downtown, knowing only that he is hopelessly lost. Leo recalls that he "rushed off the train, terrified of what these white people might do to me with no colored person around to protect me—even scold me, even to beat me, at least their touch was familiar, and I knew that they did not, after all, intend to kill me" (27). What this passage reveals is that Leo, as a child, is prone to racial bias born of fear and of stories about other blacks' experiences with whites. He does not love white people or want to be like them or with them. He sees them as a terrifying other. At this point in his life he would rather be with what is familiar, even if what is familiar is abusive. What is known is better than the great unknown. This childhood episode is a version of what the main character sees as his mother and father's "ghetto" mentality. They would rather stay where they have become known and know how things work, even when it is distasteful, than start all over someplace else.

With this in mind, Leo follows the first black man he sees in the station onto a train, picking that train only because a black man is getting on it. He gets on the train, gets as close as he can to the black man, and says nothing. Stop after stop, he rides the train.

> The train did not stop at any of the stops I remembered. I became more and more frightened, frightened of getting off the train, and frightened of staying on it, frightened of saying anything to the man and frightened that he would get off the train before I could say anything to him. . . . At each stop I watched him with despair. (27)

In an attempt to get home to Harlem, he has followed a black man to Brooklyn, a suburb of New York City proper, and a place he had never been to before. Leo's fear is the fear, literally and symbolically, that all people feel when they select a path or a course and do not know what the outcome will be. In this particular case, he has made his choice based on racial identification. His assumption is that where one black man goes, there are sure to be others, and that all black men eventually end up back in Harlem. He learns that night that this is not always the case.

Unaccountably, when he finally does speak to the man and confesses that he is lost, he finds himself wishing that the man would offer to adopt him and take him home to a new home in Brooklyn. When the man asks if he has a mama and a daddy, he longs to tell him no. "I almost said that I didn't have any because I liked his face and his voice and was half hoping to hear him say that he didn't have any little boy and would just as soon take a chance on me" (28). He learns that the man does have a son, about his age, named Jonathan, and it is because the man has a little boy of his own that the man decides to conduct Leo, personally, back to the station where Leo can get on the train that heads back to Harlem. He has turned to the man for help because the man is black, and he imagines a connection based on race. The man helps him because he has a son of his own and can imagine his son lost and how he would feel if no one helped his boy.

At this point, Leo "told him that maybe we should get off the train and that I would go back home with him" (39). Leo does not want to go back to his home. There seems to be a higher level of human relationships at work in Brooklyn than in Harlem, and Leo wants to go to Brooklyn with his new guide and be a part of that. By riding the train, Leo has already learned that black is beautiful and can be more beautiful than white movies stars, or his pale white "black" mother who is prized for her lightness. He now learns that black men can also be motivated by love and a sense of being caretakers, instead of equating "protection" with the mouth that scolds or the fist that beats.

Even at this point, Leo Proudhammer is ready to leave the ghetto, and the train is the symbolic vehicle of transport.

While riding the train back to the point at which Leo had switched train lines and gotten lost, the man asks Leo what Leo wants to be when he grows up. Leo tells him what he has never dared to tell his own family. He tells the man he wants to be an actor. Instead of laughing at him, the man appears to consider this quite seriously and says only that he is presently a bit skinny for an actor. At this moment, the train pulls into the station and the man announces, "Here's where we change" (30). He turns to Leo and says, "This train stops exactly where you going. Tell me where you going" (30). His word choice is significant in the context of the plot of the novel and in the symbolic value of this scene. On a concrete, real-world level, the man does not ask if Leo knows where he is going; he orders Leo to tell him to make sure that Leo really knows where he is going and will get home okay.

On a symbolic level, the words are prophetic. "This train stops exactly where you going" are like the words of the Cheshire Cat in *Alice in Wonderland*, where the cat tells Alice that one is only lost until one gets somewhere, and that one will always get somewhere if one heads in one direction long enough: These are words for a lost soul to live by. There is comfort in knowing that destiny has a hand in the course of one's life or that one is on course, even when one feels lost. Whatever odyssey or journey Leo Proudhammer is on, and the places his life will take him, it is comforting to think that the train will keep going, right on track, and on the right track, until the train stops, exactly where it should, in the place where he is going. There is a sense of belonging in and to one's own future in those words. Additionally the words, "Tell me where you going" provide a sense of ownership in the course of one's destiny. The direction is a choice. The suggestion is that if one knows where one is going, one is certain to get there, no matter how rough or adventurous the ride. This is the lesson of the train ride episode.

The rest of the novel confirms this thesis. For the next two hundred pages, Proudhammer has the reader join him as he re-lives various points along the time-line of his life until the present day. While the death of John Henry contains the lesson in most fictions about

John Henry, in Baldwin's novel, it is Leo Proudhammer's one-track-mind, his pursuit of a stage career, which carries the lesson.

This single-mindedness is compared to the single-mindedness of his new lover, a young man named Christopher, who is a political activist and who evaluates men only based on their potential for helping the cause of racial uplift. Christopher (whose name is perhaps meant to conjure up Christ-son-of-God imagery as the name means Christ-bearer) and Leo (the King) understand one another instantly because they are both one-track-mind men. In loving each other they learn a fuller sense of what it means to be men, or as Cora Kaplan puts it, Baldwin's work, and this is an excellent example—often revised the "ideal of masculinity" without reducing it to something "andocentric" (29).[20] Through Leo and Christopher, readers learn that manhood is not just about one's public performance as a man, whether it is as an actor or activist.

Ultimately, the lesson is that one can be a man, an important, useful, role model of a man, regardless of color or sexual preference, and that the final leg of the journey from boy to man involves forgiving one's fathers and one's brothers for trying to keep one back, down, and home. One must learn that it is not necessary to put on a big show or act like a big man just to impress other men. On the final page of the novel, Leo Proudhammer leaves Hollywood for a return visit to Harlem, on his way to a vacation in Europe where he will recuperate from his heart attack before returning to his now dual role as actor and American political activist. His broken heart is on the mend, and the return trip to Harlem to visit his father and his brother, where he does not put on any act and allows them to see him just as he is, is part of the healing process. Though both his brother and father remain stereotypes (his brother found God while in jail and is now a corner-store preacher and his dad remains a neighborhood braggart), Proudhammer has rejected all attempts to typecast him, and has become his own man. In *Tell Me How Long the Train's Been Gone*, Leo Proudhammer, the new and improved John Henry, has not missed his train and is right on track.

Similar to James Baldwin's *Tell Me How Long the Train's Been Gone*, Colson Whitehead's *John Henry Days*, published in 2001, is a full-length novel written for adult readers, not as a primer of black masculinity for children. Whitehead's text is a brilliant rejection of both the official government and mainstream popular culture's attempts to conscript black history and use it in service of an image of twentieth-century America as a time and place where racism has ceased to be a factor in public life. Set in 1996, in the predominantly white West Virginia town of Talcott during the "release party" for the United States Post Office's newest stamp in its folklore series, the John Henry stamp, Whitehead's novel demands that readers reexamine the significance of the stamp and what Talcott's "John Henry Days" festivities really signify regarding modern images of black masculinity. The question that urged the book forward, Whitehead explains was this: "What kind of monument was a postage stamp? It was so banal that it addressed something about our debased age."[21]

While the novel is difficult to summarize because it covers over one hundred years of American history asynchronously, J. Sutter, our protagonist, like Leo Proudhammer in Baldwin's *Tell Me How Long the Train's Been Gone*, is a John Henry figure. He is not "a" John Henry, but he is the next evolution of a type. Whereas John Henry worked as a temporary laborer for hire on the building of the new transcontinental railroad, J. Sutter is a freelance journalist on temporary assignment for a paper-less journal to be published electronically on the new "information highway" called the Internet. Instead of a Polly Ann figure, J. Sutter's love-interest is named Pamela Street, and she, too, is a professional temp whose most recent assignment was for an Internet company mapping the appearance and disappearance of various Web sites as part of a human-generated database-search engine, soon to be replaced by a machine known only as "The Tool" (287–90). Pamela Street is in Talcott, ostensibly to consider selling her father's John Henry collection to the town as part of their new John Henry tourist attractions, but really, she has come to bury her father's ashes in the place where the legendary John Henry met his doom.

J. Sutter has come to Talcott because he is on assignment, and because he is going for the freelance record of being able to attend all the events "the list" demands. To attend every function "the list" demands would require that the writer be able to handle day after day of jet lag, dirty hotels, airplane food, and no sustained human relationships, home life, or belongings that do not fit easily into an overhead storage bin. J. Sutter wants to "beat" the list by being able to do the impossible and actually keep pace with "the list" now that "the list" aided by "the latest advances in information technology" was "contacting its charges by mail, later by fax, then email" (54). Lucien, the man who controls the list, views the men on the list "like day workers who crowded the farmer's truck every morning for penny work" and using the database in his laptop "he monitored their progress" until he "discovered a ratio he liked" (297).

During the three days leading up to the culminating media event, J. Sutter has a near-death experience and is saved from choking by the same white stamp collector who will, on the last day of the festival, kill him. Alphonse Miggs, a small forgotten man, takes the place of the steam drill and is the villain of "this particular drama" who "waits for the cue" because "what's a hero without a villain" suggesting, of course, that Miggs and the machine were not the real villains in the historic John Henry story or what will be the story of J. Sutter's death (341). Such villains are "just a device" (342). The real villain is much more elusive.

Equally elusive, in the text, there is also a ghost, presumed to be the ghost of John Henry, that haunts the motel who is either in J. Sutter's room or the stamp collector's room, (Josi, the motel keeper's wife can't be sure as the ghost moves around spreading his influence on the unaware), and a "slow" man-child with a beautiful voice who can only sing one song, "The Ballad of John Henry," who steals what is said to be John Henry's hammer, and buries it in the earth so that it may "go back to nature" (168). Interspersed throughout the text are vignettes of other black Americans whose lives were touched and transformed by the legend of John Henry and who are, in the author's words, "adding verses" to the ballad as well as a fleeting glimpse of the story of John Henry through the eyes of John Henry himself (399).

The question posed by Whitehead's *John Henry Days* is twofold. Does the 1996 issuing of the John Henry stamp and the weeklong celebration of the man, organized by the white businessmen of Talcott to increase tourism in their part of the state really signify that America now embraces and celebrates black masculinity, or as William Strickland suggests, is it simply that, "in the modern era racism has become structurally covert and universally duplicitous. . . . It is more sophisticated" (354). Moreover, does the legend of John Henry still have a lesson accessible and applicable primarily for black men, a lesson about the choices in a man's life, and that each choice is expressive of the man himself? If man is not a machine, does he have a higher spiritual destiny than mere survival? In the final battle between John Henry and the machine, when the men in the crowd place their bets on who will win, the man or the machine, Whitehead writes, "there was more than money on the line. Each wager was a glimpse into the man who made it. There was more than wages on the line in this contest" (384). Choices, the author suggests, matter beyond the simply physical consequences of the choice. There is also the way those choices will be remembered and talked about in word and song. In addition, this dynamic spirit of song and story, Whitehead suggests, is far more important than any static visual artifact, like a statue that can be, as happens in the town of Talcott, "chained to a pickup truck and dragged off its pedestal," used "for target practice" or a stamp to be collected (265).

Whitehead observes that while the ways and means of exploitation have become more subtle, black men are still exploited by white culture, and that this exploitation complicates their personal relationships with their families, their place in the workforce, and their place in American history. Alternatively, as Hortense Spillers explains, in the latter half of the twentieth century, "we appear to be at a crossroads in trying to determine who owns African American cultural production as an intellectual property, who may speak for it, and whether or not possession itself is the always-exploitive end of kinds of access, even when the investigator looks like me" (77). Race, Spillers asserts, "travels" from "time to time," and "in a word, race haunts the air" (78). However, Spillers concludes, African American writers at the end of the twentieth century now look inward, not "as an answer or a cure" and "not as an arrival but a departure," and this inward gaze "is the mine of social production that arises, in part from interacting with others, yet it bears the imprint of particularity" (84–85).

In a February 2003 interview with *The Boston Globe*, Henry Louis Gates, noted author, scholar, and director for Harvard's W. E. B. Du Bois Institute for Afro-American Research, explained his selection of Whitehead and thirteen other writers to speak at Harvard, and his view on the writers of Colson Whitehead's generation in response to the interviewer's question about whether Colson Whitehead and Rita

Dove could really be "lump[ed] . . . together in one literary tradition" (para. 2). Gates's reply was that writers like Colson Whitehead,

> are very secure in their identity as persons of African descent. They don't have to claim it, as members of my generation did; they just presume it. So you don't read them to learn about the Black Experience in a sociological or anthropological way. You read them to learn about love, Death, Jealousy, and other universal themes. However, these young writers are familiar, I think, with the history and evolution of the African-American literary tradition. So they don't reject antecedents like Ellison so much as they "signify" or riff on them. . . . Race matters, yes—but in the realm of literature, craft matters more. Ethnic cheerleading in literature doesn't mean a thing if you can't write. (para. 5–7)

What complicates Whitehead's novel for some readers is that in Whitehead's *John Henry Days*, there are white men who are also victims of exploitation, and who respond to the legend of John Henry, but not in exactly the same way as the two main black characters, Street and J. Sutter.

Alphonse Miggs, the white stamp collector turned sniper, who will save J. Sutter from choking and then, two days later, shoot him dead as part of a shooting spree during the stamp's unveiling, responds to the legend of John Henry in this way: "What remained of the ultimate in human achievement was a stamp. It was all obsolete and preserved in adhesive elegies, limited-issue testament. He collected them all" (286). Miggs collects "the stamps of dead places" places "that had become obsolete" or "failed" or "swallowed up by larger ones" (285). What appeals to Miggs is that "John Henry's tunnel didn't stand the test of time, the roof gave in, and they built a new tunnel adjacent, according to modern specifications" (286). It is man's destiny, Miggs concludes to become "obsolete" and that no one respects the obsolete (286). Having become obsolete in his marriage and at work, Miggs decides to fight his fate and demands that, even though he is obsolete, he will be respected for his ability to make others obsolete as well, hence, the creation of the AMLF—the Alphonse Miggs Liberation Front and his dream of news coverage, "a brief story" which would "describe" his "grievances and rerun the now-familiar footage . . . violence placed in context" because of an "articulated manifesto" (360). In Miggs's mind, John Henry rebelled, but John Henry died, and the postage stamp confirms that the only message John Henry left the world was exactly the same as the other fallen, and thus failed, heroes, "the message these men gave to the world were small sadnesses," but Miggs plans to live, so that he will be able to know for sure that "the message had been heard" (360–61). Instead of a postage stamp for a dead man, Miggs is aiming for life in jail and some network coverage with a "special news report" about himself (260). For Miggs, John Henry's race is irrelevant. Miggs universalizes the figure of John Henry and thinks he identifies with John Henry's life of labor, rebellion, and eventual obsolescence by ignoring the context that created John Henry's struggles.

Whitehead includes the Miggs character to show how universalizing a black legend simultaneously grants the legend status as an integral part of "the" history of America to which all Americans may respond, while at the same time universalizing a black legend allows America to conclude that the "problem" of racism has been solved. If America "honors" a dead black man who may or may not have existed, and people both black and white respond to this figure, then, as Manning Marable has argued, America can pretend that racism no longer exists and that we are all just people. However, Marable cautions, "a spectre is haunting black America—the seductive illusion that equality between the two races has been achieved, and that the activism characteristic of the previous generation's freedom struggles is no longer relevant to contemporary realities" and while "the media, the leadership of both capitalist political parties, the corporate establishment, conservative social critics, and public policy experts, and even marginal elements of the black middle class, tell the majority of African Americans that the factors which generated the social protest for equality in the 1950s and 1960s no longer exists," there are other forces at work in the individual lives and personal experiences of black men and women that cannot be ignored (799).

It is these other experiences that Whitehead includes in his text to suggest that despite the recent white-washing of John Henry and attempts to turn him back into a universal Everyman, the legend of John Henry and his relationship to the building of the railroad still means something different to individual black Americans. According to "the Talcott Ruritan Club," John Henry symbolizes "determination" and is an object of "respect" because "the great and the strong" who are "of service to others" represent the current Ruritans of Talcott (264). This group statement, however, is far less interesting than the responses of individual people. Each black man and woman in the text responds differently to the legend of John Henry, despite the post office or the Talcott Tourism Board's attempts to control the representation of John Henry and his connection to the railroad.

John Henry is the black Adam, the father figure, the ancestor whose memory pushes forward at key moments in every black man's life urging him to persevere in the face of almost certain failure, reminding him that he is always looked upon as a symbol of his race whether he chooses to embrace that role or not, carrying with it an expectation of physical strength, and an even stronger will, the will to push the body past its physical limits. He is at once the man to be and the man not to be, and he is the ghost who cannot be laid to rest by the simple issuing of a stamp or a festival. Each man must confront this black ghost himself, and choose.

Whitehead's ghost, his John Henry who haunts the text, is more than just a literary convention representing a list of attributes. He signifies the resonating lived power of folklore that goes beyond the one-inch-by-one-inch perforated edges of a first-day issue postage stamp. Folklore, as Sw. Anand Prahlad, explains is much more than a mere "representational text":

> Rather, it is a part of the body, the unconscious and conscious mind, the spirit, the air that is breathed, the smells, sounds, sensations, and the totality of elements found in given moments of dynamic social interaction. It is a corporeally based, expressive, and artful language and system of thought of which spoken or written words are only a part. (para. 14)

That is exactly the function of the ghost of John Henry in Whitehead's text. While the post office and the businessmen of Talcott seek to package the stories of John Henry through a static representation of him on a postage stamp and as so many little "three-inch-tall John Henry" figurines sold for ten dollars a pop in a retired train car cum temporary gift shop as part of the John Henry Festival Days, the story of the real John Henry continues to impact the flesh-and-blood lives of the black characters in the novel by providing them with a historic and spiritual context for the lived experiences of their current daily lives (267).

As J. Sutter and Pamela Street bury her father's ashes in the same anonymous mass "Negro" cemetery said to be the final resting place of the legendary John Henry, Pamela tells J. that what compelled her father to collect John Henry stories and artifacts was a desire to share his version, his vision, his "revelation" of John Henry because the thing about the John Henry story was that "you could look at it both ways" meaning "his fight was foolish because the cost was too high" or "you could look at it and think the fight continued, that you could resist and fight the forces and you could win and it would not cost you your life because he had given his life for you. His sacrifice enables you to endure without having to give your life to your struggle, whatever name you gave to it" (378). To her father, John Henry symbolized the "possibility" that striving and "strivers" create out of "everyone of their hard mornings" (383). The lesson of John Henry, the elder Mr. Street believed, "was a lesson that had finally been learned at great cost" was that all strivers are John Henry, "John Henry in his infinite masks" (382).

The *John Henry Express*, the town of Talcott's proposed name for the old train caboose that will be fitted up as a museum and gift shop to house Pamela's father's treasures, Pamela decides, will be a much better representation of "the thousands and millions of John Henrys driving steel" than the "black metal" statue with "a little of the animal in him" who "looks like he's waiting for the gun to go off" dressed in "slave clothes" (262–66). For J. Sutter, John Henry's presence is best felt in the old tunnel that John Henry helped build. The tunnel "defeats the frequencies that are the currency of his life. Email and pagers, cell phones, step in here and fall away from the information age, into the mountain, breath in soot, unsettling but calming, too. The daily battles that have lost meaning are clearly drawn again, the opponents and objectives named and understood. The true differences between you and them. And it takes decades of healing and forgetting. . . . He wins the contest, but then what?" (322).

The legendary John Henry dies, of course, but does John Sutter? The ending, writes John Updike, is "frustratingly vague in its resolution" and "is either the best disguised happy ending or the most muffled tragic note of the publishing season" (89). Is J. Sutter is one of the two reporters accidentally shot by the young deputy as the young deputy shoots and kills the publicity-seeking Alphonse Miggs? The ending has prompted other critics, such as Donna Bailey Nurse, to say that *John Henry Days* "fizzles out" (para. 1). But is he dead or not? Sutter is "one dead duck," concludes Brent Stephenson:

> The duck parable at the beginning of the novel quietly establishes an important theme. The idea is that the ducks that are well bred are naïve enough to think that they are some type of royalty, but then in the end, they are slaughtered in just the same manner as the average ducks. J. is naïve enough to assume that because he reports the news, that he is immune from it, somehow separate from it, as if he transcends it. And in the end, that is what he becomes; first his choking mishap and then his death at the festival. Like John Henry, J. becomes what he does; J. becomes a headline.[23]

Greg Chagnon, book reviewer for *The Atlanta Journal*, suggests that Whitehead's intention is for the reader to entertain the notion that "being heroic in contemporary times requires a different kind of action" (para. 11). Instead of dying as a sort of "modern equivalent of the John Henry myth," J. Sutter and Pamela Street bury her father, and rather than continuing the "pattern of oppression" have the possibility of a different life (para. 9).

On the very last page of the novel Pamela and the taxi cab driver prepare to drive to the airport. Pamela has asked J. to go with her rather than stay for the finale of the festival. J. finds himself torn between going for the record and going with Pamela. As he watches her pack through the door she has left open, J. reflects, "There is still time. It will not take him long to get his little things together. They will wait if he asks. He stands there with the sun on his face deciding, as if choices are possible" (389). The reader, ironically, is left in the same position as those who bet on John Henry and the junketeers who bet on J. Sutter. Whether or not readers believe J. Sutter goes with Pamela or goes to his death is conditioned by their own understanding of the modern significance and contemporary use of the John Henry myth. Updike suggests that Sutter's "predicament" is a "very contemporary predicament, that of a talent lost in the brittle domain of irony and selling itself short in cranking out promotion pieces. . . its central character, the disgusted junketeer J. Sutter, need not be black at all" (88–89).

When asked about the ending of his novel, Colson Whitehead explained in an interview that the ending indicates his own belief that "choices might be possible. The novel, itself, has two possible endings, and readers fall into one of two camps deciding whether J. can galvanize himself and move on. J. is not really a Hamlet-like character, but *to be or not to be*, people have posed that question before."[24] In this case, the question before the reader is what choice is J. really contemplating when J. Sutter dryly comments on his own decision-making process, noting that he is debating his own decision "as if" he has a choice. Is he just pretending, to himself, that he has a choice about following or not following Pamela, or did the shared activity of burying her father bind them together as part of a more authentic John Henry experience than the stamp's unveiling could ever be, with Pamela as the real story not the puff piece. Sutter must decide whether or not "going for the record" is more important than the real challenge, the real risk of being with a woman who is not a "puff piece." After accompanying Pamela on her journey to lay her father's ashes in the same cemetery as that where John Henry was thought to reside, J. contemplates his story.

> Before he had been kidding about the story in order to get closer to the woman. He had put on paper some of the things she had said the day before but now he thought what happened today was the real story. It is not the kind of thing he usually writes. It is not puff. It is not for the website (sic). He does not know who would take it. The dirt had not given him any receipts to be reimbursed. He does not even know if it is a story. He only knows it is worth telling. (387)

In this, a real writer is born, not a junketeer, not a hack. Pamela is able, in the end, to put her father and John Henry to rest, and to move on, and she has asked J. to go with her. By leaving her hotel door open while she packs, she is, in essence, creating a liminal space for him, a threshold to cross over, and showing J. the way.

However, someone has to die. From the very first pages of the novel, when the intern reports the shooting on the last day of the John Henry Festival Days, it is apparent that in part, the novel is a mystery, not a "who-dunnit," but a "who-done-died." Josie, the motel keeper's wife, "a witch looking into bubbling murk" who sees that "the land is full of the ghosts of dead men who sacrificed to give this region life" is certain that the ghosts will "have opinions on this weekend's events" and will explain themselves forcefully (363). As she locks herself in her room and searches for her pills, even though "the pills don't help much," she hears a train enter Big Bend Tunnel, and "she hears the sound of the whistle as the engineer begs safe passage from John Henry" and wonders about the two men the ghost had visited, Alphonse Miggs and J. Sutter, if "perhaps the ghost blessed one of the men and cursed the other" (365). The festival days were "a new beginning" for the town, but this new beginning for her and her husband, and the white businessmen and women of Talcott hadn't "been paid for yet. There's some blood to be paid. John Henry spilled his, for the railroad, for his fellow workers, for Talcott and Hinton. Where will this weekend's come from?" (363). Does J. Sutter, the black John Henry figure, die, or is it someone else's turn?

Perhaps One-Eye who is tired of creating "ready-made" traditions and hopes that today "is the day he exits the List" will be the first to die, like the shaker in the John Henry story who flinched (83, 353). Perhaps the way to bury the ghost, return it to nature, as with the hungry ghost in Toni Morrison's *Beloved*, is for the blood to be shed by the villain of the piece, and as machines do not bleed, the creators of the PR machine must die, which would include Lawrence Flittings, the PR flunky, or Lucien, the Mephistopheles PR-man- extraordinaire and the creator of "The List." Lucien's boast, like Lucifer, the morning star, are nothing short of God-like as he promises the Mayor of Talcott that he, Lucien, can "release radiance":

> in my hand I have atoms, I have a sun. . . . I know the world, and it is full of light. Here and there, it leaks out, and this is where I come in. Lumens and lumens. Talcott is full of light. It is a silent star. It is a superheated solar furnace that is dark and waiting to become light. You have plans and ideas. I will give them to the world. (194–96)

According to the slightly inaccurate reporting of the intern whose story reveals the climax of the novel before the action of the novel begins, three people are critically wounded by a disgruntled postal worker who was then shot (26). The postal worker, at the end of the novel, corrects her story, reducing the kills to "two guys" plus the shooter, all three shot by the cop (267). From these small clues, there is no way to tell who, other than Alphonse Miggs, died. The frame of the text, however, beginning as it does in "terminal city" and ending with the high-flying chapter title "adding verses" that the writer, J.

Sutter, will not be among the dead. Instead of just a headline, he will, instead, write his story of Pamela, her father, and John Henry because choices are possible. "He will get the rest of the story, the parts she has not given him yet. Over time he will get the rest of the story. He already knows the ending. He witnessed it with his own eyes. But there is more" (389). Together, they will create new verses.

Sterling Brown, Terry Small, Julius Lester, John Oliver Killens, James Baldwin, and Colson Whitehead all use the story of John Henry to control, shape, or redefine their readers' responses to specific models of black masculinity. For Small, Lester, and Killens, the spirit of John Henry lives on in the sound of every train whistle, and if the texts are successful, the sight and sound of a train should summon up a dynamic memory association of the train with John Henry and collectively function as a corrective to white history and literary representations of black men. For Sterling Brown, John Henry "had what we need now," and that is the strength of heart necessary to "keep on keeping on," the pain of which can be heard in the lonesome whistle of the train and felt in every black man's heart. It is the capacity to feel this pain that makes a man a man and not a machine.

For James Baldwin and Colson Whitehead, manhood, ultimately, is a mark of and result of maturity, for all along the way, in the journey of one's life, there will be choices to be made. Being a man means being able to imagine the world in a way different from one's father and brothers and then being willing to take responsibility for the consequences of that difference. There is no one train that can carry one to this place, and one cannot become like a machine, deny the human yearnings of one's heart, and expect to live.

Despite their differences, all of these authors use John Henry and the symbol of the train to construct models of black masculinity that involve both political rebellion and a sense of spiritual destiny. The rebellion comes from the figure of John Henry and his connection to the train, not just his powerful hammer, which can easily be belittled, as in Whitehead's novel, by a fair-midway's gift shop creation of a three-inch John Henry statuette. What is important is that John Henry and those who continue to value what he represented are still hammering away at the manmade social structures of the time. The sense of spiritual power, the mystical element, comes from the symbol of the train and its historic promise to carry all passengers brave enough to take passage and board that train, from "can't" to "can." As Baldwin says at the end of his novel, "in America, nothing succeeds like success," and for twentieth-century African American writers, the train is still an emblem of the power to succeed even in the face of opposition, and John Henry remains the model of the black man with the strength of heart to make it happen (370). It is his heart, not just the hammer.

Similar to James Baldwin, ultimately what Colson Whitehead suggests is that one need not die a martyr to some cause, some contest of wills, for there is always another train, another contest, another challenge—and in the modern world, the connection between individual people, between a man and a woman, may be a bigger challenge than connecting up two tracks through a tunnel or two temporary points along the information superhighway. As long as one has heart, the ability to love, and the ability to place human priorities above mere professionalism, whether industrial or some other Internet industry, there is hope. The historic John Henry decided to battle a machine, and won, losing his life in the process; inspired by the power of the myth of John Henry to impact so many lives, J. Sutter walks away from being merely a cog in Lucien's publicity machine, and with Pamela, lives to "add new verses" about what it takes to live as a black man in the twentieth, now twenty-first, century. Living, and truly being free, is John Henry's new legacy for the twenty-first century. African American writers can now imagine a world in which black masculinity can live, thrive, and succeed rather than die.

⚜ CHAPTER FOUR

Riders of the Train: Passage, Passing, and the Great Migration

> Take your finger out of the pages, youngblood, and I will tell you about a kind of life these rails will never carry again.
> — James A. McPherson, "A Solo Song For Doc."

In "To Move without Moving: An Analysis of Creativity and Commerce in Ralph Ellison's Trueblood Episode" (1984), Houston A. Baker Jr. asserts that what may at first seem like an isolated episode or stray detail, further analysis may reveal something about the main character, the writer's aims, and the world into which the author imagines the text entering into a dialogue (224). A singular moment, event, or detail can "generate" meaning; and while advancing the story line within the text, it can also hint at the existence of "symbolic systems" external to the text and invite the reader to comment or reflect upon "such familiar social configurations as education, economics, politics, religion, and so on" (224).

When the same kind of episode, event, or detail can be found in a range of works, we then have grounds for saying that a seemingly minor event or detail is rich in meaning. The use of the train as both setting and symbol is one of these details, and a close examination of texts in which African American characters are riders of the train, as passengers, workers, or stowaways, reveals that even when their reasons to ride vary, the symbolic value of the train as an icon of power, transcendence, and freedom remains the same.

Take, for example, Richard Wright's 1937 autobiographical sketch *The Ethics of Living Jim Crow*, which was written to demonstrate the impact of Jim Crow on the development of black masculinity. Wright begins,

> My first lessons in how to live as a Negro came when I was quite small. We were living in Arkansas. Our house stood behind the railroad tracks. Its

> skimpy yard was paved with black cinders. Nothing green ever grew in that yard. The only touch of green we could see was far away, beyond the tracks, over where the white folks lived. But cinders were good enough for me, and I never missed the green growing things. And anyhow, cinders were fine weapons. . . . The green trees, the trimmed hedges, the cropped lawns grew very meaningful, became a symbol. Even today when I think of white folks, the hard, sharp outline of white houses surrounded by trees, lawns, and hedges are present somewhere in the background of my mind. Through the years they grew into an overreaching symbol of fear. (37–39)

The "natural" world of manicured lawns, well-groomed hedges, and strategically placed suburban trees becomes a symbol of the way in which white men mask their desire to do violence to black men behind a façade of "natural" superiority. Moreover, throughout the piece, the black women in Wright's life ask him to pretend that this is so, often resorting to violence themselves to beat into him the "gems of Jim Crow wisdom" in order to protect him from white male violence (38). This, of course, causes an identity crisis for the young Wright, one that he continued to explore in his later fiction as he searched for a symbol powerful enough to combat that of the green suburban lawn. He turned at last to the symbol of the train, the producer of his original cinder-weapons. Written almost twenty years later, after the writing of his autobiographical sketch and his more famous works, *Native Son* (1940) and *Black Boy* (1945), the short story "The Man Who Was Almost a Man" (1961), published in a collection of short stories the year after Wright's death, demonstrates that the power of the train is mightier than that of the white house or well-tended green suburban lawns that money can buy but which nature did not intend.

In the story "The Man Who Was Almost a Man," Wright's Dave Saunders escapes punishment for the killing of his employer's mule, mules, of course, according to Zora Neale Hurston, being symbolic of the white man's view of black men and women, and mules also being symbolic of the broken promises of the Freedman's Bureau at the close of the Civil War when the freedmen were promised "40 acres and a mule"; Saunders escapes from his life as a "field boy" by stealing a ride on a train.[1] At first, as he gazes at "Jim Hawkins' big white house," (Jim Hawkins, of course, is Wright's white enforcer of Jim Crow laws) Dave Saunders does not know what to do, but then he hears the sound of the Illinois Central and realizes that the only way to maintain his sense of pride and to "know Dave Saunders is a man" is to ride the train out of town (1916):

> The cars slid past, steel grinding upon steel. Ahm ridin yuh ternight, so help me Gawd! He was hot all over. He hesitated just a moment; then he grabbed, pulled atop a car, and lay flat. He felt his pocket; the gun was still there. Ahead the long rails were glinting in the moonlight, stretching away, away to somewhere, somewhere he could be a man! (1916)[2]

Wright's character believes that the train can and will carry him "away to somewhere, somewhere he could be a man," and whether readers concur or not with the character's point of view, it is a point of view echoed by characters in works by Albert Murray, Ralph Ellison, James McPherson, Claude McKay, Zora Neale Hurston, and many others.[3]

The success of riding the train from one life into another and what the actual experience of riding the train felt like, however, depended on whether one road as a stowaway, a worker, or as a passenger in the Jim Crow car. Not all riders of the train had positive experiences. As previously discussed in chapter one, racism and prejudice after World War I instigated another wave of migration north via the Exodus trains. Economic, political, and social mobility and equality were still the goals, and the train still the symbol of the push for the freedom to make such dreams come true. While the train continued to symbolize the fast track to freedom, because of the social and economic realities of the 1920s and 1930s, the train was also often an emotionally charged space where black and white came into contact and often conflict with each other.[4] Train scenes involving racial conflict thus became a literary convention used by white and black writers alike.

White writers primarily use the convention as an episode that solidifies racial difference.[5] For African American writers, however, these train scenes are much more complicated because of these three distinct categories of experience. Some riders of the train, often women or young adults, are passengers who must suffer the indignities of the Jim Crow cars. Racial conflict plays an important part in these stories and the resolution of the conflict shapes the characters' future.[6] Other riders of the train are workers. The main character in such stories is often a dining car or "kitchen mule" worker in an all-male environment, and because of being brought into contact with a lot of different kinds of men, both black and white, he can learn important lessons about both the limitations and the possibilities of true freedom. The third category of train riders has the main characters, again usually male, as stowaways or hobos stealing a ride on the back of an open train. These stories, most often, have the most positive results.

What links the three categories of experience, while also differentiating them from the way in which white writers use the same setting or material, is that instead of reinforcing who the main character really "is," as if that person existed inside all the time and simply needed affirming, in the African American texts there is a sense that the characters actually learn something new about who they want to be in the future. The train becomes a liminal or transitional space, an educational space, and traveling on the train as passenger, worker, or stowaway carries them across a threshold from one identity to another. The rider gains self-knowledge and an increase of personal power, though sometimes the application of the power is deferred in the cases of narratives about children, but even then, the train episode fires their desire for transformation and is thus a key component in their transformational learning process.

This specialized use of the train as a gateway from one identity to another and as an educational space owes much to the early twentieth-century association of the trains with the story of Exodus in which Jewish slaves, through arduous travel and continual hardship and conflict, become free men. The book of Exodus ends with the journey still in progress, and with the people wondering if the journey and the search for a new land will last as long as did their four-hundred-and-thirty-year enslavement. As discussed in chapter one, this association of the train with the book of Exodus comes from the practice of referring to special work trains that transported African Americans from the agrarian South to the urban, industrial cities of the North as Exodusters. Trains became increasingly contested space, symbolic of the far greater issue of the right to work, freedom of mobility, and the right to determine or create one's own identity without race being the primary factor or consideration.

According to Samira Kawash in her 1997 study, *Dislocating the Color Line*, racial identities form as a result of experiences that are forced upon one only because of race. A person would not have a racial identity if race was not a determining factor in his or her experience of living. She writes, "segregation and the legal, social, and institutional contexts in which it operates function as mechanisms that contribute to the production, ordering, and control of racial identities" (97). Segregation, from the point of view of many African American writers, was not about controlling miscegenation or maintaining the fiction of racial difference as scholars such as C. Vann Woodard have asserted. Segregation, at least from the perspective of twentieth-century African American writers, was about white attempts at producing, ordering, and controlling something as private and as personal as one's individual identity. Segregation, and the racism used to maintain the fiction of difference, created difference.

Not surprisingly, this is made very clear in works by twentieth-century African American writers who have, in a significant episode in a novel or story, characters who are passengers, train workers, or stowaways. For African American writers of the twentieth century, despite the racial conflict that often occurred on trains, the train remained a largely positive symbol and communicates to their readers a rejection of American racism, a denial of the identity assigned to them as second-class citizens as "natural," and along with that, a particular view of American history emphasizing a need for continued agitation in the cause of true freedom, a freedom which includes the right to work, the right to mobility, and the right to have an identity that is not based predominantly on race. The railroads, with their early symbolic association with the Underground Railroad as a force large enough to reject and undermine state and federal law, and their later role as the contested site of a man's right to construct his own identity, remain a powerful, though little studied, symbol in twentieth-century African American fiction.

With this in mind, it is easy to see how the train in Ralph Ellison's "Boy on a Train," a story set in 1924 and written sometime in the late 1930s, is meant to, in Baker's words, "generate meaning" (224). The boy and the train are symbolically very similar. The story begins with a description of a train as it races down a hill, blowing off steam as it goes. Looking out the window of this train, a boy points out to his baby brother all the pretty colored leaves painted by Jack Frost as they say good-bye to their life in the North and head back South. The boy's father has recently died and the mother, unable to support herself and the two boys, has determined that she must return to Georgia after fourteen years of living in the North.

By the third paragraph of the story, without ever describing the color of the boy or his family, it is apparent that they are black because of their experiences on the train, beginning with where they are placed on the train. The train car where they must ride is hot and the car is

> too close to the engine, making it impossible to open the window. More than once, cinders found a way into the car and flew into the baby's eyes. . . . The car was filthy, and part of it was used for baggage. Up front, the pine shipping box of a casket stood in the corner. . . . Bags and trunks covered the floor up front, and now and then the butcher came in to pick up candy, or fruit or magazines to sell back in the white cars. (13)

In this story, a white butcher shop owner makes extra money selling grocery store items on the train. He returns periodically to the baggage car to get more supplies. The boy and his family ride with the baggage; they are viewed as objects.

James Alan McPherson, in his history *Railroad: Trains and Train People in American Culture,* records that it was common to place African Americans as passengers in the baggage car directly behind the engine because this was an undesirable location for "regular" (i.e., white) passengers to ride because of the soot, heat, and noise. In Ellison's story, the white butcher, who periodically returns to this car to restock the goods he is selling on the train, reaches out and touches the mother's breasts. She spits in his face and tells him to keep his dirty hands off of her. Ellison includes this passage in order to show the disparity between how a black woman traveler is viewed by white men, and how she views herself and them. From her perspective, it is the butcher who adds to the "dirt" of traveling in the Jim Crow car.

As the train continues on its journey South, the boy looks out the window at the landscape and thinks about all that has happened to him that day, that year, and what might happen in the days to come. As they pass by a farm with a crooked fence, he remembers the silly children's nursery rhymes his mother used to teach him about the crooked man who walked a crooked mile. Ellison's technique of combining this memory with a flash picture seen through the train window as it speeds South suggests that from the moment they board this train, the boy's childhood is passing away. He next sees a boy walking a dog as he herds cows, and thinks to himself that it is a nice dog, and tries to remember what kind of dog it is, as if it is important to remember every detail of the setting of the life he is leaving.

From the window, he also sees a train headed North, in the opposite direction from his train, and a lump forms in his throat as he thinks about what will happen if they never go back. He longs to be picking peaches for money with his two best friends, and thinks about how the storekeeper would let them eat some of the peaches. At this point he sighs, and "the train whistle sounded very sad and lonesome" (14). The train engine continues to personify the boy's feelings, first blowing off steam and now sounding sad and lonesome.

As the train continues further and further South, various white people enter the Jim Crow car to attend to their dogs (pets rode in the Jim Crow car) at rest stops, or to remove baggage, deliveries at the various stations, and, of course, to remove the coffin with the dead man being shipped back South for burial. It is at this point in the story that the mother's composure breaks down and she cries. Her voice trails off into a tortured moan that blends with the sound of the train, and tears stream down her face. James turns his eyes to the train window.

> The train was moving again, and he wondered why his mother cried. It wasn't just that Daddy was gone; it didn't sound just that way. It was something else. I'll kill it when I get big, he thought. I'll make it cry just like it's making Mama cry! The train was passing an oil field. There were many wells in the field; and big round tanks, gleaming like silver in the sun. One well was covered with boards and looked like a huge Indian wigwam against the sky. The wells all pointed straight up to the sky. Yes, I'll kill it. I'll make it cry. Even if it's God, I'll make God cry, he thought. I'll kill Him; I'll kill God and not be sorry! The train jerked, gaining speed, and the wheels began a clicking ragged rhythm to his ears. (20)

The boy is unable to understand what it is, exactly, that causes his mother's fear, pain, hurt, humiliation, shame, and sadness. He recognizes, of course, the part white people play as the tools to accomplish those things, but he cannot figure out what it is that animates the tools, making white people act as they do. There is a force that engineers the whole thing, he decides, and it is that force he wants to confront and make pay for his mother's pains. In many ways, his feelings are reminiscent of Melville's Ahab, who wishes to push through the pasteboard mask to find whatever force it is in the universe that makes or allows bad, painful things to happen, and to kill it, even if it is God.

Without knowing exactly why, the boy identifies the white man's pursuit of rich, black oil as the force that is behind his mother's pain, and vows to hurt that force, that system—to disrupt it, hurt it, make it cry and kill it, no matter how big it is, even if it is the force that brought him into existence. Furthermore, one could argue that greed and the pursuit of wealth did bring slavery into existence, and that when Mammon (money) becomes one's God, slavery and the abuse of other people's bodies, and then a lasting history of racism and wage slavery, are the direct result. Barbara Foley suggests that an awareness of this is the purpose of this story, both aesthetically and politically. The story allows the reader to "explore what it feels like to view the world through red lenses—or, at least, the dark pink lenses of the Popular Front era" (326). Foley reads the text as being anti-capitalist first and foremost, and about race only in conjunction with class.

The reader, however, realizes things that the boy on the train cannot. The story ends with the train jerking into high gear, gaining speed, and becoming a rhythm in his ears that matches the words, "I'll kill it." The words become part and parcel of the sound of the speeding train, and soon the words melt into the sound. He looks out the window at all the for-sale signs and advertisements. Although Ellison, the author, does not choose to have his child narrator make the connection between all the for-sale signs and his current situation, the adult reader can see this as reinforcing the oil fields passage, a critique of an America where everything, even the quality of a child's life, has a price tag on it and is for sale. In this respect, Ellison's story relies on the same technique employed by William Blake in his chimney sweep poems from the "Songs of Innocence and Experience," in which the narrator's innocence is visible only in light of the reader's experience of the immoral secular world. The boy makes "a wish never to forget" and whispers to himself, "This is 1924, and I'll never forget it" (21). He then looks out the window, "resting his chin on the palm of his hand, wondering how much farther they would have to ride" (21). Although the child means how much further in geographical distance, the adult reader, again, realizes this wondering parallels other concerns, such as civil rights. How much further does black America have to go to be at home in America? To what lengths must they go to ensure economic and social equality and security? How much further must they go?

Toni Morrison's *Sula* (1973), also set in the 1920s, contains a train episode in which another mother, headed South to visit her old home, is insulted by a white man, and, as a result, the daughter's sense of personal identity and of the kind of person she wants to be is forever altered. Set in November of 1920, as the last of the World War I black soldiers were trickling home from victory abroad only to find that race relations at home had not improved, Helene Wright and her daughter Nel must make a trip South, back to the home of Helene's youth to visit Helene's ailing surrogate mother. It will be Nel's first journey by train and her first time South of the Great Lakes region where she lives. Morrison repeatedly refers to their final location as South, perhaps capitalizing on her readers' feelings about what the South signifies.[7]

In the story, the mother prepares for the trip with misgivings. She is not worried about the trip; what occupies her mind is returning to the place where her biological mother was known by all to be a Creole whore. She has spent a lifetime cultivating good taste, dignity, and grace. She fears that a return to her old home might prove a battlefield and that her honor will be questioned because of her own mother's lack of honor. She prepares for the imagined battle with the folks from home as a soldier might, constructing a suit of women's armor out of deep brown wool and expensive, tasteful velvet for the sleeve cuffs, collar, and pockets. Her "best protection," however, she tells herself, will be "her manner and her bearing" (19).

It is both painful and ironic, then, when the battle occurs in a place and at a time she least expects it. Late for the train, Helene and her daughter must run along the track to catch it, and they mistakenly enter the wrong coach. Instead of immediately leaving the coach reserved for white passengers and risking missing the train, Helene and her daughter walk on through to the colored car. As she enters the colored car from the white car, a white conductor comes toward them and blocks their way. He knows that they have not entered the colored car through the colored door. As Patricia McKee explains, "with one slip," Helene "begins to lose control of her existence and slide back into an identity with her mother, a Creole whore" (8).

Morrison describes the incident in great detail so that the reader can imagine the scene in its entirety. The chill of the day is contrasted with the "light skim of sweat" that glistens on Helene's face as she is forced into a confrontation with the white conductor (20). Her daughter, Nel, stands at attention, struggling to hold the heavy basket of food packed for their journey to New Orleans. He calls the mother "gal," and instantly her defenses dematerialize. "Gal" was the word the men called her mother, the whore. "Gal" was the word they called her until her grandmother rescued her, took her away, and raised her to be a lady. That one word, "gal," causes

> all the old vulnerabilities, all the old fears of being somehow flawed gathered in her stomach and made her hands tremble. She had only heard that one word . . . Thinking he wanted her tickets she quickly dropped both the cowhide suitcase and the straw one in order to search for them in her purse. An eagerness to please and an apology for living met in her voice. "I have them. Right here somewhere, sir." (20)

A single word, a label, what one is called, picks a hole in her armor and makes it possible for a history of doubts to assail her.

Even though Helene should not, she finds herself wondering if his summation of her, in the careless application of that one word, is correct. She then feels even more flawed for this weakness. She begins to believe her weaknesses are real and that her imagined flaws exist and are plain for everyone to see. She hopes, somehow, that if she can please him, make him look at her in a different light, she will then be a different person, and not this generalized "gal."[8] He is the cause of her discomfort, and yet it is to him she turns "for compassion," as the other black riders in the car avoid making eye contact with her, thinking that they are sparing her additional humiliation or pain by not "observing" what is happening (21).

At this point in the episode, her language changes to match the conductor's low language in which all g's are dropped and double negatives abound. She tries to defend herself by using his language. "There wasn't no sign," she tells him, to which he replies, "We don't 'low no mistakes on this train. Now git your butt on in there" (21). He stands there, running his eyes over her body, and then, Morrison writes,

> Then, for no earthly reason, at least no reason that anybody could understand, certainly no reason that Nel understood then or later, she [Helene, the mother] smiled. Like a street pup that wags its tail at the very doorjamb of the butcher shop he has been kicked away from only moments before, Helene smiled. Smiled dazzlingly and coquettishly at the salmon-colored face of the conductor. (21)

Perhaps best understood as a modified sort of Stockholm response, a situation in which kidnap victims grow to value and need their victimizers' approval and value themselves only as an extension of their kidnappers' power, Helene wants the conductor's approval and uses sexuality to try to get it. A coquette, not a whore, Helene uses her one power, her beauty, to try to make the man like her. She is flirting, not selling, and it is her attempt to have some sort of impact on him or to in any way control his responses to her. She does not recognize that in this respect she is acting like her mother. This is not a conscious decision or strategy on her part; it is a memory reenacted from childhood about how a woman exerts control over men, white or black, and gets her way. Morrison's comparison of Helene's behavior to that of a street pup, however, indicates that in no way will the ploy be successful. Even if she treats the conductor like a man, he will never treat her like a woman. In his mind, she can be no better than some man's "bitch."

Painful as this episode already is, the scene, however, does not end there. Morrison shifts perspective and reveals what the scene looks like through the eyes of both the daughter and the other black passengers on the train. Nel looks away from her mother and watches the black passengers watch her mother.

> The two black soldiers, who had been watching the scene with what appeared to be indifference, now looked stricken. Behind Nel was the bright and blazing light of her mother's smile; before her the midnight eyes of the soldiers. She saw the muscles of their faces tighten, a movement under the skin from blood to marble. No change in the expression of the eyes, but a hard wetness that veiled them as they looked at the stretch of her mother's foolish smile. (21–22)

Here Morrison's Helen-of-Troy figure becomes Medusa and the black men are turned to stone. Like the petrified men of Southern fictions, these returning black soldiers cannot hope to reproduce a new social order with women such as this. When the conductor leaves, Helene looks for a black man to lift her bags onto the overhead rack for her, but "not a man moved" (22). The black men do not act like gentlemen and help her with her bags because she has ceased to behave like a lady. Demonstrations of black masculinity seem to be predicated on the actions of black women. The suggestion is, of course, that black men cannot be men when black women act like "gals." A man can only be a man when he has a woman to be a man for.

Nel watches the black passengers watch her mother and finds that she cannot meet her mother's eyes:

> In the silence that preceded the train's heave, she looked deeply at the folds of her mother's dress. There in the fall of the heavy brown wool she held her eyes. She could not risk letting them travel upward for fear of seeing that the hooks and eyes in the placket of the dress had come undone and exposed the custard-colored skin underneath. . . . if she were really custard, then there was a chance that Nel was too. (22)

In that instant, the heavy brown folds of expensive material are all that remain of the mother Nel thought she knew. The train's heave births a new revelation for Nel. Nel's journey, as Elizabeth House points out, has long-lasting effects (99). In that instant she experiences her first real bout of psychological mother-child identity separation. She wishes NOT to be like her mother for the very first time. Her identity construction begins with this rejection of her mother and a resolution never to be like her mother, dependent on a dress or manners for a sense of self. She vows that her sense of self will also not be determined by or changed by how others perceive her.[9] Nel's identity is thus shaped by her mother's identity being obliterated by the white train conductor's century-old assumptions about black women. "It was on that train, "Morrison writes, "shuffling towards Cincinnati, that she [Nel] resolved to be on guard—always" (22). By the time Nel and her mother reach New Orleans, this resolve has firmly taken root. Though negative, this incident on the train has been both the birth-place and, in a sense, the birth mother of Nel's new identity: She no longer views herself as an extension of her mother to be molded or manipulated under the impression that mother knows best.[10] The train incident, as Patricia McKee points out in "Spacing and Placing Experience in Toni Morrison's *Sula*," is the incident that "sets limits" and helps Nel to reject duplicating her mother's slip into a "generalized identity," that of being "just another black woman in sexual complicity with a white man" (9).

In terms of the episode's significance in the novel, the scene is clearly an important one in Nel's identity construction, particularly in regard to sex, sexuality, and her understanding of true womanhood. Ralph Ellison's short story, "Boy on a Train," previously discussed, depicts a similar incident, but because the child character is male rather than female, his response is slightly different. He vows to "kill it," whatever the "it" is that makes it possible for the pink-faced white man to touch his mother. Nel vows to be on guard against herself, blaming her mother more than she blames the salmon-faced conductor. In both cases, however, the children vow to remember their first train trip and this lesson that they have learned by coming into contact with white men in a segregated Jim Crow car. This experiential learning or training will influence the type of adults they become. The boy is training himself to respond with righteous anger and potentially with violence; the girl is training herself to take responsibility for all that happens to her, to be on guard against an enemy within herself.[11]

There are positives and negatives to both children's decisions. The boy has committed himself to being an active hero who will take arms against the world if need be. This decision is both positive and negative depending on how violence is played out. The girl has committed herself to personal discipline and responsibility, which is a good thing, but it can become a bad thing if one holds oneself responsible for "sins" that are really beyond one's control, such as someone else's inappropriate lust. As passengers on a train, both children are passive. This is primarily a negative thing, and their experiences on the train are negative, perhaps because they are both riders on trains headed South. However, what they learn has some positive aspects mixed in with it, and their identities form around these nuggets of truth that each child feels that they have found by riding the train and remembering this first trip, this first initiation into the world of

Southern white men. In twentieth-century African American fiction where the main character is a passenger on a train, the train may be able to return them to the place from which they departed, as in Nel's case, but they will never be the same now, having once taken this journey.

Where the main character is an adult train worker, the train is also an educational space, a sort of moving classroom, and is still symbolic of the push for freedom under the guise of passive subservience. The train whistle and the rhythm of the wheels still speak a message without words and voices the feelings of the black narrator. In Claude McKay's *Home to Harlem* (1928), for example, the main character, a returning soldier named Jake, first learns about pan-African history and the African Diaspora while working as kitchen help in a train dining car.

McKay's Jake bears a startling resemblance to some of Ernest Hemingway's returning soldiers in his now classic collection of war aftermath stories, *In Our Time* (1925). In fact, the name of McKay's soldier is the same as Hemingway's protagonist in the 1926 novel *The Sun Also Rises*. However, while Hemingway is celebrated for his "prolonged examination of violence" and the quest for a personal morality in the face of "victimization in war, love, hunting, fishing, bullfighting, and writing," or anything involving "human interchange" (*Columbia Literary History of the United States* 850), McKay's use of similar themes has been faulted as brutal realism that portrays African Americans as both violent and overly sensual. McKay is accused of creating a work that "pandered to the worst stereotypes of Afro-Americans held by white America" (Cooper's foreword to the reissue of McKay's *Home to Harlem* xviii). In fact, W. E. B. Du Bois wrote that the book "for the most part nauseates me, and after the dirtier parts of its filth, I felt distinctly like taking a bath" (qtd. in Lueth 43). Contemporary critics, however, such as Elmer Lueth, find in the book a "more complex presentation of Black life than seems apparent at first glance" (44).

In contrast to Hemingway's Jake or his other returning soldiers, McKay's returning soldier comes home to urban Harlem. There can be no quiet camping scenes or slow return to everyday life beginning with breakfast in one's mother's kitchen while Dad heads off to work as in Hemingway's "Soldier's Home." Instead, McKay's Jake lands in

New York with a limited supply of cash, a suitcase, and a new suit, a situation more akin to a man being released from serving a term in prison than a soldier returning home.

As Alladi Uma points out, however, a scene like this is not written expressly as nationalist black propaganda to encourage black anger or anti-white sentiments: "McKay does not write propaganda but his writing itself becomes a voice, a voice which will awaken the consciousness, not only of himself but of those around him.... To him as for any African American it is necessary to use writing as a means of self discovery and self assertion" (25). As Uma suggests, *Home to Harlem* is Jake's exploration of an "emerging self" and this exploration of identity is largely inspired by his work on the train (25).

Working for the railroad in the kitchen becomes the only way he can get out of the city after his return, and Jake enjoys watching the Pennsylvania countryside as the train travels west. His fellow workers are a mixed group of African Americans, including dignified older men whose "wives moved in some sphere of Harlem society, and their movements were sometimes chronicled in the local Negro newspapers" (127). Others are light-skinned mulattos who refuse to associate with the darker-skinned train workers. Though classed as one group by the white train stewards, the African Americans are a diverse group, and Jake learns much about the different pathways his life could take by coming into contact with this diverse group of men. Eventually, Jake teams up with a French-speaking man from Haiti, nicknamed "the professor," a young man who was a student at Howard University, who teaches him the history of Haiti and, more importantly, teaches Jake to believe, by example, that a black man is capable of learning anything a white man can if given the same opportunity for education.

Each night, at the end of their respective shifts, as they get ready to bed down for the night, the professor teaches Jake something new about black history. He begins with the history of Haiti (which McKay spells Hayti) and its revolution under the leadership of Toussaint L'Ouverture. For the first time, Jake sees a black man as a world-class hero and wishes that it had been in Toussaint's army that he had been a soldier instead of the mud and muck of Europe. As the nightly lessons continue, he learns that the history of Africa he had always believed to be true, that "Africa was a jungle and Africans bush niggers, cannibals . . . monkey-chasers" was a lie, and that Africa was actually a country with a history and culture as old as the Romans with kingdoms in Abyssinia and beyond (134). Jake was amazed to learn that slavery was not a condition limited to those of African descent and that the Jews and the Saxons had also been slaves. He learns too that King Solomon of the Bible had a black wife, having married the Queen of Sheba who was as black as night.

This new information fills him with a sense of pride, and yet, also for the first time, a sense that not all black men are really men. Some men, like the head cook on the train, have capitulated and internalized white racism against themselves and their own people. This idea that certain black men have internalized white racism is, as David Goldwebber points out in his essay on McKay's conversion to Catholicism, a common theme in McKay's work. According to Goldwebber, McKay "warns black Americans to beware of the materialistic Protestant god of progress" and associates such progress with "bigotry, slavery and greed," suggesting that the Protestant work ethic has become corrupted and that it is Protestantism that causes internalized racism and makes black men hate themselves and devalue their own history (12). This is clear in the text when the head cook calls the professor's words all "nonsense" that will get in the way of Jake doing an honest day's work on "the white man's train" (139, 160).

The professor, Ray, is a different kind of man from any Jake has met before, and knowing Ray makes Jake want to be more and to feel like more is possible. While the other men he has met make him feel as if his current situation is all that life is or can be, Ray's histories make Jake feel that life is larger and has roots that run deeper than he had suspected. Jake begins to feel like there is a past that is different from the present, and hence a future that is potentially different as well. He is learning to see his place in history through different eyes as a result of moving through time and space, both figuratively and literally, each night on the train. Jake says to himself, "We may all be niggers aw'right, but we ain't nonetall all the same" (159).

Eventually, Ray, the "professor," decides that America has failed him and signs on as a mess cook for a boat headed to Australia. Jake decides to give up working for the railroad as well. Although Ray feels America is too small, too limited, too racist to offer him true freedom, Jake, though changed by his experiences with Ray and working on the railroad, has not yet given up on America. In the final section of the novel, Jake renounces his philandering ways; finds Felice, the girl of his dreams; rescues her from a bad relationship; and insists that she give up her modified version of whoring and come with him. The final pages of the novel show Jake at the subway station, waiting for Felice to arrive. She is late, and they need to catch the subway to the train station before the train departs. Jake decides that whether she shows up or not, he will board that train. She arrives, breathless, at the last minute, and all is well. They will head west, via train, to begin a new life in a new city, a new Adam and Eve of sorts headed to a new urban frontier.

Home to Harlem thus ends, ironically, with a leave-taking. This, Lueth suggests, points out that there is "no limitation of the potential of Blacks" and that the life of 1920s African Americans, regardless of what the social scientists claimed, "is not the prejudiced and deterministic 'straightjacket' it initially appears to be"(50).[12] This is, as Lueth rightly points out, because of the train. The train is the place where Jake first learns to think of himself as more and to want more, and the train also becomes his chosen vehicle by which to begin that new life. The reader's focus, at the end of the novel, should be on the horizon, at that place where the train tracks seem to converge from two into one, and disappear into the great unknown. There is the suggestion, the hope, that he and Felice will be successful because she believes in him, and he now believes in himself, without, as Lueth points out, needing to "bleach the Negro soul" which, Lueth concludes, means that one "cannot help but think that Du Bois' decision to take a bath was premature" (51).

In James Alan McPherson's short story, "A Solo Song: For Doc," from his 1969 collection of short stories, *Hue and Cry*, the author also explores how working on a train and train travel participate in identity formation. According to Calvin Reid, these stories were inspired by and based on McPherson's experiences "as a dining-car waiter for the Great Northern Railroad in the 1960s" when he "would ride the trains out of the south to Chattanooga, along the Mason-Dixon line" (36). In this particular story, the education of the main character occurs directly because of his exposure to a diverse group of other black men while in service on the train so that when he gets older, he attempts to pass along that education to another young man. This, McPherson suggests, is how young men really become men. Manhood, McPherson suggests, as did Sterling Brown, is about service without servitude and pride without boasting. Manhood is persistence, not passivity, and of having something to do as opposed to someone that one loves. Manhood is not about sexuality or selfishness; it is about doing things right.[13]

In McPherson's short story, black manhood is a dying art, and it is symbolized by the trains, and by the waning popularity of the passenger trains. "I am dying, youngblood," the old waiter tells the summer college boy waiter,

> and so is this business. Both of us will die together. There'll always be summer stuff like you, but the big men, the big trains, are dying every day and everybody can see it. . . . We made this road. We got a million miles of walking up and down these cars under our feet. . . . The Old School died with Doc, and the very last of it is dying with me. What happened to Doc? Take your finger out of the pages, youngblood, and I will tell you about a kind of life these rails will never carry again. (151–53)

So begins an old waiter's story of an even older waiter as he tries to teach a summer worker, a college boy, how to be a man's man. The college boy, with his fingers in the white pages of the railroad's service staff guidebook, has just been introduced to a better guide. Rather than the dry pages of directives issued by the company, directives that cover every aspect of service so that all service is uniform, his guide is from the older generation of men who, in a sense, wrote the book on service because for them, there was no guidebook. They invented it; it came from a deep sense of self-respect. It was not an act put on for show like a pair of cheap white kid-gloves.

He first describes Doc as a man who "fell in love with the feel of the wheels under his feet," a man who "got the rhythm of the wheels in him, and learned, like all of us, how to roll with them and move with them" (153). Riding the rails becomes a metaphor for, as the old cliché goes, rolling with the punches. Being a waiter on a moving train requires that one be able to keep perfectly in balance, even across the bumpiest stretch of track. Again and again, McPherson's narrator will point to the delicate almost dance-like quality of the balancing act required to keep everything upright, in place, on time, and on target. In his article on McPherson, Calvin Reid refers to these men as "the elite black railroad waiters during the golden age of the passenger train" (36). In effect, what these elite black waiters performed was a metaphor for life. It takes strength and agility to balance competing needs and demands when the road or track ahead is twisted or is not smooth. As the "ideal" waiter, he maintains his precarious sense of balance in an unbalanced world, and makes it look easy and beautiful.

It is from Doc that the old waiter now telling the story learned to be a man. "There were no rules in those days" (155), he tells the young waiter and points to the black book, a guide to providing wait staff service on trains that the railroad now makes all the waiters read and follow. He tells the young man that those rules were written by white people who were trying to duplicate what can never be duplicated, as if it were the rules that made the men and not the men that made the rules, as if a man can be ordered to be either graceful or to have taste or class. The younger generation, the waiter says, merely acts the part and provides surface service, which is truly servitude for money. The members of the older generation, he says, actually were graceful, tasteful, and also possessed more class than their passengers, hence they could provide service with dignity and without servitude. The old waiter suggests here that the younger generation has a different attitude toward work and toward how work and identity are connected. For the younger generation, a job is just a job, and shoddy work is not seen as a personal reflection of who a man is. For Doc, any job he does with dignity becomes dignified. It starts within and radiates to the outside visible world.

The old waiter tells the young man that in his generation a man did not go looking for a job with dignity already attached to it and step into a ready-made identity. Instead, a man found something for which he had an affinity, and then applied himself as would any dedicated artist.

> There were no Civil Rights or marches or riots for something better in those days. In those days a man found something he liked to do and liked it from then on because he couldn't help himself. What did he like about the road? He liked what I liked: the money, owning the car, running it, telling the soldiers what to do, hustling a bigger tip from some old maid by looking under her dress and laughing at her, having all the girls at the Haverille Hotel wait-

ing for us to come in for stopover, the power we had to beat them up or lay them if we wanted. (158)

He liked, the narrator concludes, "running free" (158). This freedom includes some questionable activities such as "pimping" for the big white farm girls who do a little hooking on the side and who "could take on eight or ten soldiers in one night" (158). For his part in opening up a club car at various stopover stations and giving the girl use of the club car, the narrator received 60% of the profits. Such activities, though morally questionable, and perhaps an imitation of the white gangsters of the time, give him a sense of manhood and a feeling of being powerful and free. To leave train service would mean a revision of how he sees himself because it would leave him without the means of acting out his own fantasies of what it means to be a powerful man. Though certainly a flawed definition of manhood, for him, there is dignity in this.

The narrator tells the young man that the beginning of the end came when airplanes began to replace the trains as the passenger vehicle of choice. The railroad workers unionized to protect themselves from layoffs, and from that point on, the white managers seemed intent on firing the black waiters and doing away with luxury dining car service. Because of the union, they could not get rid of them except if they were repeatedly written up for giving bad service.

At this point, the story becomes a story of Doc versus the company. The company is out to get Doc and to retire him and all he represents. The battle plays out in the dining room where the seventy-three-year-old Doc, like a John Henry figure, battles corporate America's rule-book of service. Unable to read, Doc cannot digest the mimeographed new memo stating that the lemon fork must pierce the meat of the lemon and be served on a bread-and-butter plate with no doily. A week ago, the rule had been that the fork tines must pierce only the skin of the lemon, and be served on a bed of crushed ice. "Haven't you seen the new rule?" the inspector asks again and again, "Haven't you *seen* it?" (170). Unwilling to admit that he cannot read, Doc, in his fortieth year of service, lies and says, "I didn't check the book yet" (170). The inspector replies, "Then that's *two* rules you missed," and then, as if to drive home the point, "Two rules you didn't read" (170). Doc is removed from service and dies.

Were the story to end here, it would be possible to read this in much the same way as some of the mis-readings of the John Henry story. One could argue that McPherson is suggesting that the old ways are dying out because, like Doc, they are not suitable for the new and improved future. Because Doc is unable to adapt to the new world, he goes the way of the dinosaur. One could argue that this is a nostalgic look back at the artistry that is lost with modern efficiency and standardization.

However, the story does not end here. In the fourth and final segment of the story, the narrator wonders if he should take his pension and retire or keep riding the rails until he dies in service or is taken out, the way Doc was, by a crafty inspector hell-bent on ridding the rails of all senior wait staff and replacing them with temporary workers. In the end, the old waiter basically tells the young waiter that it is up to him to make a difference and to make the old waiter's story end differently from Doc's. In the end, it seems as if the young waiter might actually be the author, James Alan McPherson, or someone very much like McPherson. "You have a good story," the old waiter tells him, "but you will never remember it. Because all this time you have had pussy in your mind, and your fingers in the pages of that black bible" (173). There is a challenge in that, to remember, and to pass along the story of Doc, and indirectly the story of the nameless older waiter. The story within a story is passed on to the summer schoolboy waiter who too readily reads rule books written by white men for black workers but who is willing to stop reading in order to hear a good story.

The reader, like the young waiter, hears the story within a story, and is challenged to remember it and, problematic as it is, value it, and the construction of manhood it celebrates, as well. Although the days of the "big trains" and the "big train men" have passed, there is a suggestion that if they are remembered, not nostalgically as obsolete fossils, but as role models of excellence, the younger generation stands a chance of growing up from boys to men. It is not how Doc died that should be remembered, but how he lived. "I'm searching for codes that might work for black people today," McPherson told Calvin Reid in his 1997 interview with *Publishers Weekly*, and in "A Solo Song For Doc" despite the sad ending, the code Doc lived by is one that McPherson believes provides a model of excellence.

For many readers, however, McPherson's story is problematic because of the treatment of women. Although the old waiter cautions the young man not to fixate on "pussy," the words he uses to describe women are offensive as is the celebration of the even older waiter's success as a pimp. In many ways, this story suggests the necessity of James Baldwin's attempts to revise the "requirements" of black manhood and the stereotypes that accompany it. The train provides the instructional space for lessons in manhood; unfortunately, in this case, manhood seems to be achieved, in large part, at the expense of women.

Nevertheless, as passengers and as workers, riders of the train come into contact with other people, and this contact educates them about other ways of living and also often brings them into situations where their identity is forced to undergo some major reconstruction. This is true, too, for those who are not passengers in the Jim Crow cars or workers in the dining car. In fact, for those who are stowaways, or train hobos and roustabouts, the train is an overwhelmingly positive symbol of freedom, growth, mobility, and the power to mold one's own sense of self and identity.

Ralph Ellison has several good train hobo stories in which the narrator, a young black man, learns valuable life lessons and learns to see himself and others differently as a result of catching a ride on the back of a train. These stories were not written as an intentional series or collection, and yet, because of the importance of the train as both a plot device and a symbol, the stories feel like part of a series. "Hymie's Bull," "A Hard Time Keeping Up," and "I Did Not Learn Their Names" are all about the adventures of a nameless young black man riding the rails as a stowaway.[14]

In Ralph Ellison's "Hymie's Bull," the narrator explains the dangers of hoboing. In addition to the physical dangers of catching a speeding train, white "bulls," security men hired by the railroad, often threw unofficial riders off the speeding train or clubbed them badly. In the story, the narrator explains that he and the other black riders steered clear of the bulls whenever possible, and occasionally teamed up with white hobos, because their destinations seemed similar. The suggestion is that as stowaways the men are bonded by an experience more significant than race. One night, however, the narrator teams up with a white tramp, Hymie, who, when a bull lashes out at him, turns the tables on the bull and kills him. Even though Hymie kills the bull, the black riders of the trains are the ones who suffer the consequences of Hymie's miscalculated temper.[15] "They don't care who did it," says Ellison's narrator, "because the main thing is to make some black boy pay for it" (83). In this story, the train provides the setting for a valuable lesson about racism. There is, however, also word play about the "price" of the ticket and the hidden "costs" of riding the rails that black stowaways pay. There is also, possibly, the suggestion that "Hymie," a name often associated with Jews, in this case is the specific cause of this price hike. Hymie's inability to control his anger causes a backlash against the black riders of the train.

The lesson the traveling narrator learns in "A Hard Time Keeping Up" is twofold. Part of it is that black men need to stick together and need to stop behaving as if they were forever running a race against each other. The other part is that even when one is part of a minority group, one has a difficult time "keeping up" with the changing pace of life. Old stereotypes are changing, and sometimes even the people who are part of the community do not realize it.

The narrator and one of his hobo friends step off a train, in the middle of a snowstorm, in the wee hours of the morning. They go to the black part of town, where they meet a friend who takes them into a bar. In the bar, they see a girl who looks, for all practical purposes, white. The narrator and his traveling companions argue about whether or not the girl is "a fay chick" slumming it in a black bar, or, as the narrator asserts, "one of us" (101). The girl hooks up with a big, beautiful black man, named Charlie, a man the narrator describes as "a big bastard," a "buck nigger," and speculates that "he was the kind they had kept at stud" during the days of slavery (104). While watching the man swagger about the bar, the narrator wonders why a whole band of such men never got together to accomplish anything good. Instead, each simply swaggered in his own small way, attracting women. The narrator then wonders whether or not the slave owners "must have trained something out of us during slavery like they do wildness in a hunting dog" (104). Instead of working together, black men, he reflects, "are all lone wolves, each trying to fight it out alone—like the guy in Birmingham who stood off a whole police force by himself" (104). It is heroic, tragic, but also pathetic and impotent.

The two roustabouts and the local man leave the bar and begin walking through the snow, arguing about whether or not the white-looking girl is going to cause problems. Suddenly there is a disturbance behind them, involving gunfire. "Then we saw the big guy. He was headed in our direction and was running like the anchor man on a relay team and when he passed through the circle of light he was naked and there was red on the front of his body, which rippled and shone in the light" (105). The narrator and his two companions follow the streaking black man around the block and back to the bar. The cops arrive, there is a lot of confusion and yelling, and no one is, at first, sure what has happened. The story the locals in the bar tell the cops is that no one has been hurt and that the whole evening's adventure was simply part of a bet; the man with the gun bet the big guy, Charlie, that he could not drink a whole Singapore Sling and then run naked around the block without getting sick. The blood, they tell the cop, is really just catsup that the girl threw on her man when the man with the gun fired as the starting shot, and that she had done it just to scare him. To prove her point, she wipes away the catsup.

Disgusted and yet "very damn much relieved" the narrator and his friend decide not to stay in this town and head back to the railroad to catch another train (109). They are disgusted with the practical joke, done at the expense of the beautiful big man, but they are relieved that the scene played out before their eyes was not one of true violence. The events seemed to fit well-known patterns, but instead, the tragedy was actually comedy, and the narrator realizes an important fact about himself. He realizes that he had been theorizing about what had happened based on his own stereotypes about black men and bar life. He had expected tragedy and so that was what he originally saw. With the changing pace of black life, he will have to re-think some of his own stereotypes if he wants to keep up, and he then hops the next train out of town. The train, here again, is a vehicle of education, in this case, providing travel opportunities that place the narrator into new situations. Though not a worker on the train, these riders of the train experience the educational aspects of domestic travel.

Perhaps the most significant of Ellison's train stories is "I Did Not Learn Their Names," in which the train, again, becomes the vehicle through which the narrator's sense of who he is expands as part of an almost Hegelian dialectic: conflict, resolution, growth of a new sense of self. The narrator shares a moving train car with an elderly married couple and does not realize until morning that they are white. The narrator and the elderly white couple are illegally hitching a ride on a Santa Fe freight train headed north to St. Louis. When they go to sleep "it was pitch-dark in the car," but when the narrator awakens, it is light enough to see that the old couple is white, and the narrator is black (91). The narrator braces himself for the old couple to make racist comments, all the while telling himself that the old people will only be expressing "passively what they had been taught" (92). He begins to plan his reaction. "I was nasty sometimes, because to be decent was to appear afraid and aware of a place. And since when you were decent they thought you were afraid, and that you were expressing those qualities that even their schoolbooks said your race possessed, I was almost always nasty" (92).

Instead of "cussing" him out, which is what he expected the old man to do because he, a black man, had slept in the same train car as the white man's wife, the old man offers him some cold beef and mustard sandwiches wrapped in wax paper. He takes the sandwiches, but does not say thank you or sir because, "Saying sir was too much a part of knowing your place. I had learned that on the road you really had no place; you were all the same though some of them did not understand that" (93).

His response represents what Chikweyne Okonjo Ogunyemi identifies as "a strong, positive blackism" representative of the "new generation, proud of its black identity" (23–24). The "old black order" was "marked by its aping of white ways and its longing for white approval" full of characters who were ambivalent toward or denied their blackness, thus becoming an "invisible outsider in white society" (24). Ogunyemi asserts that in Ralph Ellison's short stories, this is clearly not the case, and "a new generation, proud of its black identity" can "establish a future in which people aid one another in a spirit of togetherness" (24). As Bernhard Ostendorf notes, "ironically this makes him [Ellison] a forerunner of the very cultural nationalism whose militant fringe now rejects him as an Uncle Tom" (196).

In this story, the young black man learns three new lessons. The first is that not all white people are racists. The old couple perk up instantly the minute he mentions that he is going to school because their son had gone to school for four years in Amherst, Massachusetts, and had had a black roommate for all four years who was "a fine fellow" (94).

It is then that the old couple explains why they are traveling as hobos and the narrator learns his second new lesson. Five years ago, they were wealthy, but their son ran away from his life with them in Texas, got arrested, and has spent the last five years incarcerated in a prison in Joplin, Missouri. Tomorrow he will be released. "When we had money, we lost our boy. Now the money is gone, and our boy will be back with us. We are very happy," the father tells the narrator (95). From this confession, the narrator learns, in Michael Moon's words, about how unreliable racial stereotypes about people's lives really are because of the "mixed fluidity of race and social roles in the histories of the West" (25). Moon suggests that it is Ellison's well-documented Oklahoma heritage and experiences as a young man hoboing on the trains that have provided him with "these uncanny, stereotype-shattering characters," who "were of a piece with the actual social communities that produced and circulated these narratives of crossing" (25).

He does not learn the third lesson until the next day. After parting from the old couple, the narrator gets pulled off the train by some white guards looking for girls whoring out of the train cars and is thrown in jail. While waiting for his friend Morrie to contact the school officials who will eventually come and get him out, he finds himself thinking "of the old couple often" and discovers that "I was sorry that I had not learned their names" (96). He realizes that he had treated them as stereotypes, not individuals. In the dark, all people are just people, but even in daylight when they could see him, the old couple still treated him the way they would have one of their son's friends, sharing their limited supply of food with him, and making polite, and yet real conversation. He keeps waiting for them to respond to him with racism, but they do not. Instead, they share the intimate details of their travels and ask him to do the same. There is an intimacy that comes with travel that is accelerated, and it is only in retrospect that he realizes he never learned their names.

In this story, riding the rails has brought him into contact with whites on an equal basis as well as the standard contact with white authority figures that results in racial conflict. There is in the bread and the meat the old couple offers as nourishment for his body the recognition of a common humanity and a sense of being one human family. It occurs in that shared moment of transition that comes with being displaced and in motion. It is the riding of the rails that makes such a moment possible for the narrator of this story.

As passengers, workers, or stowaways, the characters that ride the train in twentieth-century African American texts learn valuable lessons, not only about who they are, or who the world says they are, but also about who they want to become. The train is used as a literary vehicle carrying them not only across geographical space, but also as a liminal or threshold space into a new sense of self and identity. They are changed, not by the destination, but by the journey. As passengers, they experience a stimulus for change. As workers, they learn to work with others and to learn from and care for each other. As stowaways, they break the rules and break through the social conventions designed to keep them in their place. The train provides both the setting and the symbol of these transformative experiences and provides the impetus for feeling that change is possible, both internally and in the world at large.

An interesting variation on these uses of the train as literary vehicle and liminal space is James Weldon Johnson's multiple uses of the train in his fictional account of what happens to a man when he journeys not only across chronological time and geographic space but also across the color line. In the 1912 edition of *The Autobiography of an Ex-Coloured Man*, Johnson's narrator's journey begins on a train and is described as "an endless journey" where the narrator, as a child, "knelt on the seat and watched through the train window the corn and cotton fields pass swiftly by" until he fell asleep (6). He eventually arrives in Connecticut, and spends his boyhood in "a little cottage" that his white father had "fitted up almost luxuriously" (6).

As Donald Goellnicht notes, Johnson is intentionally parodying an aspect of the traditional slave narrative in which an "escape to freedom, usually involving a dangerous journey from South to North," results in "hard-won freedom by means of a daring escape" (para. 27). Johnson's text is not really an autobiography, but, as Kathleen Pfeiffer notes, "because the book first appeared anonymously," the book was "understandably first construed by its initial readers as the genuine autobiography of a light-skinned black man who had successfully passed into white society" when Johnson himself was not light enough to pass (403). In fact, unlike his narrator who can easily avoid the dangers of white violence against black bodies, such as the lynching of a black man for consorting with a white woman that occurs at the end of the fictional autobiography, in his real autobiography, *Along This Way*, Johnson shares with his readers the details of his work with the National Association for the Advancement of Colored People to support the Dyer Anti-Lynching Bill that went before Congress in 1922, and his own near-lynching experience in Florida while still a young man.[16]

Johnson and a woman writer from New York had agreed to meet at a train station. The woman was late, Johnson boarded the train, and then saw her from the window, just as the train prepared to leave. Leaping from the train, he followed after her until he caught up with her, and then the two walked to a nearby park and began to discuss their writing (166). Soon, they are accosted by a mob, and while the woman slips away, Johnson is seized and charged with "being out" with "a white woman" (167–68). She returns and Johnson is able to tell the magistrate that "the lady with me is white, but not legally so" (169). Johnson is freed, but in his autobiography he records that "for weeks and months the episode with all of its implications preyed on my mind and disturbed me in my sleep" as he relived, yet again, his experience with the "band of murderous bloodthirsty men in khaki" (170).

The nameless narrator of Johnson's text, however, experiences very little childhood danger. While still in grammar school, he learns that his birth represents the coupling of his mother, the former "sewing girl" of his father's mother, and that the narrator was the product of their "unsanctioned love" conceived during one of his father's trips "home from college," but that now he and his mother had to be sent North because his father "was about to be married to a young lady of another great Southern family" (42–43). The narrator has thus been sent North, as Goellnicht explains, "to save his father from embarrassment" (para. 27).

In contrast to Ellison's "Boy on a Train" story, in which the train ride provides the setting and symbol of the main character's first rejection of the forces at work in America that seek to commodify his body and his labor, Johnson's narrator, the "perfect little aristocrat" with his ten-dollar gold piece strung rung his neck like a pampered pet's collar, is unaware of what the journey North costs his mother in terms of personal pain and sleeps through his first journey North. Ironically, it is the journey South that is uncomfortable and fraught with peril for Johnson's narrator.

After the death of his mother, and the selling of the home and piano provided for them by the narrator's absent white father, the young man has enough money for two years of college, takes the proceeds, and boards a train headed South. As Carlyle Van Thompson notes, this journey South rewrites Du Bois's trip. Whereas "Du Bois' southern journey leads to an emotional and spiritual connection with the souls of black folks, the Ex-Coloured Man recoils in horror at the abject poverty and wretched conditions of black people" (158). This time, as he "peered through the car windows" he finds himself "disappointed" (52). Instead of "the luxuriant semi-tropical scenery" he had imagined he sees "the red earth partly covered by tough scrawny grass, the muddy, straggling roads, the cottages of unpainted pine boards, and the clay-daubed huts" which "imparted a burnt up impression" (52). Upon his arrival, he is taken through the rain and mud by a train worker to an uncomfortable lodging house owned by a "big, fat, greasy-looking brown skinned man" who rented beds to the Pullman porters (53).

The second night, his college money is stolen by one of the porters, and then this same porter offers to sneak him aboard a train headed to Jacksonville where, the porter tells him, with his complexion he "won't have any trouble to get a job in one of the big hotels" (64). Again in a quasi-comic parody of older slave narratives, the narrator heads deeper into the South by stowing away for "twelve hours doubled up in the porter's basket for soiled linen" (65). The shelves of clean linen are placed on top of the basket of dirty laundry so that all the passengers can see are the shelves of clean white linen. The narrator describes the basket in the same terms one might a casket, and says that during the long journey he "had grave doubts about reaching my destination alive" because "the air was hot and suffocating and the smell of damp towels and used linen was sickening" (65). Unaccustomed to any sort of discomfort, each "lurch of the car over the none too smooth track" causes the narrator to feel "bumped and bruised," and this results in effete feelings of nausea (65). In comparison to all the hardships and dangers detailed in the many slave narratives of daring escapes North, the narrator's voluminous complaints about a mere twelve-hour journey South seem comic in comparison.

With many slave narratives to choose from, Johnson used the story of Henry "Box" Brown to play with the notion of the nameless narrator's attempts at, in his words, "getting practice" at being black (74). As Gary Ashwill explains, Henry Box Brown's narrative used "resurrection imagery to a degree unusual in slave literature, underscoring the crucial role of Christianity in Brown's experience," and when Brown's twenty-seven-hour ordeal in the coffin-shaped box is complete, he describes his "achievement of freedom as a kind of rebirth, a resurrection from the grave of slavery" (102). Similarly, Johnson's narrator uses birth and rebirth imagery and identifies his arrival in Jacksonville as his "entrance into the race" (74). His "theory of what it was to be coloured" which he had "formulated" while in Connecticut, was now "getting practice" as he enters, for the first time, "the freemasonry of the race" (74). For the next three years, he plays at being black. He works in a factory, and as a "hail fellow well met with all of the workmen at the factory" he learns "from their example" to "be careless about money" and to "join them in their pleasures" (83–84). He felt such "joy" in working in the factory with the workmen while also being accepted into the "professional and well-to-do class" of blacks because of his education, musical talents, and complexion, contemplates marrying the local colored school teacher, raising a family, and working in the cigar factory for the rest of his life (82–88).

This plan, however, is derailed by the closing of the cigar factory, and without so much as a good-bye scene with the young schoolteacher, he heads to New York with some other factory workers as part of the exodus of young, black, male southern workers headed North. In New York, in the company of his former factory mates, he learns to play pool, shoot craps, and gamble. He also becomes familiar with the presence of the various types of whites who "were out sightseeing or slumming" in the black part of town, and one, in particular, catches his attention, a white woman called "the widow" who paid for the diamonds and exclusively tailored clothes worn by her black companion (107). During this same interlude, because of his abilities on the piano, the narrator catches the attention of a wealthy millionaire who becomes the young man's patron. Hired to play "rag-time transcription of Mendelssohn's *Wedding March*" or anything else the millionaire wants, the narrator becomes another kind of kept man (119). This parallel is made painfully clear when the widow turns her attentions from her original partner to the narrator. The narrator does not want to be seduced by the woman because he knows she is only using him to make her black companion jealous, and yet, he is powerless to resist her, just as he put up no resistance to being the millionaire's hired hands (122).

The situation ends badly when the woman's former paramour "whipped out a revolver, fired" and the "first shot went straight into her throat," while the narrator, rendered speechless, merely looks on in horror (124). Instinctively, he flees, dazed, and wanders about the city until his benefactor chances to see him wandering along Fifth Avenue (124). After telling his millionaire patron of the night's events, the narrator's patron decides that the two will sail for Europe in the morning (125). Rescued from the consequences of his involvement in the biracial affair, by the white quasi-father/master figure who pays his salary, in Europe, the narrator lives quite happily for the next year and a half.

In comparison to his train ride south, his train ride from Havre to Paris "ran very smoothly" and "the toy-looking engine, the stuffy little compartment cars, with tiny, old-fashioned wheels," he says, "struck me as being extremely funny" (127). Soon he begins "to appreciate the stuffy cars for their privacy" and while he "watched the passing scenery from the car window," concluded that Paris "seemed too beautiful to be real" (128). For a while, life in Europe seems perfect, and his patron bought him "the same kind of clothes which he himself wore, and that was the best; and he treated me in every way as he dressed me, as an equal, not as a servant" (130). For a while, he tries to view his patron as a sort of father figure rather than an employer or master. In Paris, however, his perspective on his own situation changes as a result of a chance sighting of his biological father, father's wife, and their daughter, his half-sister, at a performance of *Faust*. It is then that "the desolate loneliness" of his "position" became clear (135). The tragedy on the stage pales in comparison to the tragedy the narrator feels is his lot in life, "and in the darkness of one of the scenes" the narrator "stumbled out of the theatre" (135).

The narrator's sense of being a man without family, without roots, without connection deepens until the point when the narrator determines to reenter the world as "a coloured composer," who will give "voice to all the joys and sorrows, the hopes and ambitions, of the American Negro, in classical musical form" (147). Unrecognized in the theater by his biological father, he will give voice to his mother's silent joys and sorrows as he performs his version of her music, certain that he "should have greater chances of attracting attention as a coloured composer than as a white one" (147). The narrator parts with his millionaire, receives a good-bye gift of five hundred dollars, and heads back to the United States and back to the South.

Tucked into the last fifty pages of Johnson's text is a fairly lengthy and somewhat artificially rendered interlude staged in the smoking car of a train as the train passes through the Jim Crow South. As Eric Sundquist notes, in this scene, a scene that calls to mind Homer Plessy's historic train ride, unlike Plessy, Johnson's narrator does not announce that he is "really" black and instead enjoys the white privileges of the smoker car, becoming, to use Carlyle Van Thompson's terms, a sort of "racial voyeur" while indirectly requiring the reader to do the same (178). Just as Plessy did, Johnson's narrator easily passes for white, and listens in as a Jew from Florida, an Ohio professor, a former Union soldier, and a cotton-planter from Texas debate "the Negro question" and conclude "the nigger" will never "be the equal of the white man, and we ain't going to treat him as an equal" a sentiment which brought "a general laugh and good feeling" from the men in the smoker car, and only the Ohio professor refused to join in a shared drink (164). The narrator, still passing for white, drinks.

As the narrator continues his travels throughout the South, he reports that he found himself "sometimes amused on arriving at some little railroad-station town to be taken for and treated as a white man, and six hours later, when it was learned that I was stopping at the house of the coloured preacher or school-teacher, to note the attitude of the whole town change" (172). All the while, like an anthropologist, the narrator is "trying to catch the spirit of the Negro in his relatively primitive state" (173). After one particularly moving visit to a town, a town in the midst of a religious arrival, where many souls will be born again, the narrator finds himself anxious to get to work on what he is sure will be a great contribution to the history of American music. However, "instead of going to the nearest and most convenient railroad station," the narrator decides to spend the evening in the company of a local school teacher who had, by "strange coincidence" been at student at "one of the Negro colleges . . in which Shiny was now a professor" (182).

While the two are preparing for sleep, the event that forms the final catalyst for the narrator's decision to step over the color line explodes, and a rumor spreads that a black man had committed a terrible crime (185). The narrator, certain that his "identity as a coloured man had not yet become known" follows the crowds to "the railroad station" where a crowd of white men gathered (185). At noon, the black "wretch" was dragged into town to the accompaniment of "a terror-instilling sound known as the rebel yell" (186). Quickly, "a railroad tie was sunk into the ground, the rope removed, and a chain brought and securely coiled round the victim and the stake" (187). The narrator watches, in silence, as the man is burned alive at the stake, and before he can even process the full horror, he finds himself "looking at a scorched post, a smoldering fire, blackened bones, charred fragments sifting down through coils of chains" with "the smell of burnt flesh, human flesh" in his nostrils (187).

The narrator reports that after witnessing the event, he "was as weak as a man who had lost blood" but that he was also, now, a man with a "general plan well fixed" in his head (190). As a result of witnessing the burning of the black man tied to the railroad stake, in the very same town as the religious revival, the nameless narrator decides to be born again as a white man. His decision was not based upon discouragement or fear, he tells his readers, but because of shame, "unbearable shame. Shame at being identified with a people that could with impunity be treated worse than animals" (191). Thus, before the sun sets on another day, the narrator forsakes the South and "the Negro race" and returns to New York, the "great witch at the gate of the country" with "her alluring white face," who tempts "those who come from across the seas to go no farther" and crosses over the color line (89). The novel ends, a dozen pages after the narrator's decision to live as a white man. He gives up his aspirations as a composer, goes into business, marries a blonde, has two children, a girl with dark hair and a golden-haired son, and becomes "an ordinarily successful white man who has made a little money" (211).

In each instance where the train usually functions as a vehicle for self-discovery, Johnson's narrator learns the wrong lesson. His perspective is tragically skewed by the world's perception of him. However, while Johnson's narrator is only vaguely concerned that he may have "sold" his "birthright for a mess of pottage" Johnson's use of the train as a literary symbol and trope makes sure that the reader is not left in doubt of the author's true intentions regarding the lesson for the reader (211). As many critics have observed, the black man crucified on the railroad tie serves as a sort of mirror double for the narrator, a "dark double" and the narrator's sensation of having "lost blood" is directly tied to his renunciation of his mother's blood following the lynching-burning of his "dark double" (Thompson 180). However, because so much attention has been paid to the merits of the novel as what Herman Beavers refers to as "a sociological study," many readers miss "the greater importance of the book" (40).

Focusing on how the mechanism of the symbol of the train operates can help a reader to see that while Johnson's narrator appears to escape the usual fate of the "tragic mulatto," Johnson does not intend for his readers to view the narrator's actions as manly, heroic, or noble. Whereas the motif of "passing" is used in novels such as Harriet Beecher Stowe's *Uncle Tom's Cabin* to "condemn American society as hypocritical, since it is only through passing" that characters can "find what the mythology of the United States promises: personal access to a particularly American form of success: financial security, social prominence, personal independence" (Pfeiffer 417), in Johnson's text, passing is "a tragic betrayal of his black heritage" (Thompson 188). The stories of Henry Box Brown and Harriet Tubman, the work ballads of John Henry and the even older spirituals and work songs, all the many stories of the various riders of the train, the music men and the stowaways, go up in smoke with the narrator's renunciation of the black figure on the railroad tie.

⊕ CHAPTER FIVE

"Two Trains Running": Making Choices

> One ever feels his twoness,—an American, a Negro;
> Two souls, two thoughts, two unreconciled strivings;
> Two warring ideals in one dark body, whose dogged strength alone keeps it from being torn asunder. — *W. E. B. Du Bois,* The Souls of Black Folk

> There are always and only two trains running.
> There is life and there is death.
>   Each of us rides them both.   — *August Wilson,* Two Trains Running

> The Monkey speaks *figuratively*, in a symbolic code; the lion interprets or 'reads' literally and suffers the consequences of his folly.
> —Henry Louis Gates Jr. "`The Blackness of Blackness': A Critique of the Sign and the Signifying Monkey"

No study of African American uses of the train in twentieth-century literature would be complete without an examination of the stories in which the train is both a vehicle of death and the harbinger of the possibility of a glorious resurrection, for, as indicated in the discussion of Johnson's fictional *Autobiography of an Ex-Coloured Man* in the previous chapter, choice and free will are attributes of all train texts. Characters, even those with limited choices, still have the ability to choose which track their life will take. No one is destined or railroaded into any one particular life. In African American literature, even when the deck is stacked against them, train stories are not the stories of victims.

Rather, in African American literature, readers who focus only on the scenes of death in which the train is the vehicle bringing death, the setting for a violent death, or the vehicle by which a character has made his cowardly or ignoble escape from the responsibilities of manhood miss the latent promise of resurrection that is also inherently associated with these trains. Despite the perspective created by many twentieth-century textbooks or anthologies of American literature, twentieth-century African American literature is not a literature of victims in constant futile protest against an unstoppable force that forever crushes their chances of success in the modern world.

Instead, in texts by twentieth-century African American writers who use the train as literary symbol, the train clearly represents "two thoughts, two unreconciled striving, two warring ideals," and thus the train has both a literal function and a symbolic importance.[1] The literal function causes some readers to find poetic justice or irony in a character's death or misfortune. This is a misreading. The promise of the train in these stories is that of resurrection or rebirth, if not of the actual character, then of the spirit of a people that exists beyond the confines of any temporal grave, and support for such a reading occurs all throughout the texts.

For example, in Zora Neale Hurston's *Jonah's Gourd Vine*, the main character, John, a former preacher, is killed by a train after committing adultery with a girl young enough to be his daughter. While it is tempting to read this as an example of divine retribution, Zora Neale Hurston suggests that the train symbolizes the possibility of God's mercy, even when that mercy seems undeserved by the standards men set up for their communities and by which they then judge one another. The train is the hand of God, that comes to carry a man home to the Lord, even when the white courts and the church-world have passed legal judgment on that man and called him a sinner. Though the community expects the Christian God to destroy the sinner, God, the text seems to suggest, has his own universals and is not interested in upholding the values expressed by the rulings of white judges or nominally Christian church councils.

The shared attitudes of the white court and the black church, in Hurston's text, indicate a critique of the church. Even between antagonist groups, such as these, people, Eric Lott suggests, adopt an attitude of "assumed sameness," meaning that they believe that everyone's behavior can be judged by the same code of conduct and believe that it is okay to judge their fellow man because they "believe what is right is right for everyone" ("After Identity" 668). The title of Hurston's text indicates that she does not believe this to be so, referring, as it does, to the biblical story of Jonah's gourd vine.[2] Hurston's text seems to suggest that God is not as interested in punishing man, as are men in punishing one another. God in the end of the text does not kill John to punish him; God uses the train to bring John "home," so that John does not need to live with the painful emotional consequences of his adultery.

Support for this reading of the final train scene comes from an examination of the book as a whole, and a close look at what the train has signified throughout the entire text. Instead of God or Christ being represented as a white man with a beard, it is the train that is invested with the power of the divine. The train, like God, is beautiful, dangerous, and difficult to understand. When the main character of *Jonah's Gourd Vine* first sees the train, he does not know what it is. What he sees is a "great eye beneath the cloud-breathing smokestack" that "glared and threatened" (15). Of the train, John says, "'hit sho look frightenin,' and his candor took the ridicule out of the faces of the crowd, 'but hits uh pretty thing too'" (15). Although the crowd originally judged John a fool, his powers of perception are great, and they recognize the truth of his observation. This first episode with the train shows how John, even though inexperienced and unschooled, sees God clearly, while the experienced town crowd does not. This first train scene sets up the theme of the novel. The masses, the crowd, the secular world believes that it has earned the right to judge God's greatest creation, man. The crowd believes it has the right to select its own heroes and then police them. In the end, however, only God, the novel teaches, can judge man. Moreover, only John seems to hear this because he is listening without a preconceived notion of what is being said.

As the crowd thins out, an old man approaches John. John is still watching the train as it disappears over the crest of the horizon. The old man and John then speak:

> "You laks dat old train Ah see," the Negro said to John, watching him as he [*John*]all but fell down into the railroad cut, trying to keep sight of the tail of the train.
> "Yeah, man, Ah lakted dat. It say something but Ah ain't heered it 'nough to tell whut it say yit. You know whut it say?"
> "It don't say nothin'. It jes make uh powerful racket, is all."
> "Naw, it say some words too. Ahm comin' heah plenty mo' times and den Ah tell yuh whut it say." (16)

This is the first sign of John's ability to hear the word of God in the world of men and of John's ability to hear things that other men do not. Though it is boastful, it is a boast based on certainty. John is certain that there is a message in the sounds of the train and is certain that he will be able to translate the train's message into something that other people can hear and understand. Though he does not, at this time, recognize that it is his destiny to be a prophet, even now he is marked as different because already he can hear something in the sounds of what for other men is simply the everyday sounds of the train.

John, however, is not a saint.[3] In fact, John is a very flawed man. He womanizes his entire life, and his pride gets him into fights again and again. His pride, perhaps, is at the root of his womanizing as well because the women he sleeps with while he is married to Lucy bolster his sense of manhood. Lucy, periodically, will make mention of the fact that their children are starving or that she had to beg food from her family, while the other women in John's life make no demands on him beyond what he can readily provide, sex. John is also a bit of a rolling stone. He is full of potential and ability and yet, in the first part of the novel, seems unable to stick to any one occupation. Each time he starts a new job, he remains at it only until he excels, and then, bored, he gets into woman trouble or a fight, and then must flee. Periodically, however, there are suggestions that he has been chosen for a higher purpose worked into the language of the text. These suggestions of being chosen, as in the John Henry stories, are often associated with the railroad.

For example, during one of his roustabout phases, John leaves Lucy and signs on with a railroad building camp.

> On the nights that he stayed in camp he was the center of camp life. He could chin the bar more times than anyone there. He soon was the best shot, the fastest runner and in wrestling no man could put his shoulders to the ground. The boss began to invite his friends out to watch the fun. John won his first match by pinning Nelson Watson from another camp to the ground, but his greatest stunt was picking up an axe by the very tip end of the helve and keeping the head on level with his shoulders in his out-stretched arm. Coon could muscle out one axe, but John could balance two. He could stand like a cross, immobile for several seconds with an axe muscled out in each hand. (61)

With his arms outstretched, Hurston, here, is suggesting that John is a sort of black Christ figure. He is depicted as a sort of supreme being, the perfect blend of human attributes and strengths that make him the sort of man that women admire and men want to be. Human accomplishment occurs, for the most part, within a certain range of expectations. Hurston's John accomplishes things just beyond the usual range. This makes him a hero to the men in the camp, and in the context of the novel, he seems chosen for greatness.

What his greatness will be is not yet clear to John. While Hurston has provided clues in the early part of the novel that John's greatness is in his power to perceive the presence of God in the world of men and his ability then to speak of it, a talent which makes him a vehicle for the word of God, John still does not realize this potential. Again he cheats on his wife, and again, he gets in trouble for fighting and must flee.

In terms of the plot, at this point in the novel, John has just beaten Lucy's brother almost to death for her brother's attempt to repossess John and Lucy's marriage bed in payment for the debts Lucy incurred while John was away womanizing. As John and Lucy lay in bed, the bed John refused to give up, he compares his marriage to Lucy with a train. He is the engine, he tells her, and she the caboose, and even when they seem miles apart, they are still hitched. Each time he turns a corner, he can see her with "dat piece of red flannel she got hung 'tween her jaws" which he says is "equal tuh all de fistes God ever made and man ever seen" (96). She has a power over him that no beating can ever hope to have. The caboose, which some see as the least important part of the train, is the part which lets the engine see its speed and its trajectory as the train rounds perilous corners. In reverse, though, when the train must slow down, retrace its steps, and head back, it is the caboose, not the engine, that tells the train when to stop and when to start.

This passage is significant for two reasons. First, it is the first time that John associates himself with being a train. As Gary Ciuba asserts, the train is the primary symbol John uses in his "quest for selfhood through the medium of language" (1). He is beginning to associate himself with the train, and the train is already emerging as a symbol of God's presence in the world through the objects man makes. It is also important because it shows that John has become aware that, although he is the engine, he is not all-powerful. As the engine, he is the servant leader, the horse that pulls a more significant carriage.

It is at this point that John takes his first train ride. John heads to Florida to disappear into an all-black town where he hopes to make enough money in order to send for his wife and children. On this first train ride, John figures out what it is that the train has been saying since day one: The riders of the train are bound for glory.

> To him nothing in the world ever quite equaled that first ride on a train. The rhythmic stroke of the engine, the shiny-buttoned porter bawling out the stations, the even more begilded conductor, who looked more imposing even than Judge Pearson, and then the red plush splendor, the gaudy ceiling hung with glinting lamps, the long mournful howl of the whistle. John forgot the misery of his parting from Lucy in the aura of it all. That is, he only remembered his misery in short snatches, while the glory lay all over him for hours at a time. He marveled that just anybody could come along and be allowed to get on such a glorified thing. It ought to be extra special. He got off the train at every stop so that he could stand off a piece and feast his eyes on the engine. The greatest accumulation of power that he had ever seen. (104)

This passage is very significant because it reveals both the lesson of the text and the limitations of John's skill of perception. John sees that the train is bound for glory, and that although they are not worthy, all the riders of the train are bathed in glory. He marvels that "just anybody" can "get on such a glorified thing" (104). His first instinct is exclusion. There should be some way of keeping other people off. This signals the limitations of John's understanding at this point in the text. He has not yet learned that no man would ever be worthy of God's glory, that God's glory is always a gift. Fixated on the power, his misses the spiritual message. In fact, upon his arrival in Eatonville, Florida, "the Negro mayor filled John with almost as much awe as the train had" (107). The "Negro mayor" represents power, but he is still not quite as awe-inspiring as the power of the train.

After Lucy's arrival, John is called to serve the Lord and becomes a pastor. Popular as a pastor, he uses his congregation as a springboard into politics, becomes mayor of Eatonville, and eventually, Moderator for the State Association. Assured now of being, in his own words, "a big nigger," John becomes over confident. Although at various points in his life he has learned that the engine is not the most important part of the train and that the feeling of glory comes from riding with his fellow passengers in a greater state of luxury than any one man could ever earn, because he is human, he forgets this lesson. Driven by his own lusts, and not the will of God, John sins against his wife, his community, and his own better nature. When the trains begin to say, "North," John does not hear. "The wind said North. Trains said North. The tides and tongues said North, and men moved like the great herds before glaciers" (147). The Great Migration is here compared to a terra-forming crisis event, the Ice Age, and the suggestion is that the entire climate and landscape of the South is about to change, and that the men of the South must move on or die with the South.

Soon, John's congregation is down to half its size, and the church wardens decide that what is needed is new leadership from the pulpit. A guest preacher is invited to battle John for the pulpit, and while John is speaking, John understands what it is the train really means. The theme for the battle is the wounding of Jesus which is found in Zachariah 13:6. God asks Jesus how the wounds came to be in his hands. The question posed for the churchgoers via this reading is where would you have been when they killed our Lord? Would you have been screaming for his blood or begging for his mercy? No one, it seems, fought to save the Lord.

Even so, John tells his congregation, God still loves man. God has placed Jesus at "de throttle of de well ordered train of mercy" (178). However, as Jesus streaks toward Earth, there is, in the distance, the sound of another train approaching, and it is, "De whistle of de damnation train dat pulled out from Garden of Eden loaded wid cargo goin' to hell ran at break-neck speed all de way thru de law all de way thru de prophetic age all de way thru de reign of kings and judges— plowed her way thru de Jordan and on her way to Calvary" (180). This other train is the damnation train. Man's first sin set its wheels in motion, and from the time of Adam and Eve, man has been on a one-track road hell.[4] Only Christ's blood can derail the damnation train, hence the origin of Christ's wounds. When man takes it upon himself to eat of the tree of knowledge of good and evil, and takes it upon himself to judge good from bad, right from wrong, the train begins its journey. With each false judgment, each false law and king, the train picks up speed until only Christ's body can derail it.

John tells his listeners that this scene is acted out over and over again, even today, and that time and time again, these "two trains of Time shall meet on de trestle and wreck" (181). Who wounded Jesus? They do. Again and again. Each time they board the damnation train. But the choice, he tells them, is theirs. They must choose between the two trains of time. One brings eternal life, the other death.

Before they can choose, however, they must be able to read or decode what the two trains symbolize, and this is what John tries to do for his congregation based on his own lived experiences. As Ciuba says,

> From his adolescence in Alabama, John has sought to comprehend the cryptic significance of the vehicle that loomed before him. When he actually rode the coach to Florida, he came closer to understanding this sign. . . . But he compromised such spiritual dynamism so that power gave way to pride, and glory to disgrace. The conclusion of John's sermon used the image of the train to make the track of salvation history intersect with his own journey to interpret himself. (15–16)

Ciuba suggests that John is still more interested in himself than his congregation, but this is not so. John uses the train here to cast himself in the role of Jesus, into the role of one who is judged by man, when only God should judge, wounded unto death, and then brought home to God. The sermon also foreshadows John's death. Ciuba suggests that with this last sermon, John is writing his own ending, which is not accurate. Were this accurate, the novel would end soon after, and that is not the case. Part of Hurston's point, and one John himself understands, is that God, not man, gives grace and mercy. Man cannot, no matter how eloquent, write his own ending or control how others will interpret his death.

John walks out of the church and out of his life as a preacher. His wife Lucy has died. His second wife has divorced him. His children have all grown and have gone off to other parts of the country. He is the grandfather to grandchildren he has never met. He is no longer a big man in town. He moves to a nearby city and becomes, symbolically enough, a carpenter. In this capacity, he meets a wealthy widow, marries for a third time, and prays that God grant him purity. For one year, John is true to his marriage vows, but then, during a brief trip back to Eatonville, he finds himself in bed with a girl young enough to be his daughter. He has sinned again.

As he heads home, he contemplates his life. Lucy and his third wife, Sally, both offered him "faith and no questions asked" (200). At this moment, he begins to understand the value of such a gift, and that it is a gift, something he had never earned. It seems to him, as he is driving his car home, that the car is moaning the word "ho-o-ome" (200). John can feel that cry for home in the ache of his heart. He "drove on but half-seeing the railroad from looking inward" (200). Here Hurston is suggesting that John has begun an inward journey toward a spiritual home. The physical railroad is about to transform into a vehicle for the spiritual.

As John crests the trestle, his car stops. In the distance, a train engine wails a warning whistle, but John does not hear it. All he hears is the word home, repeated over and over again. In the context of the novel, the word *home* means Sally and his physical home, but because of his inward reflections about the past fifty years of his life, and his need for God's forgiveness and his desire for purification, there is also a sense that home means his heavenly home with God. The train does not stop and "strikes the car squarely and hurled it about like a toy" (200). John is killed instantly. The manner of his death calls to mind John's earlier sermon about the two trains of time, how the damnation train and the train of mercy shall meet and wreck on the trestle of time, and how Jesus shall have mercy on those in his train; they shall be carried by the hand of God into the kingdom of heaven. John has sinned repeatedly. Mankind would judge and condemn him for his sins. The text suggests, however, that God does not. In death, John receives the gift of God's mercy, and the train is the *deus ex machina* that provides John with a happy ending.

To ensure that readers understand this, Hurston has the novel end with John's funeral during which the preacher warns the congregation not to judge John. "He wuz uh man, and nobody knowed 'im but God" (202). The suggestion here is that only God can judge a man because, like Jonah in the biblical story, man always judges too harshly and without mercy or forgiveness. Though John has committed sexual sins, he has also been a vehicle for the word of God, and at the end of John's life, God calls him home. The train that takes John's life is the hand of God, the train of mercy, carrying John home. The train is a symbol of the hand of God at work in the world of man.

In Amiri Baraka's "Dutchman" death is also associated with the train, although in this case, tunnel vision damns the white female lead character to a living death of forever being trapped onboard an underground train going nowhere while the black male lead character gambles on defiance, and readers are often left wondering how to read his death at the end of the play. The play takes its name from the myth of the Flying Dutchman.[5] According to legend, the Flying Dutchman is a ghost ship piloted by a white Dutch ship captain who gambled with devil, staking his soul for safe passage around the Cape of Good Hope (Africa) on the roll of a dice. The Dutch captain lost his roll. The ship and all souls on board were lost, damned to sail aimlessly about the sea, playing dice with the devil for eternity, unless, legend says, someone can beat the devil at his own game. Critical responses to the play are as varied as they are numerous. The play has been read as an inversion of the Beauty and the Beast myth, a mapping of one layer of Dante's Hell, a reworking of the Adam and Eve story, the Adam and Lilith story, the Adam and the snake story, just to name a few.[6]

However, critics do not and cannot seem to agree about what Clay's death signifies at the end of the play. According to George Piggford the play "functions as a warning—both to heretical blacks like Clay who help support the Gothic nightmare of black oppression through inaction and to whites . . . that the revolution is coming" (155). Others, such as Craig Werner, read the play as a call to action, with the threat of murder extended only to whites, not blacks. "The devils, the money worshippers; must die. The black everyman must kill them in the name of life" (38). Kathryn Lee Seidel suggests that the purpose of the play is to represent how "white America has preyed upon the best of black men," whereas Jeff Epps views the entire play as a devil's game of chess (88).[7] Still others read in Clay's death and Lula's triumph an indictment of American culture as "a world of ghosts" (Casimir 308). The play, Werner Sollors tells us, "is Lula's and aesthetic protest's last stand. She is only the physical victor in the end of the play; spiritually she has been exorcised" (131). With such critical controversy, when one looks at just the two main characters in the play, it seems impossible to say with any certainty what exactly Lula's triumph and Clay's death signify if one focuses only on the characters and ignores the setting and the symbol of the train.

Thus, one useful point of entry into a real understanding of the text and what Clay's death signifies is to examine the setting of the play and to determine why the entire action of the play takes place on board a subway train. As Savas Patsalidis notes,

> The entire play takes place within the oppressive realm of the subway train that visualizes in a theatrical context the characters' imprisonment in limited and limiting roles. This prison-like topos is all there is. There is no outside. All stage signs are contained . . . reminding those involved that there is someone always watching. (103)

Patsalidis asserts that Baraka uses this "prison-like set," this "impersonal train" to animate a world vision similar to that which Foucault maintains in *Discipline and Punish* with the train as representative of "the unrestrained presence of the System. . . . anything outside this power is sacrificed to symmetry and homogeneity" (112). According to Patsalidis, Clay is killed when, in anger, he steps outside his "role" as a college-educated, middle-class black man who attends parties at which black and white people mix socially without conflict, and expresses his true feelings about "ofays" and what it means to be a black man in America.

Patsalidis's observation about the train, though not developed in a direction supported by a broad range study of African American literature, is still useful because it addresses a key issue, which, despite the history of Jim Crow, other commentators too often overlook. Why set the play on a train? What is it that the train symbolizes? The train, in this case, is a public space, and there is the possibility of equal interaction in a public space. However, rather than signifying the presence of "the System," or the limiting roles mandated for African Americans by some external power, in fact, the train is a space that provides exactly the opposite. History itself teaches this lesson. In the early part of America's train history, trains were often contested spaces precisely because they were public.[8] This scenario can be seen in stories by both black authors, such as Ralph Ellison and Toni Morrison and white authors, such as Flannery O'Connor or Thomas Wolfe.[9] Both black and white writers have seen the train as a place where people of different cultural or racial backgrounds come into contact, and that contact potentially disrupts or threatens one's sense of identity. Conflict indicates that the "System" is not secure in the permanence or righteousness of its power.

The train itself here symbolizes American history. American history is like the Dutchman's ship: It is damned to keep repeating itself. Joel Williamson, in fact, uses the image of the Flying Dutchman in *The Crucible of Race* to make his point about black-white relations in America. The problem in American culture, he argues, is that the North committed a "great sin" in destroying slavery and yet not destroying "the culture that slavery had generated" (43). "The result," he says, "was to doom a whole people to the fate of the Flying Dutchman, to abandon them to pursue a culture whose primal base, whose very reason for existence, had been forever lost, to ride a social ship that could never find haven or harbor" (43). Lula, the white woman in the play, tries to suggest that there are two separate trains of thought, trains of history "smashing along through the cities entrails," on a collision course, but the play itself shows that there is truly only one train. Life and death, mercy and damnation, black and white, all ride the same train.

Lula represents a type of racism that Ralph Ellison defines as a racism born of "petulance, exasperation and moral fatigue" ("What America Would Be Like Without Blacks" 577). She symbolizes all those who long for a blackless America, and who, because they recognize the impossibility of such a desire, commit themselves instead to controlling representations of blackness in America, even if they must lie to do so. "I lie a lot," Lula tells Clay. "It helps me control the world" (2128). Ellison calls this conflict over representation to be one of the great "tragic themes of American history," a theme made visible in

> Black Americans' ceaseless (and swiftly accelerating) struggle to escape the misconceptions of whites, and the continual confusing of the black Americans' racial background with his individual culture. Most of all, I refer to the recurring fantasy of solving one basic problem of American democracy by "getting shut" of the blacks through various wishful schemes that would banish them from the nation's bloodstream, from its social structure, and from its conscience and historical consciousness. ("What America Would Be Like Without Blacks" 578)

Lula represents all those who wish to banish black history and black lives from the nation's conscience. "We'll pretend that people cannot see you," Lula says to Clay (Baraka 2132). However, Clay does not wish to be one of Ralph Ellison's "invisible men," nor does he wish to be the man Lula keeps insisting he is. Clay represents those who "struggle to escape the misconceptions of whites" (Ellison "What America Would Be Like Without Blacks" 578). Lula has what Ellison calls "a white man's inadequate conception of human complexity" which she will use to try to reduce Clay into what she insists upon truth ("A Very Stern Discipline" 737). Alternatively, as Ellison says, "There is another reality behind the appearance of reality which they would force upon up as truth" ("A Very Stern Discipline" 737). Black men and women must refuse to accept white clichés about black life (Ellison 726).

This is what makes Clay such a threatening figure for Lula. She misreads him from the start. Her first sight of him is framed through the window of a train. As the train sits in the station, he is staring out the window at nothing in particular. Lula insists that his glance "had caught her ass" (2127). He tells her that she is mistaken, and that he was thinking of more metaphysical things, but she refuses to believe him and insists that he admit he was staring at her with pointed, very specific sexual desire. "Staring through train windows is weird business," he tells her. "Much weirder than staring very sedately at abstract asses" (2127). While Clay refers to the metaphoric possibilities that gazing out a train window conjure up for him about beginnings and endings, departures, and arrivals, Lula refuses to believe that he was thinking of anything deeper than sex, and sets out to prove herself correct by seducing him. "Would you like to get involved with me, Mister Man?" she says, and flings herself into his lap (2129).

This begins a rehashing of all the sexual fantasies and, as W. E. B. Du Bois put it, "inter-racial sex jealousy and accompanying sadism" spouted about black men and white women since the 1880s (*Black Reconstruction in America* 699). These stories, Martha Hodes tells us, followed a fairly standard pattern of "a series of false accusations of rape followed by certain, violent death for the man" (176). Despite voluminous proof that white women were often the agents or aggressors in pursing relationships with black men,[10] white male response remained the same: "The black brute is luring in the dark," George Winston wrote, " a monstrous beast, crazed with lust," who must, like an animal, be "taken down" (qtd. in Hodes 201). In Baraka's text, however, it is "Lula the Hyena" who is both self-proclaimed beast and aggressor ("Dutchman" 2130).

When the train first pulls out of the station, Lula and Clay are seated side by side. A journey of a different kind than Clay anticipated has just begun. Lula has successfully distracted Clay, at least enough to get him to engage in conversation. She begins by telling him who he is. She tells him that he is from New Jersey, lives with his parents, is growing a beard, reads Chinese poetry, drinks lukewarm tea, and has a skinny black friend who uses a fake English accent to get girls. He is surprised that she knows so much about him and asks if she knows his friend Warren. She tells him that she does not need to know him or Warren to know who they are because, as she has just successfully shown, they are a type (2131).

Suspecting that despite her denials, she is a friend of Warren's and that they are both on the way to Warren's party, he plays along with her bantering. Their bantering mimics the acceleration of the train. Lula insists that he play act with her and pretend that they are boyfriend and girlfriend, and then draws for him a picture of how the evening will go, what the other partygoers will think, and how the evening will end. Each time he gives in to her request that he pretend to go along with some portion of her skit, the physical action accelerates. Just as a train pulling out of station slowly accelerates to great, almost unstoppable speeds, so too does Lula's version of their shared history. Clay goes along with it until she grabs his crotch (2131). "Watch it now," he tells her. "You're gonna excite me for real."

Instantly, she removes her hand, slumps in her seat, and refuses to look at him. At this moment, her behavior is similar to that of the "typical white" as described in John Oliver Killens's book, *Black Man's Burden* (1965). In this novel, Killens argues white people spend their psychological, social, and cultural energy creating myths about black people, and the greatest of all these is that "the master must always make himself believe in the undying love of his slave" (8). When Clay reveals that he was just playing along with Lula, humoring her in fact, she is outraged. He is a black man; she is a white woman. According to all the clichés she believes in and by which she defines herself, he is supposed to want to sleep with her. As numerous critics have observed, for so long, the construction of white female identity has been "dependent upon images of black men as bestial" (Hodes 198) and the white woman as "the flower of civilization" that the black man must "pluck" to assert his full manhood (Wiegman 93).[11] Chikweyne Okonjo Ogunyemi calls this the "stereotypic romance between the white woman and the black man" and suggests that it is a result of "the potpourri nature" of American culture (29). In Ogunyemi's reading of the play, Clay falls for Lula's seduction because he is "a typical black, educated middle-class man, one of many on a journey through American history" (29).

Baraka himself says that black men have been brainwashed into believing that a white woman is "one of the most significant acquisitions of white society" (222). He asserts that such couplings

> take place usually among the middle class of one kind or another—usually the "liberated" segment of the middle class, artists, bohemians, entertainers, or the otherwise "famous." Liberated here meaning that each member has somehow gotten at least superficially free of his history. For the black man this would mean that he had grown, somehow, less black . . . . There is a whole social grouping of white women who are body-missionaries, and feel themselves elevated through such acts. . . . For the black man, acquisition of a white woman always signified some special power the black man had managed to obtain within white society. (223)

As is perhaps obvious from the inflammatory word choice, Baraka himself had just separated from his wife, a white Jewish American woman, and now he very much condemned such marriages as examples of false liberation.[11] Though Baraka did not in his early years shun what he later termed the "body-missionaries," by 1964, he felt that his main character, Clay, should.

This rejection accelerates Lula's actions. She uses words and her body in order to try to force him to behave according to the stereotype she has constructed for him. Lula becomes hysterical, calling Clay an "escaped nigger" who has "crawled through the wire" and begins to bump and grind against him (2135). "Come on, Clay. Let's rub bellies on the train. The nasty. The nasty. Do the gritty grind, like you ol' rag-headed mammy. Grind till you lose your mind. Shake it, shake it! OOOOweeeeeeee! Come on, Clay. Let's do the choo-choo train shuffle" (2136).

Imitating the sound and motion of the train, Lula makes as if she is humping Clay as he pulls away from her. She has insulted his mother and turned the train into a euphemism for carnal relations, as if all of American history were simply about sex and miscegenation.[12] At this point, she is trying to make him angry, trying to get him to lash out and to act like another black stereotype: the violent, angry black man. "Red trains cough Jewish underwear for keeps!" she yells at him. "Clay, you got to break out" (2136). She demands violence of him in response to obscenities that make sense only to her.

Baraka, though, rejects this stereotype. Clay does not instantly find solace in anger. Baraka's Clay, at this point in the text, escapes becoming a caricature of the "angry" black man. The "angry" black man, Ellison explains, "He rants and raves against society, but he is actually one of the safest Negroes on the scene. Because he challenges nothing, he can only shout 'taint' to some abstract white 'tis,' countering lies with lies" (727). Lula has made him angry, angry enough to want to kill her and to want to become the stereotype of the violent black man, but, with effort, he controls himself. He tells her he is angry enough to kill her and "all these weak-faced ofays squatting around here staring over their papers at me. Murder them too. Even if they expected it" (2137). However, he does not. He tells her that he understands her stupid stereotypes, the savage and the Uncle Tom, but that she cannot make him be a stereotype. No matter how angry she makes him, he will not kill her.

> Simple as that. I mean, if I murdered you, then other white people would begin to understand me. . . . If Bessie Smith had killed some white people she wouldn't have needed that music. She could have talked very straight and plain about the world . . . . Murder. Just murder! Would make us all sane. . . . Tell this to your father, who's probably the kind of man who needs to know at once. . . . Tell him not to preach so much about rationalism and cold logic to these niggers . . . . Don't make the mistake of talking too much about the advantages of Western rationalism . . . with no more blues, except the very old ones, and not a watermelon in sight. . . . all of those ex-coons will be stand-up Western men, with eyes for clean, hard, useful lives, sober, pious, sane, and they'll murder you. They'll murder you, and have very rational explanations. Very much like your own. (2138)

At this point in the play, Clay has not only rejected Lula, he has rejected the stereotypes she believes in and participates in maintaining as well. His manhood has not been achieved via sex with a white woman; he has asserted his manhood quite eloquently with his own words and asserted his own perspective of western history. He has not played the part of an Uncle Tom nor has he allowed her to railroad him into performing some stereotype about black men and violence. Though he is angry enough to kill and does slap her across the mouth at the start of his soliloquy, he does not use excessive violence against her person.[13] She has misread him from beginning to end.

As he packs up his belongings and prepares to get off at the next stop, Lula stabs him in the chest, twice. Her view of the world as segregated, of an America with two separate histories, of her own importance, is one that cannot exist if Clay is free to exit the train and get on with his life while she cannot escape. She kills him in her fight for control over how black men will be represented in American history. Clay has threatened her with his suggestion that the final destination of the train that she is on is her own destruction. With Lula, and those like her in charge of the train, her eventual death is assured. Superficially she will remain in control for a while longer but not a long while.

As Ogunyemi suggests, Baraka has painted Lula as an outdated cliché or stereotype herself, one on the verge of extinction, and "the will for survival is sometimes predatory" (30). The play closes with the train again departing the station, and a young black man walking down the aisle, looking for a seat. An "old Negro conductor comes into the car, doing a sort of restrained soft shoe, and half mumbling the words of some song" (2139). In response to Lula's penetrating gaze, the conductor tips his hat and moves on, and Lula begins her spiel with the young man. While the old man is content to channel his strong feelings into a comical soft shoe and some half-fragments of a song, Lula, and those like her, are not sure that the young black men of the 1960s are. While on the surface they may be content to write poetry and read Chinese philosophy, Lula fears what may lurk under the very stereotypes she insists are true. Vigilantly, she rides the trains, policing them as best she can, a damned ghost from a bygone era. However, her powers are already waning. She has killed Clay and thrown his body from the train, but as in the old legend from which the play gets its name, her journey will never end. It is she, not Clay, who is the Dutch ship captain. It is she, not Clay, who has gambled her soul away to the devil and who is damned. She is a ghost from a once permissible past, and Clay, as she tells him herself, "a ghost of the future" (2132).

Throughout the text, when not insulting him, Lula has alluded to Clay as a ghost or a spirit and herself as an old God, one that predates time. They are, we are told, part of what she and Clay decide to label "a corporate Godhead" (2133). With "knifelike cynicism," the stage directions tell us, she also calls Clay "My Christ. My Christ" (2133). "You must be Jewish," Clay says to Lula, as Baraka slowly sets up a re-enactment of an even older story: that it was the Jews who betrayed and killed Christ (2135). Examining the play "Dutchman" alongside Baraka's poem "Note from the Underground," in which a Lula-like figure begs a black man to "save me save me save me save me save me" to whom he whispers, "you're not worth it"; and his other poem "Clay," which begins "Killed/by a white woman/on a subway/in 1964/he rose/to be the first Negro congressman from Missouri," Sollors concludes that Baraka intends for Clay to be read as a Christ-figure (132–33). Equally important, Sollors's insistence on reading the poem "Clay" alongside "Dutchman" suggests that Baraka predicts Clay's resurrection. Like a Phoenix rising from the ashes, so too does Clay rise up from the subway grave and subaltern position in American politics to control a southern state.

The importance of the train as a symbol of the divine, of something that can be driven under ground, but never derailed, supports Sollors's interpretation. "Man, this subway is slow," Clay tells Lula, but like the train in the gospel songs, the songs in which, Clay tells Lula, black people "sing curses at you in code," like the midnight sabre black train of Hayden's poem which haunts the swamps, the train has a direct connection to the will of the divine, and Clay, in one form or another, will return (2134 and 2138). No matter how many Clays Lula kills, there will be another Clay, and another, and another:

> The train apparently stops and all the others get off, leaving her [Lula] alone in the coach. Very soon a Young Negro of about twenty comes into the coach, with a couple of books under his arm. When he is seated she turns and gives him a long slow look. He looks up from his book and drops the book on his lap. Then an old Negro conductor comes into the car, doing a sort of restrained soft shoe, and half mumbling the words of some song. He looks at the Young man, briefly, with a quick greeting. . . . The conductor

continues down the aisle with his little dance and mumbled song. Lula turns to stare at him and follows his movements down the aisle. The conductor tips his hat when he reaches her seat, and continues out the car. (2139)

Critics too often focus on the murder Lula has just committed and miss the significance of these final stage directions, thus interpreting the ending as indicative that Lula is a force that cannot be stopped, when in fact it is the return of the repressed, the never-ending tide of young black men, who cannot be stopped.[15] Lula cannot kill them all. However, all too often critics with a particular political agenda focus on Clay's death, as if in death he becomes another anonymous statistic.[16] Stage directions, though, divert attention to an alternate reading.

Lula, as she herself says in the very first scene, is getting older: "My hair is turning gray. A gray hair for each year and type I've come through" (2129). The young black men are not getting older. Just as Clay was described as a "twenty-year-old Negro," so too is the "young Negro of about twenty" who comes into the coach (2126 and 2139). Despite her attempts at creating an America free of black men, Lula was "alone in the coach" for only the very briefest of moments before, just like the old cliché about the train, it isn't too long before another one comes along, with "an old Negro conductor" singing songs she now knows are but "coded curses" (2138–39). The train only "apparently" stops; try as she might, Lula cannot control what C. Tsehloane calls "the final destination of train America"(47).[17] Clay is a "ghost of the future," not the past, and as such, it is not one that she can put to rest.

August Wilson's *Two Trains Running* continues this theme. The white ghosts of the past are finally exorcised and the playwright looks forward to an America rich in possibility for black men and women of all ages. In an interview with Mary Bogumil, Wilson explains that the image of two trains running preceded the writing of the play itself and that in drafting the play,

> there were two ideas in the play, or at least two ideas that have confronted black America since the Emancipation, the ideas of cultural assimilation and cultural separatism. These were in my mind the two trains running. I wanted to write a play about a character for whom neither of these trains were working. He had to build a new railroad in order to get where he was

> going, because the trains are not going his way. That was the idea when I started out exploring. (112)

As the play began to take shape, Wilson came to a better understanding of what the new railroad would look like and discovered that there would always be two trains running. According to Wilson, "There are always and only two trains running. There is life and there is death. Each of us rides them both. To live life with dignity, to celebrate and accept responsibility for your presence in the world is all that can be asked of anyone" (Wilson *Two Trains Running* author's note).

In the 1930s, Zora Neale Hurston suggested that there were two trains running: mercy and damnation, the train driven by man out of the Garden of Eden, and God's train of mercy with Jesus at the throttle. In the 1960s, Amiri Baraka suggested that there is, in fact, only one train—one America, one history, but that white segregationists and racists were intent on making black history, black truths, black men and women, invisible—intent, but damned to failure. In the 1990s, Wilson again suggested that there are two trains, and that at various times, we find that we have ridden both. There are things that we do, decisions that we make, that smack of death, for they lead us down a certain path to destruction. However, then there are other things we do or decisions we make that add to the dignity and grace of life. Man's life is thus a series of train rides, of departures and arrivals, to points and possibilities yet unknown.

Set in 1969 Pittsburgh, in Wilson's play, according to Lisa Wilde, "memory has been given a voice" (74). The play is not about Martin Luther King, Kennedy's Camelot, Malcolm X, the Black Panthers, the Vietnam conflict, or any of the "great" moments in American history. The characters, Mary Bogumil asserts, "represent private lives away from the public spotlight whose limited prospects are as much a part of the African American experience as the impassioned oratory and defiant slogans the history of that era celebrates" (95). The play is part of what John Lahr refers to as August Wilson's "mission" to chronicle, decade by decade, black American history (52). What the train represents in this play is the connection to the past, and the power to right wrongs from the past.

In the past, the main character, Memphis, tried assimilation. Next he tried separatism. What finally works for him is a refusal to settle for less than what is rightfully his and a political climate that makes that stance viable. Only then is he able to go back to where he came from and attempt to right old wrongs. As Lahr puts it, Wilson's plays ultimately always have as part of their resolution a demonstration of "the individual's interaction with the community, not his separation from it" (53). Instead of a timeline of progression, Wilson creates a circle of life in which a step forward, ultimately, takes one back to the beginning where things first went wrong so that one can begin again.

Chronologically, much of what is important in the play occurs before the play begins. Memphis is from Jackson, Tennessee. Thirty-three years before the play begins, Memphis bought a small farm there for which he still has the deed in hopes of being accepted as a farmer. A white man, Jim Stovall, sold him the land because it had no water on it. Determined to make a success of his venture and enter the farm market on equal footing with the white farmers in his area, Memphis dug a well sixty feet deep until he found water. After that, Stovall wanted the land back, claiming a clause in the contract made the deed null and void if Memphis found water. This, of course, was not in the original deed Memphis had signed. "Went down to the court to straighten it out and come to find out he had a bunch of these fellows get together to pick on me" (72). Jim Stovall and his gang grabbed Memphis's mule and

> cut his belly open. He kinda reared back, took a few steps, and fell over. One of them reached down, grabbed a hold of his dick, and cut that off. I stood there looking at them. I say, "Okay. I know the rules now. If you do that to something that ain't never done nothing to you then I know what you would do to me." (73)

The judge found in favor of Stovall and ordered Memphis to settle with John Stovall. Stovall was ordered to return the money, and Memphis to vacate the premises. Memphis returns home to find his farm burning. Instead of staying to fight it out any further, he abandons his hopes of assimilation, leaves town, and begins to live the life of a drifter and a failure.

Memphis stays away until the day he receives word that his mother is ill. He "called the train station and found out the schedule" but did not have enough for the train fare (59). Flat broke, as always, a drifter, as always, while he is in the process of trying to borrow enough money for the train fare, his mother dies. Suddenly,

> Everything changed. I felt like I had been cut loose. All them years something had a hold of me and I didn't know it. I didn't find out till it cut me loose.... You couldn't hold me down. It look like then I had somewhere to go fast. I didn't know where, but I damn sure was going there. (60)

He borrows fifty dollars, goes back home for his mother's funeral, and returns to Pittsburgh a different man. Somehow knowing that his mother still lives in the town that has witnessed his defeat had made him feel held back. Her death releases him because now they cannot hurt him through her. At this point in his story, however, he is still not eager to go back to Jackson. Periodically he fantasizes about going back to Jackson and demanding that they respect his original deed, but when the play begins, that is still just fantasy.

Memphis currently operates a diner in a segregated part of town. Segregation is what Wilson referred to as the second train that does not lead to any desirable destination. In his all-black area, Memphis has made a success of himself and his diner is now worth, by his estimation, $25,000. The city has issued an order that they are buying up the downtown area in order to improve it and that he must sell. As Memphis prepares for his court date, the residents of the neighborhood speculate about whether or not he will get what is due to him. Memphis himself is unsure about whether or not he should settle for less or sell early to someone else who would be able to get a better price from the city than what he anticipates they will offer him as a black man. Inspired by a young convict named Sterling who refuses to accept less than his due in a rigged lottery and by the local "idiot" who refuses to accept a chicken when the butcher offered him a ham to paint a fence, and the advice of a medicine woman who says, "if you drop the ball, you got to go back and pick it up. Ain't no need in keeping running, cause if you get to the end zone, it ain't gonna be a touchdown," Memphis and his lawyer go into their court date determined to refuse to accept less than what Memphis feels he deserves (109). The city offers him $35,000, ten thousand dollars above what he had valued the property. In celebration, Memphis goes down to the Brass Rail, the train depot bar, and plans his return to Jackson. "That's what I'm gonna do. I'm going back to Jackson and see Stovall. If he ain't there, then I'm gonna see his son. He is enjoying his daddy's benefits he got to carry his daddy's weight. I'm going back up to Jackson and pick up the ball" (109). The Brass Rail, the train depot bar, has as its name a combination of the phrase "brass ring," which is an old expression referring to an object just beyond reach, but for which we are all supposed to keep reaching, and the rails of the railroad, itself a sign of dreams. "Brass," also, according to railroad slang glossaries, refers to "railroad officials" (Beebe 219). Many train bars also used to have a brass rail around the top of the bar so that drinks did not slide off the bar while the train was in motion. In any event, the train is the vehicle on which one travels in pursuit of the brass rings of dreams, and a symbol, itself of the choices one has in life: to run or return, to flee or fight. Inspired, Memphis is now committed to returning home, to "pick up the ball" he feels he once dropped, and to demand payment for what is rightfully his.

In Wilson's play, ordinary people can make mistakes, be afraid, fail, and yet improvise and make changes; they are not necessarily trapped or limited by the things that life has done to them in the past. It is possible to make a return trip, to go back to the place and point in time where things started to go wrong, and to fix them. Despite all the examples in real life that indicate the opposite, in the world of the play, you get more than one shot at having a happy, successful life. The message of the play is this: you get what you settle for, so if you have settled for less in the past, it is time now to go back and get what you earned plus interest.

The play ends with a funeral, and yet the characters who remain seem inspired by Hambone's death and Memphis's rebirth and begin to ask for more of life. The play concludes with Sterling stealing a giant ham from the butcher who had refused to pay the local idiot the promised ham. Sterling places the ham on Hambone's coffin. Memphis sends Risa to the florist to get fifty dollars worth of flowers, with a card that says "it's from everybody who ever dropped the ball and went back to pick it up" (109–10). Thomas Wolfe may insist that one can never go home again, but August Wilson suggests that this is not so. For many writers, life is depicted as a time line, and a series of events carries you further and further away from a point of origin. There is no turning back. In Wilson's play, life is depicted as a train ride with a return ticket available. A single failure or shortcoming does not make up the sum of one's whole life.

Implied in Wilson's play is a lesson about national history and the American dream. As Houston Baker suggests in *The Journey Back*, part of what coming to terms with black life in America means is coming to terms with the South, with the history of slavery, with Jim Crow, with the agricultural world that preceded the great Northern migrations, with the autobiographical reflections and poetry of eighteenth-century black Americans, with early records of the journey from Africa to America.[18] Unlike the re-invented black bourgeois daughter in Alice Walker's "Everyday Use," who adopts a fake back-to-Africa sense of blackness and returns home only to collect artifacts, such as a quilt made of Confederate and Union army uniform scraps, which can prove the existence of black female "artists" in her family, and who wants photos of her mother's shack that she can put on her New York city apartment wall to show how far she has come from that place as proof of her internal difference from other, more common black people, Baker and Wilson suggest that to be healthy, whole, and happy, black Americans must not be afraid to go home and revitalize their old homes, to look back to their Southern homes and agrarian traditions, and feel a sense of pride, purpose, and belonging. The Northern cities promised freedom from Southern racism, but at the cost of one's agrarian, southern traditions. Perhaps, Wilson suggests, the time has come to reach for the brass rail and use that return ticket, leave the city behind, and head home to the South. As Wilson suggests, "There are always and only two trains running. There is life and there is death. Each of us rides them both." To live life with dignity and responsibility, one must not be afraid of the return trip, even when that journey back seems to invite death or court disaster. The train, here, becomes the vehicle for the return of the repressed, the journey back that in the mind's eye appears as a train racing straight into the mouth of a place one thought of as Hell, but also happens to be the place one calls home.

In 1901, W. E. B. Du Bois could not imagine a return home that did not kill his black protagonist. In his short story, "The Coming of John," John's return home via the Jim Crow car crushes his spirits, and his homecoming results in his eventual destruction. Nearly ninety years later, August Wilson is able to imagine a different sort of homecoming for his black protagonist, although the return home still exists outside the text itself. In the Du Bois story, the train becomes a symbol of the broken promise of the American dream and the conflicted nature of Du Bois's time. In Wilson's play, the train is instead a symbol of possibility. Collectively, Hurston's, Baraka's, and Wilson's texts demonstrate that while death is always a possibility, so too is life. Moreover, Wilson's use of the train as metaphor for a way of looking at life suggests the possibility that the train is, at long last, approaching an acceptable final destination.

♰ CHAPTER SIX

Around the Corner and Down the Track

> Trains—you hear those men talk about trains like they were their first lover—the names of the trains, the times of the trains! And, boy, you know, they spread their seed all over the world. They are really moving! Perhaps it's because they don't have a land, they don't have a dominion. You can trace that historically, and one never knows what would have been the case if we'd never been tampered with at all. But that going from town to town or place to place or looking out and over and beyond and changing and so on—that, it seems to me, is one of the monumental themes in black literature. . . . Curiosity, what's around the corner, what's across the hill, what's in the valley, what's down the track. Go find out what that is, you know! And in the process of finding, they are also making themselves.
> —Toni Morrison, "Intimate Things in Place: A Conversation with Toni Morrison," by Robert Stepto, May 19, 1976

Albert Murray's *Train Whistle Guitar* (1974) is a novel in which references to the Underground Railroad, the Tubman tradition, the John Henry tradition, train mobility, a spiritual coming of age, leave-takings, home-comings, life, death, and train symbolism all combine, revealing, as Morrison sums up, that in "in the process of finding," very often, those who ride the rails are also "making themselves." Thus, in the final analysis, the emphasis of twentieth-century African American literature that uses the train as a literary symbol is on the positive, the heroic, the creative, the genesis of a new world order, not the social protest texts or sorrowful tales of victims that all too often seem to dominate the slim chapters of anthologies "reserved" for the study of black American writers.

The study of African American literature does not need to be the study of victims. As Albert Murray explained to Mark Feeney in a 1993 interview for *The Boston Globe Magazine*, "When white intellectuals see a dark-skinned person, they want you to be belly-aching" (71). Alternatively, as Murray explained in an interview with Gene Seymour, "White folks love being cussed out and told, 'you've done this to me, you've done that.' Because you've defined yourself to them as a victim" (56). As Murray pointed out in still another interview with Marvin Gelfand, in his own writing Murray consciously and with forethought "counterstates" the "conventional black nonsense" that black boys grow up without possibilities or pride or role models of heroic possibilities. Murray states:

> For in fact, the kids are/were always taught to be heroic. I counterstate the sociology . . . I extend Mann's Joseph stories, Nick Adams in a story like "In Our Time" and *Portrait of the Artist as a Young Man*. Luzana Cholly, the guitarist, is Odysseus, Beowulf, Roland and all the heroes to Scooter. Auden talked about the "true ancestor" whom you don't find by going back along a straight line. . . . Those images and metaphors make you see possibilities. (Gelfand 10)

Odysseus, Beowulf, and Roland are all epic heroes, and their stories are the timeless legends of their people's origins. Murray's argument is that his character, Scooter, has available to him the same kinds of epic heroes, regardless of what the sociologists, both black and white, would claim about the legacy of slavery.[1] Quoting Auden, Murray suggests that one's "true ancestor" need not be one's parent, or even a blood relation (qtd. in Gelfand 10).

Thus, this study of twentieth-century African American writers who use the train and associated railroad legends and history will conclude what might serve as a model text, encompassing all the themes associated with the train as symbol, for close study by students and scholars of African American literature. As a close read of Murray's text in light of this entire study of the train as symbol clearly indicates, black men and women, and students of African American literature need not be railroaded into an acceptance of any stereotypes about black life in America, even when those stereotypes are reinforced by the well-intentioned inclusion of black slave narratives into textbooks or history courses that focus on the repeated victimization of minorities in America. There is a long and ongoing history of heroism, self-discovery, and self-expression in African American literature that gets ignored when students of literature are trained to identify key themes or symbols based on canonical white American literature and the field of literary criticism which has been so long dominated by white male readings of texts produced by other white males. Instead, according to Murray, a black man or woman's literary ancestors can just as easily be based on the history they wish to privilege and the heroes, the representations of human possibility, they wish to honor. Murray explains that it was the "great books of the world" that inspired his thoughts about

> human possibility, not what some dumb-assed white guy thought a colored guy should be doing and feeling. . . . Ralph [Ellison] said something similar to this in his essay responding to Irving Howe—you know, when her talks about being much wider than the narrow box of social protest that Howe wanted to put him in . . . because it was all a fairy tale, and if you can't make it a fairy tale it doesn't come to anything. The bluesteel, rawhide, patent-leather implications of fairy tales—that's what my writing is about . . . . My perception is that whatever self you create is mythical. The downtrodden, that's a myth. The heroic, that's a myth too." (qtd. in Pinsker 212–14)

Murray clearly believed that no man was limited by the facts of his life; a man's only limitations were the one's he insisted on for himself due to a failure of imagination, an unwillingness to respond to the stories of human possibility, and a refusal to create a life in this image for oneself. Stories about flying Africans, Harriet Tubman, John Henry, and others can thus form the base for the stories one will live, tell, and believe about one's own life. It does not matter if there is a direct line of inheritance. Even if one learns the stories from books instead of from some oral tradition, these stories are still stories about, according to Murray's reading of Auden, "the true ancestor." The link is imagined or self-created, and that, according to Murray is the power and value of myth. It "saves" like nothing else because it cannot be demolished by the facts of history that stand between the original "epic" and the now. Revisionist history is nothing to be ashamed of and instead can be very beneficial because belief provides, even when that belief is based in imagined connections, folklore, or fairy tales, as psychoanalyst Bruno Bettelheim asserts, very beneficial psychological effects and serve an important moral function, particularly for children. Such revisionist stories can

> carry important messages to the conscious, the preconscious, and the unconscious mind, on whatever level is functioning at the time. By dealing with universal human problems, particularly those which preoccupy the child's mind, these stories speak to his budding ego and encourage its develop-

ment, while at the same time relieving preconscious and unconscious pressures. (qtd. in Beckson and Ganz 85–86)

Fairy tales, fables, folklore, or revisionist history may, on the surface, seem like mere children's stories, but in fact, they are, as Murray makes clear, an integral part in identity formation.[2] Murray's characters, in fact, combine children's stories like "The Little Engine That Could" with oral history, folklore, and revisionist history to ensure that universal human problems are addressed and solved in a way that encourages the healthy development of a sense of self in a world that insists on coloring-coding some selves as black and some selves as white. Murray accomplishes this not by calling attention, again and again, to the existence of black selves defined in opposition to white selves; but rather, Murray's protagonist, Scooter, grows into healthy manhood via the stories, real, imagined, or as part of a revisionist history, that become a part of the lenses through which he views the world and himself.[3] His stories are the stories of Gasoline Point, Alabama, a little town created to serve the needs of the "L&N timetable" and the trains "en route to St. Louis, Missouri and Kansas City by way of Meridian, Mississippi" (3).

Furthermore, as Murray makes clear in his text, even revisionist history is grounded in actual history. Because the train is the town's raison d'etre, the train possesses magical qualities. It created the town thus creating life. That is a fact of history. However, in Murray's text, these qualities are not associated with whiteness or with the railroad industry. It does not seem as if the railroad corporate structure has any impact on the town at all, from Scooter's perspective, even though the town exists as a service station for the railroad. Instead, it seems as if the train itself simply decided one day to stop there, at what was once a briar patch in Alabama, and like a rabbit, simply decided to make its temporary home there, on occasion, during a run from here to there. The train seems to be at home in the landscape the same way a rabbit in an Uncle Remus story might be. When it comes, it runs near a "meadow of dog fennel," then past the "jimson weeds as well," and "along the curving roadside from the sweet gum corner to the pump shed," which is the same path Scooter often takes (1–2). There are blackberry slopes hidden by honeysuckle thickets, pecan orchards, sunflowers, and a chinaberry tree "as tall as any fairy tale beanstalk" (2–3).

Much of the time, the train tracks cannot be seen, nor the "AT&N cut, which you couldn't see either," but "whose night whistles you could sometimes hear as sometimes after midnight you could also hear the M&O, the GM&O, and the GM&N" (2–3). Like the rabbit dashing into a briar patch in a folktale, the train darts in and out of Scooter's sight, and becomes a multifaceted symbol of the mysteries of the outside world, the future for which the present is only a glimpse of things to come, and the vehicle of both leave-takings and home-comings for the roustabout heroes. The song of the train becomes part of the roustabouts' songs, the old people's stories, a way of marking time and place, and becomes, for Scooter, associated with perseverance, courage, and generosity of spirit.

Murray incorporates white texts into his text without apology. The novel begins, as does James Joyce's *Portrait of the Artist as a Young Man*, in the mind of a young child, and one of the first train "stories" mentioned in the book is a children's story, "The Little Engine That Could." In the Watty Piper edition of the text (1930), the one Scooter would have read, a little red engine is pulling a train of toys and good things to eat up over a mountain in order to deliver them to worthy children waiting on the other side. The little red engine, however, burns itself out, leaving the toys and treats stranded on the mountain.

Various engines come by and the toys ask for assistance. They state their noble purpose, their need, and the worthiness of the children on the other side, but engine after engine refuses to aid them. The first is painted gold and is too dignified to pull toys and milk. Another is too old, and another has work to do that is, he tells them, much more important. Finally, a little blue engine stops and offers its service before even being asked. It agrees to pull the train up over the mountain, and as it does, it chants the now famous phrase, "I think I can I think I can I think I can," over and over.

The message of the book, for all children, is to have self-confidence, to attempt difficult tasks, and to think positively while doing so. For Scooter, the story of the little blue engine that could, carries extra weight because of the way Scooter associates the color blue with black masculinity. For Scooter, the excuses the bigger engines give—that they are too important, too busy, or too tired to help those in need—are familiar social excuses that those in authority often give as justification for ignoring need. A real man, the story suggests, tries his hardest and pulls more than his own weight. This story is thus reminiscent of the old John Henry myth. Manhood is measured by a willingness to try, even against the odds and even when what one is attempting is not valued by anyone but the small group of people it helps.

This, Walter Mosley argues, is the fate of the black hero. The black hero's deeds, no matter how bright the flame burned, were "never recorded in *serious* works of history" and instead have been remembered only in oral stories where their memory has "moved forward like ancient men carrying fire in the night and burning their bodies to protect their burden" so that the next generation might warm themselves by this fire (237). For Scooter, the story of the little-engine-that-could resonates because the little blue engine helps people and serves a purpose that the more important engines find unworthy. The little blue engine's heroism is not appreciated by the engines, but it is celebrated by the children. In *Train Whistle Guitar*, Luzana Cholly fulfills a similar function. He is Scooter's first self-selected male role model, and he is the kind of man that the world outside of Gasoline Alley would call a villain, but for the children and some of the townspeople, he is a hero, the kind of black hero Walter Mosley celebrates as "a man who will stand up against bone-cracking odds with absolute confidence. He's a man who won't accept even the smallest insult. And for a people whom insult is as common as air, that's a man who will bring joy."

For the children, who are told what to do by their parents, school teachers, aunts, uncles, and every other adult in town, Luzana Cholly would perhaps be exactly the right kind of hero, black or white, but his blackness is secondary in the story to his association with "the gray-patina of freight train engines and railroad slag. Because in those days, that was a man's color even as tobacco plus coffee was a man's smell" (6–7). The gray-patina and railroad slag color is also described as being "blue steel," the color of a ".32–20 on a .44 frame" carried in an "underarm holster" (6–7). Guns and railroads are the color of manhood, and the "blue steel is the color you always remember when you remember how his guitar used to sound" (6–7).[4]

Murray, a man Henry Louis Gates Jr. calls the "King of Cats," sees the blues as part of a theory of identity (70). As he explains in an interview with Louis Edwards, the "jazz musician" is "central to my whole literary, philosophical system of American identity" (47). In *Train Whistle Guitar*, Luzana Cholly plays the blues, lives the blues, is the blues and the blues and the sounds of the train work in tandem. Scooter says,

> I still can't remember any point in time when I had not already seen him coming up that road from around the bend and down in the L&N railroad bottom. Nor can I remember a time when I had not heard him playing on his guitar as if he were also an engineer telling tales on a train whistle, his left hand doing most of the talking including the laughing and signifying as well as the moaning and crying and even the whining, while his right hand thumped the wheels going somewhere. Then there was also his notorious holler, the sound of which was always far away and long coming as if from somewhere way down under. . . . I myself always thought of it as being something else that was like a train, a bad express train saying Look out this me and here I come and I'm on my way one more time. (8)

Cholly is both the engineer and the train, and, as the adult version of the little-engine-that-could, he is the kind of hero Walter Mosley would appreciate, a man who keeps on keeping on. Scooter decides that he wants to be like Cholly, and be the sort of man who was "going somewhere to do something you had to have nerves as strong as rawhide to get away with" (9).

Scooter and his friends see the blues and trains as integral parts of their passage into manhood.[5] Luzana Cholly was "forever turning guitar strings into train whistles" and his music seems to tell the boys that one day "we too would have to grab ourselves an expert armful of lightning special L&N freight train rolling north by east to the steel blue castles and patent leather avenues of Philamayork" (15–16). Philamayork, the boy's accidental conflation of Philadelphia and New York, based on their misunderstanding of the train conductor's call, is a place that seems to be calling them. The train, the music tells them, is the vehicle by which they will travel to the world of men. However, just as the boys have misheard the conductor, so too do they misunderstand Luzana Cholly. He does not want the young boys to follow in his footsteps.

Although playing the blues and riding the rail were, for him, the only options for freely exploring manhood, he does not encourage Scooter (whom we later learn may actually be his biological son) or Scooter's friends to start their lives as men by running away from home in the boxcar of a freight train headed North. "Oh no you don't oh no you don't neither," he tells them when he catches them dogging his trail, and personally escorts them back to town (27). Over a meal of tin can food, Cholly explains his reasoning to the boys. Scooter recalls,

> He said that the young generation was supposed to take what they were already born with and learn how to put it with everything the civil engineers and inventors and doctors and lawyers and book keepers had found out about the world and be the ones to bring about the day the old folks had been prophesying and praying for. The three of us just sat there looking across the water then. And then we heard the next northbound freight coming, and he stood up and got ready; and he said we could watch him but we'd better not try to follow him this time; and we promised, and we also promised to go back to school the next morning. (30)

Cholly, of course, means two things when he says the boys should not try to follow him. Literally, he means that they should not try to follow him on his train journey. Symbolically, he means that they should not try to follow in his footsteps and should instead go further, by going a different way. The new way is school and education.

The physical journey, Cholly seems to be suggesting, is no longer as important as the one that will happen as a result of getting an education. At least, that is Cholly's hope:

> *Make old Luze proud of you* he said then, and he was almost pleading. *Make old Luze glad to take his hat off to you some of these days. You going further than old Luze ever dreamed of. Old Luze ain't been nowhere. Old Luze don't know from nothing.* And then the train was there and we watched him snag it and then he was waving goodbye. (30 original emphasis)

In this passage, Murray chose to italicize Luzana Cholly's words to signify their importance. For the older generation, all opportunities were rumored to be in the North and a man could earn a kind of respect in his Alabama community by going North, earning enough money to buy patent leather shoes, returning home, telling some good stories, and then heading out again.⁶ A man was a man according to the stories of his own adventures and the meager tokens of success he could carry on his person.

What Cholly wants for the boys, the next generation, is for them to journey up through the social and economic ladder and make inroads into the previously forbidden occupations, a journey that can be undertaken only through extensive education. Instead of going geographically further, Cholly wants the boys to go qualitatively further in terms of what they shall be and how they shall live. For Cholly owns no home, has no wife, and if in fact Scooter is his son, has no way of providing a home for the boy or the boy's biological mother.

This part of the novel both does and does not mirror Murray's own life.⁷ Murray was, it is true, adopted, and, like Scooter, was not told he was adopted. Like Scooter, Murray found out he was adopted by overhearing an adult conversation while the adults supposed he was asleep. Unlike Scooter, however, Murray's biological parents were far better educated and financially placed than the parents who raised him. According to Henry Louis Gates Jr. the parents who raised Murray did not finish the ninth grade and were common people while his birth parents were from "an entirely different social stratum."

> His natural father, John Young, came from a well-established family in town. His natural mother had been attending Tuskegee as a boarding student and working part time for John Young's aunt and uncle, who were in the real-estate business. When she learned that a close encounter with John Young had left her pregnant, she had to leave town. . . . As luck would have it, a cousin of hers knew a married woman who, unable to bear a child of her own, was interested in adopting one. (76)

In discussing his birth with Gates, Murray compared it to a fairy tale. "It's just like the prince left among the paupers" (76). In the novel, Scooter's biological mother, Miss Tee, fits the Tuskegee student model, but Murray has radically redrawn the biological father figure in order to make him a more masculine and more romantic figure. Whereas Murray's biological father had conformed to the expectations of bourgeois culture in every aspect but a little adultery, Scooter's biological father is his own man. Cholly makes his own money, his own way, and his time is always his own. No one owns him, and he owes no one. He is not a salesman dependent on having other people like him.

Also, Luzana Cholly has a place of mysterious honor in the culture that Murray is trying to present. He is an almost archetypal figure, what Lawrence Levine calls the "black bad man," "bluesmen," or "hard man," or "outlaw" figure who is "hard, unyielding, remorseless" (408–10). These "hard men" are the kind of men who can take care of things when things get hard. Levine explains that these men are the heroes of black folklore and that the "classic qualities of the black bad man" include sexual virility, an association with the blues, and mobility, a mobility often made possible by escape via train (410–13). Even the law is afraid of the black bad man (414). Thus, when Cholly tells the boys that he does not want them to be like him, it is very significant. Little Buddy thinks that Cholly is just trying to protect them because Cholly still sees them as little kids who could get hurt by the hard life, but Cholly's words, his almost pleading tone, makes an impression on Scooter. Scooter still admires Cholly, and he still wants to be like him, but the tone, the "almost pleading" tone in Cholly's words, makes Scooter consider the possibility that there is something more, something better that is beyond Cholly's reach, but that he, Scooter, just might, someday, achieve (30).

Although the two promised Cholly they would go to school, they have a difficult time keeping their promise. Scooter receives extra reinforcement about the value of school from a well-respected lady in town, Miss Tee, the woman he eventually will learn is his biological mother. Despite her praise and Cholly's extracted promise, the boys again skip school because at this point manhood and the classroom still seem at odds, particularly for Little Buddy, who tells Scooter that school may be the thing for Scooter, but for Little Buddy, the "real" world is his "goddamn school" (39). Scooter, who is a good student, has been doing his reading of the unnamed children's classics (perhaps *Treasure Island* and *The Adventures of Tom Sawyer*), and so the two boys skip school to hunt for pirate treasures in the swamp. The swamp, Buddy says, is their "smoke-blue destination," the place where they can experiment with being men (37). Instead of treasure, they find a dead, bloated body floating face down in the swamp. They think it is the body of a white man, but the body is so blue and bloated from being in the river that it is impossible to tell. As Samira

Kawash has noted in her discussion of the symbology of dead bodies, "neither black or white are immune to its [death's] effects; black and white bodies drown indifferently" (203). This is a very important moment for the two boys because both instantly see that the kind of adventures they have been longing for lead, most certainly, to death, and in this case, a particularly unattractive death.

Instead of the glamour of outlaw danger, they see and smell the stench of the corrupted body. In death, instead of fame, there is a complete loss of identity.[8] Frightened, the boys pretend that they hear someone coming and run from that "someone" so they do not have to admit to themselves or each other that they are running from the corpse. No sooner do they run away into the woods than they see a posse of bootleggers arrive, grab hold of the body, strip it naked, and then weigh it down with stones and sink it in the very center of the swamp's stinking ooze.

For days, the boys mull over what happened and what they saw, and this event undermines their confidence in the beauty of steel-blue masculinity if that is the end result and final resting place for that particular brand of masculinity. What disturbs the boys most is that no one will ever know for sure what happened to the man, and his body will never be claimed by those who loved him. The swamp swallowed him up whole as if he had never been born. His "smoke-blue destination" is the anonymity and ignoble rot of the swamp. The image of the drowned man sticks with them forever (37).

Soon after this episode in the swamp, Scooter becomes more and more interested in the stories of what he thinks, at the time, are his own lost relatives as he looks for direction and purpose in his life. One story, in particular, that stands out in his mind is the story of his mother's grandfather. His mother's great-grandfather was a slave and used to tell his children stories about his escape from slavery. Scooter's mother now tells these stories to Scooter. The stories are never about slavery; the stories are always about his escape. Recollecting his mother's telling of the tale, Scooter

> [c]ould see it all and I was in it too, and it was me running through the swamps, hearing them barking, coming, and it was me who swam across the creek and was running wet and freezing in the soggy shoes all the next day. Hungry and cold but not stopping even when I didn't hear them anymore, and not hopping a freight either, because they would be looking for you to

> do that. . . . Because that is what Mama always said, who knew it from her grandfather too, who knew it from his father when there was no hope of foot rest this side of Canada, which was also called Canaan, which was the Promised Land, and I also knew all of that was about something called the Underground Railroad, which ran from the House of Bondage to the land of Jubilo. (66–67)

The bootleggers' swamp ends in death, but the swamp in his mother's story, leads to the land of "Jubilo" (Jubilee). Scooter's mother is such a good storyteller, and Scooter himself has such an empathetic imagination that he finds himself as part of the action whenever his mother tells the story of the Underground Railroad.

Other people in the family also tell Scooter stories about the Underground Railroad and the heroics necessary to ride that metaphoric rail, and Scooter begins to doubt if the symbolic train requires more bravery than the skill and expertise necessary to roustabout the rails. He temporarily forgets about Cholly's plea and again begins to associate manhood with mobility. His Uncle Jerome, a preacher, reinforces that as he tells Scooter that back in the day, "the freedom road was a road through the wilderness," and that there was no easy road to freedom (67). Jerome pontificates about the necessity of being a real man and reasserts the connection between manhood and the blues by referring to all the things that are blue and are part of a man's search for freedom. Jerome tells Scooter, "the color of freedom was blue. The Union Army came dressed in blue. The big hand that signed the freedom papers signed them in blue ink which was also blood" (67). This emphasis on the color blue as the color of American manhood is part of Murray's theory about American identity and the blues, but it is also a constant reminder of the blue steel trains, guns, and toughness required for boys to become men.

However, Scooter tells us, "then it would be education again" (68). Part of the toughness required that the women push for, and that some of the men reinforce, is education. In this text, education is depicted as a revolutionary act of daring, an act requiring stamina, strength, and skill:

> They didn't ever get tired of talking about that. . . . the old days when they used to have to hold school whenever and wherever they could. Wherever they could spare the time from working the crops and wherever there was a teacher. Then later on I was the one they meant when they said the young

generation was the hope and glory. Because I had come that far in school by then; and sometimes it was Geography and sometimes it was History, and sometimes I had to tell about it, and sometimes I had to get the book and read it to them. (68)

As Scooter reads from the books, quite often, the women and some of the old men there with them, will correct him. In actuality, they are concocting revisionist history as they "correct" the textbooks.[9] The textbooks, they tell Scooter, forgot to tell about the "jet-black roustabout right in there with old Christopher Columbus" and "them royal black Ethiopians" with their "cities of iron" (69). White folks, they tell him, need to hear that, the left-out history, but more importantly, they need to hear how well he can read the Declaration of Independence, and how well he can explain the Constitution, and here him "preach" it. "White folks need to hear some talk like that," one of them says, "that's freedom talk" (69). Their hope is that instead of ending up sunk in a swamp, or merely fleeing through one on the way to Canada, that Scooter will be the kind of man to take a stand, an educated man, who will one day arrive in glory in Washington, DC, and help run this country.

Slowly, as Scooter gets older and older, the meaning of the train and the blues changes. Instead of escape, the train and the blues come to symbolize possibility. While it "remains the same old blue steel network of endlessly engaging and frequently enraging mysteries and riddling ambiguities which encompass all the possibilities and determine all the probabilities in the world," those possibilities have expanded (107).

As the book draws to a close, Scooter goes off to college via train and returns home only for holidays and funerals. It is in this final section of the book that he learns his parents are not his biological parents. This revelation comes as he dozes with his head in his mother's lap, and the old people are reminiscing and gossiping. He wakes up because he hears one of the old women ask if he is Miss Tee's child and feels his mother's "stomach was vibrating again and I felt the sound start and heard it go and then it came out through her mouth as words" (180). The information he is about to hear is a rebirth of sorts, hence the labor imagery. "She brought him into the world but he just as much mine as my own flesh and blood. I promised her and I promised God" (181). Scooter is now awake, but keeps his eyes closed. As the conversation turns to which man "spermed" him, "Mama's stomach and voice said against and above my spinning head and ringing ears" that she never asked who the father was, never intended to, and wished "everybody else would just keep their mouths out of it" (181).

For Scooter, this is a pivotal moment. He has just learned that the man and woman he called Mom and Dad for over twenty years are not his biological parents. However, with his great power of empathy, he also feels himself her child, almost as if he is being born that very night, as she states publicly that he is hers not as if he were her own flesh and blood but "as much mine as my own flesh and blood" (181). The difference in her word choice is subtle, yet quite significant. "As if" would imply a conditional relationship based on a comparison, a metaphor. "As" indicates a transubstantiation. He is as much hers as her flesh is hers and her blood is hers. Their relationship has gone beyond the metaphor. Her love, her pride in him, her life lived for him has made him hers. The metaphor, the word, has been made flesh. He is hers. However, he is also, that night, now someone else's child as well. This sets him apart, makes him feel differently about himself, and frees him, somehow, to become his own man. Other unknown parents mean other unknown possible selves. He is secure in his relationship with the parents who have raised him, and somehow, their love makes him feel that his biological parent must also have loved him very much in order to have placed him in just the right spot in the "briar patch" (*Train Whistle Guitar* 4).

When he brings up his parentage with Little Buddy, it turns out that everyone in town had always known and that Little Buddy had simply never told him.

> Shoot man, you want to know the truth? Shoot man the reason I didn't even need her to make me swear? Because man that's as good as giving you the inside claim on old Luzana and old Stagolee and old Gator Gus and them and all that. Because man you welcome to Old Lady Metcalf and all that old school stuff. But shoot man. Goddam. Not that. (182)

As Little Buddy explains it, Scooter's life is just like a fairy tale. By having an unknown father, his father could be, as Gates has said of Murray, the "King of Cats," the hero of all their boyhood adventure stories, the son of somebody famous. With an unknown father,

Scooter could be the son of somebody dangerous and brave, hidden away in Gasoline Point, Alabama. Instead of being viewed as a bastard, the absence of a known father makes all the heroes in the world potential fathers. Moreover, because everyone in town suspected that Miss Tee was Scooter's mother, the stigma of the "motherless child" does not apply either. Instead, Scooter has two mothers: the one who loved him enough to give him up to have a secure two-parent home and the one who provided that home.

At the end of the text Scooter recalls not the possible epic fathers, but his two mothers, and upon reflection decides that he had somehow always known that both women were his mothers. He recalls how as a child Miss Tee was the one to whom he went "hop-skipping up the steps with my certificate and the top prize" when he did well in school, and that she would always tell him how very proud she was, but would then tell him to go to his mother, whom she called Miss Melba, first, for Miss Melba should "always be the one to see things first," (182–83). Each time, he would say, "I forgot," and "when I looked back from the gate she was waving and smiling and there were tears in her eyes" (183). The book ends there.

In Albert Murray's *Train Whistle Guitar* trains are first associated with a particular kind of dangerous black masculinity. Luzana Cholly, the key black man in the text, is a John Henry, Stagolee, Railroad Bill, Gator Gus, kind of bluesman and train roustabout, who makes his living gambling and playing music as he travels from town to town, an expert at hitching a stolen ride on a train. A proud man, he nevertheless cautions the boy who may be his biological son away from following in his footsteps; instead he pushes education as the new way for a man to make a real name for himself and to make something of himself, to go someplace and really arrive. Scooter's guides along the way are the women who tell him stories about the past, such as his mother (who like Harriet Tubman was never able to bear children of her own) with her stories about their relatives and the Underground Railroad, and Miss Tee, the family friend who is, he eventually learns, his biological mother, who pushes him to excel in school.

Scooter has what at first seems like two trains running, two mutually exclusive options heading in contrary directions. He can hitch a ride on the old ways, the train ways, and follow in Cholly's footsteps as does his friend, Little Buddy, or he can be a school boy, as Miss Tee wishes, but for a long time, that lacks charm and importance until he learns how the stories his mother tells and the history books he reads in school intersect. Education slowly becomes seen as something manly and important, and as his childhood dreams of steel-blue guns and bootleg treasures in the swamps fade, he slowly begins to replace them with geography and history, which become his new tools for success. What Scooter learns to do is to combine the spirit of the roustabout into his educational goals and prospect for achievement. It is the spirit, not the lifestyle of the blues and the train roustabout, Luzana Cholly, he inherits. He will travel to places Luzana Cholly would never be able to go and would never be welcome, and he will not have to steal his way there or home. There is the suggestion, at the end of the text, that Scooter is ready, willing, and able to take his place as a first-class passenger on a brave new track to the future. The train, its whistle, and the sound of old Cholly's guitar will live on in Scooter's words as he becomes, in the novels that follow, a man like Albert Murray himself, a powerful thinker, a man of depth, a master of words and inspiration.

When critics try to sum up the importance of Albert Murray's work, or comments on his insistence on specific African American icons like the train, or African American metaphors for identity, like the blues, they often find themselves tongue-tied because scholars, like readers, are still more familiar with the traditional slave narrative and social protest tradition as a way of reading African American literature instead of breaking free of the imposed structure of the American literary canon and reading the texts as literature—which is what Murray demands of his readers. Speaking of Albert Murray and his contributions to the field of literature, Henry Louis Gates Jr., who as a young man often visited Murray the way one might a revered and honored griot, had this to say:

> You could say of him what he said of Gordon Parks: "Sometimes it is as if he himself doesn't quite know what to make of what he has in fact already made of himself." Sometimes I don't quite either. On the one hand, I cherish the vernacular; on the other, I've always distrusted the notion of myth as something deliberately added to literature, like the prize in a box of Cracker Jack. (81)

Murray, Gates says, "has always spelled trouble for critics and artists of every description, for icon-breakers and icon-makers, for friends and foes" (81). Gates concludes, however, that he, himself, learned "a great many things" when he would "sit with him in his apartment" and that summed up, "they amount to a larger vision" of a world that the younger generation does not have the passion to create, to live in, to maintain because "we live in an age of irony, an age when passionate intensity is hard to find outside a freshman dining hall, and when even the mediocre lack all conviction" (81). When looked at in isolation, the train in *Train Whistle Guitar* might be, as Gates suggests, "like the prize in a box of Cracker Jack," but when studied along with the other twentieth-century African American texts which use the image of the train as a significant symbol, it becomes clear that this particular "notion of myth" Gates so distrusts is present all throughout the works of twentieth-century African American writers.

The image of the train is deliberately added to the literature, but for good reason. More than setting, more than plot conveyance, the train serves a symbolic purpose for the African American writers who deliberately choose to incorporate trains and legendary train people into their texts. For these writers, the images of flying trains, supernatural train "conductors," strong train men, and train riders who can steal away home, are images symbolizing various aspects of a necessary inward journey toward a redefinition of self. Instead of an external columbiad or jeremiad, what these twentieth-century African American writers are interested in is the inward journey toward a reformation of identity that must come if a formerly discriminated and oppressed people are ever to be spiritually, mentally, and emotionally free. The train is the symbol of that journey, and its contested history as a symbol of, as Whitman says, the "motion and power" to change a nation, a symbol of the Underground Railroad, its association with the great John Henry, and the economic opportunities it provided both as an employer and in terms of mobility, make it a logical choice for writers who are interested in creating a sense of history and tradition where there might otherwise be silence.

"Auden talked about the 'true ancestor' whom you don't find by going back along a straight line," Murray was fond of saying (Gelfand 10). The same holds true for symbols. "Images and metaphors make you see possibilities," Murray explained in the same interview (Gelfand 10). When a writer believes that a century needs more images and possibilities, perhaps it is the job of the modern writer to create believable myths and symbols from the cloth of history and cut them to fit, like bits of fabric in one of Faith Ringgold's many quilts.

As for the future, will the image of the railroad continue to be used by African American writers of the twenty-first century? By and large, the future of the train as symbol remains shrouded in mystery, much like the angel seat in the final pages of Leon Forrest's *There Is a Tree More Ancient Than Eden*. However, for as long as there are black modernist writers, those interested in myth-making and magical views of history in which the past and the present connect through the tangible transport of a quasi-celestial train, the staying power of the train as symbol will remain. "Trains . . . the names of trains, the times of the trains!" Toni Morrison explains, and goes on to identify exactly what it is that powers the hearts, minds, and spirits of the black men and women of the trains. Harriet Tubman and John Henry meet Nathaniel Witherspoon and J. Sutter, flying high with Faith Ringgold's children and the poetry of Robert Hayden. They all meet again, somewhere, out there, beyond the horizon, beyond the last visible outpost of "civilized" society. What the train symbolizes, Morrison concludes, is the spirit that guides men and women to be more than any machine, and yet, is the impetus of mechanical creation. "Curiosity," Morrison concludes. "What's around the corner, what's across the hill, what's in the valley, what's down the track. Go find out what that is, you know! And in the process of finding, they are also making themselves."[10] Though the train has long ceased to be a symbol of the modern and the modern world, it remains a powerful symbol of a necessary inward journey, a journey that cannot be rushed, and, once started, cannot be stopped.

☥ NOTES

Introduction: The Train as Symbol in African American Literature

1. In *The Machine in the Garden: Technology and the Pastoral Ideal in America*, Leo Marx cites example after example of how white American painters and writers used the image of the train. He calls it an "endlessly evocative image," a motif which "has served again and again to order literary experience" and which "appears everywhere in American writing" as "a cardinal metaphor of contradiction, exfoliating, through associated images and ideas, into a design governing the meaning of entire works" (229). As Marx explains, for the white artists and writers he cites, the train shows "the clash of opposed states of mind: a strong urge to believe in the rural myth along with an awareness of industrialization as counterforce to the myth" (229).
2. See *Harriet Tubman: Anti-Slavery Activist*, by M. W. Taylor, 107.
3. This line translates as "Led by joy, pulled there," trans. Richard McLamore. See "'Two Trains Running': The Train as Symbol in Twentieth-Century African American Literature" by D. Zabel (Diss., 2001, 5).
4. The term *flying Africans* refers to one of the many myths and legends of the African Diaspora and will be discussed in greater detail in chapter two. In brief, it refers to stories about African captives who, rather than submit to a life of slavery, either jumped off the slave ships and, according to witnesses, flew away; or as a second version of the legend states, the captives, Ibos from eastern Nigeria, once set ashore in America or the Caribbean, rejected their future as slaves, and walked out into the ocean until they were out far enough to see the way to fly back to Nigeria. For more on *flying Africans* see Virginia Hamilton's *The People Who Could Fly* and Langston Hughes and Arna Bontemps's *The Book of Negro Folklore*.
5. The ending, writes John Updike, is "frustratingly vague in its resolution" and "is either the best disguised happy ending or the most muffled tragic note of the publishing season" (89).
6. For more on the Brotherhood of Sleeping Car Porters and Maids see *From Slavery to Freedom*, by John Hope Franklin and Alfred A. Moss Jr. (382).

Chapter One: The Impact of the Railroad on African American Life

1. See, in particular, sections on Faith Ringgold, Robert Hayden, Leon Forrest, and Nikki Giovanni in chapter two. In contrast to Whitman's description of the train and train cars, in the works of African American writers, the train

and train cars instead take on the personality of Harriet Tubman, a woman who was rarely described as "merry" or "obedient."
2. For a more complete explanation of the naming of the Underground Railroad, see Siebert (44–45). According to Siebert, mystified slave catchers explained their inability to track and retake missing slaves on the existence of an underground railroad that both hid and transported escaping slaves. Though no actual railroad underground existed, the name seemed an accurate reflection of the powerful network white Southerners presumed they were up against, and the name stuck. Abolitionists turned what was meant to be a negative nickname into a positive symbol of their organization.
3. See Grissom's *The Negro Sings a New Heaven,* Johnson and Johnson's *The Book of Negro Spirituals Including the Book of American Negro Spirituals and the Second Book of Negro Spirituals,* and Work's *American Negro Songs and Spirituals.*
4. For more on key Civil War battles involving railroads see Stover (60–61), Franklin and Moss (199–236), Gordon (127). For an in-depth discussion of the strategic use of the railroads during the Civil War, see Turner's *Victory Rode the Rails.*
5. For more on this see Ayers (92–100). Ayers gives example after example of incidents where black passengers purchased first-class tickets, were ushered to the Jim Crow car, took legal action, and won their cases.
6. For more on Homer Plessy's case see Sundquist (225–435). For a detailed examination of the economic politics involved in the case see Olsen's *The Thin Disguise: Plessy vs. Ferguson.*
7. For more on the "transmission of secrets in African American culture" see Tobin and Dobard's *Hidden in Plain View.* See also Gates's *The Signifying Monkey: A Theory of Afro-American Literature* for a theoretical explanation of how nineteenth-century black American uses of antecedent texts or forms constitute "signifying" and the purpose served by this double-edge language.
8. Born slave, as an adult Henry "Box" Brown escaped to freedom by shipping himself to freedom in a packing case, traveling for twenty-seven hours on an express train "disguised" as a box of freight. According to Brown's narrative, the box was "three feet one inch long, two feet six inches high, and two feet wide" (59).

Chapter Two: Flying Trains and the "Tubman Tradition"

1. See the lyrics to the KSR ONE song "Ah-Yeah," in which Moses, Solomon, Jesus Christ, Harriet Tubman, Sojourner Truth, Nat Turner, Marcus Garvey, Malcolm X, Bobby Seale, and others are represented as the "spiritual form" of God coming again and again "to a people that was lost" inspiring them throughout history. This spirit of God now speaks through the singer KSR ONE, and even if he is attacked or killed, "on the wheels of steel my spirit flies away" and enters into new bodies, thus continuing to "bring the truth"

while speaking through "the code the devil cannot see through." Tubman is one of the black manifestations of God and the train imagery is apparent all throughout the song as part of "the code" the "devil" (re: white people) "cannot see through."

2. According to Gara, the Underground Railroad was much publicized by both abolitionists and proslavery Southerners, each attempting to use the Underground Railroad as a tool for propaganda. The "fugitive issue" became very heated and "fired the public imagination" with mental images of hundreds of thousands of escaping slaves streaming out of the South under the cover of night, headed North (114). Abolitionists used Underground Railroad propaganda to illustrate their point that now was the time for the emancipation of the southern slaves, and that the Southern insistence on the happiness and childlike contentment of the slaves was a lie. Abolitionists depicted escaping fugitives and the underground of Quakers and abolitionists who aided them as heroes. Stories of the Underground Railroad created for the abolitionists "a larger and more receptive audience than they had ever before enjoyed" (114). Southerners used Underground Railroad propaganda in an attempt to prove their point about the necessity of the passage of the Fugitive Slave Act (114). Gara's text discusses how such stories about the Underground Railroad potentially hurt would-be fugitives and quotes Frederick Douglass and his objections to this kind of propaganda. Gara asserts that the Underground Railroad was primarily a vehicle of propaganda, not liberation (147–63).

3. See Jeffrey Ruggles's *The Unboxing of Henry Brown*, which, as the title suggests, focuses on themes of containment and release. Brown said that the idea to ship himself to freedom in a coffin-like box came directly from God (27). That is was feasible was because of, as Ruggles notes, "the improvement in transportation brought by the railroad" and not the mythic Underground Railroad (27).

4. James views "othermothering" as a very positive thing. She argues that "othermothers" show the African American community at its best as it shows an "acceptance of responsibility for the welfare of non-blood related children" (44). Other feminists disagree with James's celebration of "othermothering" as a "possible Black feminist link to social transformation" (44). Some feel, as Carol Stack and Linda Burton have shown, that "kin-scription: demands that caretaking of others "supersede personal goals" and that such an emphasis on "self-sacrificing and hard work," while designed to "insure the survival of the collective," forces the one who is doing the caretaking to suppress their own natural human desires (36). Also interesting in terms of looking at the texts in which the Tubman figure kills her "children" rather than let them live a life of slavery is Stephanie Shaw's article on "Mothering under Slavery in the Antebellum South," in which Shaw provides example after chilling example of slave mothers who killed their children because they loved them too much to let them live as slaves, although as Toni Morri-

son's Sethe learns in *Beloved*, perhaps it is the slave owner, and not the child, whose throat a loving mother should slit.

5. Morrison's *Song of Solomon* is full of twentieth-century "flying" African Americans whose flight resembles suicide. On the day Macon Dead is born, an insurance man attempts to fly from Mercy Steeple. When older, Milkman Dead returns to the South and learns of the myth surrounding his family's history. His paternal great-grandfather, Solomon, supposedly was able to fly and flew back to Africa to escape a life of slavery. At the end of the novel, Milkman Dead leaps into the air "as fleet and bright as a lodestar" as he, like his great-grandfather before him, "surrendered to the air" and learns to "ride it" (337). A powerful book, for political pragmatists the ending is unsatisfying because despite his deep spiritual awakening, Milkman Dead, in the end, is dead. In the flying *train* stories, the main characters do not always end up dead. Death is a possibility but not the de facto outcome.

6. After looking more closely into the life of Tubman's authorized biographer, Sarah Bradford, Jean Humez has expressed serious concerns about the Bradford biographies of Tubman. Humez suggests that this allegedly "mediated" autobiographical text reveals much more about Sarah Bradford's needs than the true character of Harriet Tubman. For example, Humez points out that in the 1865 interview notes, Bradford includes Tubman's comments that, although she had always believed herself to have been chosen by God for a special mission, her decision to become a conductor on the Underground Railroad was made because she had been cast off by her "faithless husband," and was so upset that she decided she could die but once, and that her heart at any rate was now dead, hence she could commit herself to the cause of the Underground Railroad. In the 1886 version of the "as told to" autobiography, however, Bradford does not mention Tubman's personal reasons for having no fear of death. Humez suggests that this could be because Bradford did not want to "tarnish the saintly and self-sacrificing image of Tubman," but also suggests that it could be because of Bradford's own experiences with a faithless husband; Bradford's husband deserted her for another woman, following which Bradford threw herself wholeheartedly into the cause of abolition (178). Humez's suggestion is that Bradford decided what to include in the "autobiography" based on Bradford's own feelings about events in Bradford's life. Humez suggests that the notes of the interviews present a far more accurate portrayal of Tubman than the popularized Bradford autobiography. Though still largely dependent on the nineteenth-century Bradford texts, more recent biographies of Tubman include Dorothy Sterling's *Freedom Train: The Story of Harriet Tubman* (1954), M. W. Taylor's *Harriet Tubman* (1991), and Ann Petry's *Harriet Tubman: Conductor on the Underground Railroad* (1995).

7. There is, of course, no way of knowing this for sure, but it is interesting to note that it was important to her early biographer that Tubman's talents and abilities in no way be credited to even the tiniest drop of white blood. In terms of Tubman's historical context, this makes sense. As George

Fredrickson points out, the 1850s saw an explosion in the field of ethnology and many scientists of note, including Harvard's Louis Agassiz, were converted to the notion that by blood and biology, "Negro inferiority" was a "practical fact" (81). An example of the type of arguments put forth by "American School of Ethnology" is Dr. John H. Van Evrie's assertion that "God has made the Negro an inferior being not in most cases, but in all cases. There never could be a Negro equaling the standard Caucasian in natural ability" (93). Thus, in cases when African Americans did show intelligence or ability, those talents were credited to the "improving" presence of white blood. This, perhaps, explains Tubman's biographers' insistence on the purity of her blood. I am indebted to Clare Eby for bringing this point to my attention.

8. Turner's mother was a North African, captured when a teen, who had only been in the United States five years when she gave birth to Turner. According to legend, she tried to kill Turner when he was born so that he would not be raised a slave, but she was prevented from doing so. See Sundquist (62).

9. See Siebert (44–45) for the various stories about the naming of the Underground Railroad.

10. While many prominent black men became orators or speakers in the North and in Europe, risking capture, particularly after the passage of the 1850 Fugitive Slave Act, very few returned to the South and were active in the day-to-day activities of the Underground Railroad. While they were officially "part" of the Underground Railroad, in that they worked to provide financial assistance, or served as "agents" who provided clothes, food, or shelter to escaping slaves, very few escaped slaves actually served as conductors—the people who went back into the South to lead other slaves out of slavery. For an explanation of the difference between "conductors" and "agents" see the introductory materials that accompany Faith Ringgold's *Aunt Harriet's Underground Railroad in the Sky*.

11. Though not mentioned by name in Ringgold's text, the shoemaker in *Aunt Harriet's Underground Railroad in the Sky* is most likely Thomas Garrett, the Quaker shoemaker. Garrett is famous for his commitment to the cause of abolitionism. Garrett owned a large shoe store in Wilmington, Delaware, an important station on the Underground Railroad because of its proximity to the Mason-Dixon Line. Garrett's shoe shop had a false wall behind which fleeing slaves could hide. When they left Garrett's shop, each runaway was given a pair of shoes, often the first pair they had ever owned. According to Underground Railroad records kept by William Still, Garrett helped 2,700 slaves to escape before his shoe shop was seized and his bank account depleted to pay fines for his part in aiding the fugitives. When the presiding judge told Garrett that he hoped this would finally teach the now sixty-year-old Garrett not to interfere "with the cause of justice by helping off runaway Negroes," Garrett answered, "Friend, thee hasn't left me a dollar, but I wish to say to thee that if anyone knows of a fugitive who wants a shelter, and a friend, send him to Thomas Garrett!" (Taylor 45–46).

12. For a good overview of Nat Turner's religious and political views see Sundquist's "Signs of Power: Nat Turner and Frederick Douglass," in *To Wake the Nations* (27–112).
13. For those unfamiliar with Jewish folklore, a golem is a creature, created of earth, that can be called forth to do battle with a people's enemies. Golems are not to be summoned for individual squabbles; they should only be summoned when God's chosen children are under attack as a people. Once summoned into existence, the golem cannot be called back or off until it wipes out the entire field of battle. Often, it will take out both the good and the bad in its single-minded efforts to destroy the bad. Therefore, the golem is only activated in times of great need. Golem stories were originally very secret stories and were not written down or shared with goyim (derogatory term for the non-Jewish), but now golem figures appear in television shows and movies such as *The X-Files* and (though altered into a negative character that serves the villain of the piece) in Kevin Smith's *Dogma*.
14. As Jane Campbell points out in *Mythic Black Fiction: The Transformation of History*, black writers often use myths that belong to all of Western civilization, but do so in a way that imbues the myth with "new significance, overturning racist stereotypes" (x). Moreover, the heroes of these mythic black fictions are not Gods like Zeus or Athena, or queens, like Helen of Troy. Instead, they are "ordinary mortals" performing superhuman deeds, "turning the seemingly unnoticed actions of everyday life into miraculous statements about the limitless power and possibility of Afro-Americans" (x).
15. In fact, this is how Harriet Tubman is presented in black rap artist KRS's 1995 song "Ah-Yeah" in which he states that "God, that's what the black man is," and that God keeps coming to earth with a message for all people in the human bodies of Harriet Tubman, Sojourner Truth, Nat Turner, Bobby Seale, but that people keep missing the revealed messages of God. Each famous figure from black history gets his or her own tag. For Tubman, he says God came as Harriet Tubman to guide "a people who was lost."
16. See Shaw's "Mothering under Slavery in the Antebellum South" for her exploration of how slave mothers disciplined their children, often in ways that seem harsh by contemporary standards, but which were designed to ensure their survival. Shaw's suggestion is that some have mistakenly concluded that slave mothers abused their children because the mothers were themselves abused, thus arguing for an extended history of child abuse in black culture because of slavery, when in fact, the discipline administered by slave mothers, though harsh, taught very specific lessons necessary for survival and prepared the children for the type of self-control and personal discipline they would need both to survive as a slave and for freedom (252–54).
17. Ellen and William Craft escaped from slavery by posing as a master and slave taking passage on a train. Ellen played the part of a sickly young white male as she was light enough to pass for white. Her husband William played the part of her slave. See *Two Tickets to Freedom* by Florence Freedman and Tonya Bolden's *And Not Afraid to Die*.

18. Seltzer also raises interesting questions about motherhood, reproduction, and the equating of bodies with machines. He suggests that the machine metaphor allows things that do not ordinarily reproduce to participate in the traditionally feminine power of creation. See both "The Naturalist Machine" and "Statistical Persons" for more on this fascinating topic.

Chapter Three: Black Supermen and the "John Henry Tradition"

1. There are literally thousands of articles, books, and Web sites devoted to the study of folklore in general and the four "folk" legends immortalized by the United States Post Office in its 1996 release of these four as part of its folk legends four-pack. For example, see Mary Pope Osborne's *American Tall Tales* and Ernest Thayer's Caldecott Honor Book 2001 winner *Casey at the Bat: A Ballad of the Republic Sung in the Year 1888*.
2. For more on this, go to the Talcott, West Virginia, Web site, maintained by the Summers County Visitor and Convention Bureau. Talcott also now boasts a John Henry Park, A Community Project of the Hilldale-Talcott Ruritan Club. See http://www.summerscvb.com/henry.htm.
3. Ginna Allison's radio documentary "Steel Drivin' Man" originally aired in November, 1995, on National Public Radio's *All Things Considered*. "Steel Drivin' Man" was made possible by a grant from the National Endowment for the Arts. Transcripts of the show are available on Allison's Web site http:// www.wormlips.com/ john_henry/radio.html.
4. Many black writers have written about the need to control the representation of black heroes, and the need to firmly position such heroes as "race men." Hazel Carby does this in *Race Men*, and Baraka writes about this as necessary and "daring propaganda" in his essay "The Revolutionary Theatre," in *Home: Social Essays* (211).
5. In 1903 W. E. B. Du Bois first attempted to answer the question, "So what does it feel like to be a problem," in *The Souls of Black Folk* (43), and since then, many African American writers have responded to that question with varying degrees of anger and pain. The "problem" of black masculinity, though currently in vogue, thus has at the very least a hundred-year history. That doesn't, however, diminish the importance of the topic. For a sampling of essays by black men about the "problem" of black masculinity, see *Representing Black Men*, ed. Marcellus Blount and George P. Cunningham (1996) and *(Speak My Name) Black Men on Masculinity and the American Dream*, ed. Don Belton (1995).
6. See Harry Allen's "Hip-Hop Hi-Tech," in *Step into a World: A Global Anthology of the New Black Literature*, ed. Kevin Powell (New York: John Wiley & Sons, 2000) 91, for his discussion of singer, scholar, actor, activist Paul Robeson's 1935 statement to the *London Daily Herald*. Robeson had played John Henry in an adaptation of Roark Bradford's musical in which Robeson's portrayal of John Henry worked against the incipient racism of Bradford's por-

trayal of the great John Henry. The musical was a commercial failure and had only a short run. Also, see Colson Whitehead's fictionalized account of the mind of Paul Robeson while playing John Henry on stage, and Whitehead's summary of the life and death of the man in *John Henry Days* (228–31) where Whitehead draws an analogy between the tragic death of John Henry and the tragic end to Robeson's life.

7. See Roark Bradford's *John Henry* (New York: The Literary Guild, 1931).
8. Anderson continues to try to prove his point that John Henry was not a railroad man and perhaps never even existed by stating that John Henry's name does not appear on any tombstone in the black cemetery near Talcott where the tunnel was built: "There is a black cemetery there, but no headstone bears the name of John Henry" (para. 5). What Anderson elects not to mention in his article "Don't Turn John Henry into a Railroad Man" is that many of the graves are unmarked in the black cemetery, particularly the graves from the nineteenth century.
9. See Clare Eby's "Slouching Toward Beastliness," *African American Review* 35.3 (2001):439–459, where she discusses depictions of African American masculinity created by white authors and how authors such as Richard Wright attempted to redefine such depictions.
10. See Leon F. Litwack's *Trouble in Mind: Black Southerners in the Age of Jim Crow*. Litwack explains that while white Southerners complained that blacks were "ignorant and illiterate," they felt threatened "by any suggestion that blacks were capable of anything more and often worked to keep blacks in ignorance in order to justify their sense of white superiority" (101).
11. See Martha Hodes's *White Women, Black Men* for a discussion of how this sort of stereotype connects to the mania for lynching and burning black men (176–208). See also Baker's *From Savage to Negro* for some particularly disturbing photographs of lynchings and burnings by the KKK of "black brutes" (131).
12. See George M. Fredrickson's *The Black Image in the White Mind* for a discussion of science, polygenesis, and how these things were used as "proof" of "innate" African inferiority (71–96, 228–55). See also Baker's *From Savage to Negro* for a discussion of monthlies, magazines, and newspapers used "scientific experts" to argue for a representation of black men as beasts (28–30).
13. See Edward Ayers, *Southern Crossing: A History of the American South* for a discussion of the representation of black men in public life (71–176).
14. See Sundquist's discussion of Florida Congressman Frank Clark's 1908 description of black men as "dirty," "greasy," and other colorful terms as he argued, in the House of Representatives, in favor of maintaining segregation on railroad cars. His impassioned speech ended with a question that has made him forever famous, at least as a footnote: "Who here would permit a Negro to marry his daughter?" (qtd. in Sundquist 439).
15. For even more graphic examples of southern negrophobia, see Joel Williamson's *The Crucible of Race,* particularly his chapter on southern white writer Thomas Dixon (140–79).

16. See Franklin and Moss for a discussion of the contributions of black soldiers during World War I and World War II (323–456).
17. For more on John Oliver Killens's politics see *Black Man's Burden*, in which Killens presents his take on the Black psyche, the Black writer, the Black mystique, and, of course, the Black man's burden (1965).
18. In "Folk Culture and Masculine Identity in Charles Burnett's *To Sleep with Anger*," Karen Chandler discusses the importance of the John Henry myth as a counterpoint to the trickster-badman figure. She argues that the movie uses these two folk stories to urge viewers "both to examine the extent to which manhood should be influenced by the heroic identities of the past and to test those qualities in men most necessary for personal, familial, and communal welfare" (300). She argues also that movies, more than any other media form, currently fulfill the "instructive and epistemological role of folklore" (300). This assertion lends external support to Leo Proudhammer's argument that it was through the movies he watched as a child that his imagination was first stirred, and from this stirring, his "sense of reality" forever changed (24). Instead of fictional stories reflecting reality, these movie stories *changed* his sense of reality.
19. This obsession with "inner" experience seems to be a common trope among critics writing about homosexual characters and contemporary gay and lesbian theory. See Robert Reid-Pharr's "Tearing the Goat's Flesh: Homosexuality, Abjection, and the Production of a Late-Twentieth-Century Black Masculinity" for a summary of critics who examine homosexuality by using an "inside/out binarism" (353). It is also interesting to note that, although Baldwin's *Giovanni's Room* fits into Reid-Pharr's assertion that, in the twentieth century, black men are the ideal "sacrificial goat," complete with biblical undertones, Baldwin's *Tell Me How Long the Train's Been Gone* does not as the homosexual character, Leo Proudhammer, is not sacrificed and does not die in service of preserving or calling into question the existing social order.
20. It is worth noting, however, that Baldwin himself was not consistent about whether or not androgyny was a good thing, as Kaplan herself points out at the end of her essay. Kaplan quotes a January 1985 article Baldwin wrote for *Playboy*, called "Freaks and the American Ideal of Manhood," in which Baldwin states "we are all androgynous. . . . male in female, female in male, white in black and black in white. We are a part of each other" (48). As Kaplan shows, in other places in his writing, Baldwin very emphatically rejected the feminization of black men (46). In *Tell Me How Long the Train's Been Gone*, however, Baldwin seems genuinely to be presenting Leo Proudhammer as a man, not an androgen, and to be suggesting that sexual preference did not make a man into an androgen. Rather, sexual preference was simply part of a man's prerogative.
21. Colson Whitehead's essay "I Worked at an Ill-Conceived Internet Start-Up and All I Got Was This Lousy Idea for a Novel" can be

found in on the Random House Web site http://www.randomhouse.com/boldtype/0501/whitehead/essay.html.
22. The Ruritans are a predominantly southern institution. A community service organization, Ruritans seek "to promote fellowship and goodwill among its members and the citizens in the community, and to inspire each other to higher efforts," to "unify the efforts of individuals, organizations and institutions in the community toward making it an ideal place in which to live," and "to encourage and foster the ideal of service as the basis of all worthy enterprise." For more information about the goals and objectives of official Ruritan service organizations recognized by the National Ruritans, see http://www.ruritan.org.
23. I wish to thank Brent Stephenson, a freshman in one of my English courses at Friends University (2003), for allowing me to share his observation about Colson Whitehead's use of parables. The parable Brent discusses here is found on page 30. "In China, they used to keep the royal ducks in this nice open area and feed them the best rice and grain. It gives the ducks a special flavor. It's like they're spicing them up before they're even dead. Only they—the ducks that is—think they're king of the hill. The landed gentry of, what is it, the mallard family, the royalty who get the best food and have the best duck lifestyle. They sneer at the peasant ducks outside the gate . . . but what they don't know . . . is that they're no better than the other ducks. They're all going to get eaten. It's just that some ducks get the better rice" (30). Brent's suggestion, to quote Killens, is that "a man ain't nothing but a man" and that despite J. Sutter's education and ambitions, he, too, will die fighting against whatever the dehumanizing machine or mechanism of his age is because that is what black men do in the novel *John Henry Days*. Whether they are day laborers or Harvard-educated writers, both are eventually consumed by the culture that assigns them their relative worth. Though Brent's reading runs contrary to mine, the use of the parable of the duck to support such an interpretation makes for an interesting alternate reading of the ending. The legend of John Henry is more tragic, Brent argues, because tragedy continues to be the path of choice for so many.
24. Dave Weich, interview, www.powells.com.

Chapter Four: Riders of the Train: Passage, Passing, and the Great Migration

1. For more African American use of this mule/man symbolism see Zora Neale Hurston's two collections of folklore, *Mules and Men* (1935) and *Tell My Horse* (1938). She also wrote a play with Langston Hughes called "Mule Bone," a comedy which laments African Americans' treatment as the mule of the world. Alternately, Gerene L. Freeman of the Yale-New Haven Teachers Institute, in an essay titled "What about My 40 Acres and a Mule?" suggests that the mule in the phrase "40 acres and a mule" symbolizes the broken promises of the Civil War contract with the newly freed African American population. "[A]cting under an edict from the War Department,

issued Special Field Order No. 15 promulgated on January 16, 1865, after Sherman had conferred with 20 black ministers and obtained the approval of the War department . . . the land was then divided into 40-acre tracts. Sherman then issued order to General Saxton to distribute the plots and processory titles to the head of each family of the freedmen. Sherman also ordered General Saxon to lend to the freedmen animals that were no longer useful to the military" (para. 15–16). President Andrew Johnson later "ordered the processory titles rescinded and the land returned to the white plantation owners" (para. 16).

2. There is a great deal of controversy about what the end of this story signifies. George McMichael has summed up the debate in the form of a question: "At the end of the story, is Dave still 'almost a man'? (248). Many read the ending of the story as one which, with graveyard humor, pokes fun at adolescence, and that Dave is still, at story's end "psychologically and physically unprepared to become a man" (248). Such a reading, however, ignores the symbolic power of the train, what trains and the long steel tracks promise. For those that "steal a ride," adventure and manhood follow, and one becomes as hard as steel by riding the rails. The train is the threshold moment. He hesitates, but then he makes the leap. He is not yet a man, shooting the mule did not make him a man, but riding the train out of one life and into another will. That is the promise of the train.

3. There are also instances of female characters who believe that the train can carry them away from the limitations of one life by taking them to a new place, such as Eva in Gayl Jones's *Eva's Man*, who goes "any place the train takes me" because it is "easier being a woman and alone in different places than it is in the same place" until she becomes partners with a domineering man whom she eventually murders and castrates by tearing his penis off with her teeth (5–6). Another example of a female character who views the train as an escape from limitation is Helga Crane in Nella Larsen's *Quicksand and Passing* who quits her job on the spur of the moment and is able to leave "today" because "they can't stop me. Trains leave here for civilization every day" (14).

4. See Leon Litwack's *Trouble in Mind; Black Southerners in the Age of Jim Crow*, 217–18, 230–37.

5. See, for example, Flannery O'Connor's "The Train," and "The Artificial Nigger," or Thomas Wolfe's *You Can't Go Home Again*.

6. There are also train station stories such as Alice Childress's "Florence," in which the racial conflict that occurs in a train station on the segregated train platforms leaves the white woman confused and angry, and the black woman resolute, determined now to send money to her daughter who is struggling to be an actress in New York. The mother had originally intended to go to New York to drag her daughter, Florence, back home. The mother's decision to help her daughter "keep on keeping on" is made in response to the white woman's offer to find a place "in service" for the girl. The train station is the perfect setting for this play because throughout the

play, various trains come and go. Some are headed to New York, others back "home," and these speeding trains come to represent the various choices the mother must make. Her choices not only affect her daughter, Florence, they change the mother as well, and once her decision is made, she stands a little taller and walks with more confidence and self-assurance. Florence was the name of Alice Childress's mother.

7. In an unpublished article on Baraka's "Dutchman," coauthored by Jeff Epps and Darcy Zabel, in which Mr. Epps analyzes the character Clay, and Ms. Zabel analyzes the character Lilith, the two conclude that the seduction scene on the train is really a devil's game of chess and fits into the Mephistopheles/Devil and Dan Webster/Devil went down to Georgia tradition. In this case, however, even though Clay checkmates the Queen (Lilith), he does not "win" the game because the devil always cheats.

8. The South of the 1920s is often associated with white Nationalism and "negrophobia." See Fredrickson (130–64 and 256–82). Also see L. Baker for a discussion of Southern Ku Klux Klan activities after 1915 when they became "retooled, officially incorporated, and efficiently organized" (130–31).

9. For an interesting discussion about how "seeing" and "perspective" are often used to objectify African American women, read Mae G. Henderson's critique of Houston Baker's "There Is No More Beautiful Way: Theory and the Poetics of Afro-American Women's Writing," in which Henderson uses Lacan's theories about "the gaze" to suggest that one of the things which distorts a black woman's image of herself is that she is "at the mercy of what the other(s) determine is appropriate" (160).

10. Ibid., 160–62.

11. As readers familiar with the text of *Sula* well know, there are other significant train incidents in the novel as well. Just as Nel's identity is formed by what happens to her mother on the train, so too, in a sense, is Sula's. Sula's mother, Eva Peace, is paid off by the railroad because she has lost her leg in an accident that most in town believe to have been a deliberate attempt to extort money from the only thing around that a black woman could extort money from without resorting to sex: the railroad. For a discussion of this "accident" see Delancey (15–18). Because the train that takes Eva's leg is not ever described, it is not discussed in this chapter, but it is interesting to note that both girls, Sula and Nel, are deeply affected by what happens because of their mothers' experiences on the train.

12. As Mary Helen Washington has observed, quite often there is a difference in the way men and women express anger and rage. Quoting Gwendolyn Brooks, Washington argues that, even though much of African American women's fiction shows women "taming all that anger down," that silence is also a form of rage, and powerful enough to rival that of their more explosive male counterparts (249–61).

13. For a discussion of social Darwinism as it was misused in reference to African Americans, see L. Baker's "Looking Behind the Veil with the Spy Glass

of Anthropology," "Unraveling the Boasian Discourse," and "Anthropology and the Fourteenth Amendment," in *From Savage to Negro* (143–207).
14. Ellison makes similar assertions. In Ellison's famous essay, "The Little Man at Chehaw Station," he retells a parable about excellence. Chehaw Station was "a lonely-whistle stop where swift north or southbound trains paused" on the way to Tuskegee (490). Ellison was once told by a teacher that whatever he did, he should do with pride and excellence, even if it was "only in the waiting room at Chehaw Station, because in this country there'll always be a little man hidden behind the stove" (490). The little man the teacher referred to is the unexpected expert who at any moment might be there to evaluate a budding artist's performance and his manhood.
15. In a 1992 address at the Whiting Foundation, Ellison explained that the job of a writer is one that does "far more than creating interesting tales based on your individual view of the American experience. Underneath your efforts you're helping this country discover a fuller sense of itself as it goes about making its founders' dream a reality" (856).
16. Ellison's character's observations are based on his own experiences, as a young man, riding the rails, and also on his understanding of American history and political events such as John Brown's raid.
17. See chapter 32 of Johnson's autobiography *Along This Way* for more on Johnson's work on the antilynching campaign, and his meeting with President Woodrow Wilson.

Chapter Five: "Two Trains Running": Making Choices

1. Du Bois's words seem an apt descriptor. For more on this "twoness," see W. E. B. Du Bois, *The Souls of Black Folk* (45).
2. In the biblical story of Jonah and the gourd vine, God demands that Jonah go and deliver a message of destruction. Jonah does not want to and tries to evade his responsibilities. At last, he acquiesces and goes to deliver God's message that the entire city will be destroyed as punishment for the city-dwellers' sins. God then, for reasons he does not disclose to Jonah, has mercy on the city and decides not to destroy it. Jonah is outraged at being made to deliver a fearful message, and then being made to look like a fool when it did not happen. To teach Jonah a lesson about mercy, God then sends Jonah into the desert. When the heat of the sun becomes unbearable, God causes a vine to grow with leaves to shield Jonah. Then, God causes the vine to wither and die. Jonah is then angry at God both for sparing the sinners and killing the vine and does not realize that God was trying to teach a lesson about why it is necessary for God to shield us from his powerful force with the gift of his mercy. The phrase "a Jonah's gourd vine" thus also refers to something that miraculously springs from nothingness in a place it has no business growing. When a character refers to John and says, "we kin chop down dis Jonah's gourd vine," he is saying that he will cut down the

thing that has grown bigger and better than it by natural rights should, and also, that he is going to have no mercy (154).

3. According to Rita Dove, the character, John, is based largely on Hurston's father's life. Hurston's father was both a preacher and an adulterer (vii–xv).

4. According to Dove, "John's final sermon is taken nearly verbatim from Hurston's field notes on a country preacher" (xi).

5. For a more complete discussion of the myth see "Flying Dutchman (Myth)," Microsoft *Encarta Online Encyclopedia*, 2000. The term *Dutchman* also refers to a stagecraft device "covering the seams where two flats are joined" and is also a seamen's term (see Casimir 304). According to D. Weisgram, "Dutchman" was also the name of the very first slave ship to bring slaves from Africa to America, and the Dutch were also the original settlers of what would 150 years later be known as Harlem (217). Werner Sollors also discusses the title in terms of the Dutch-man-of-war that first brought black slaves to North America (130–31).

6. See Heble for a reading of "Dutchman" as dramatic jazz; Patsalidis for a reading of "Dutchman" and the notion of discipline and punishment; Ward for a reading of "Dutchman" as a reworking of Dante's Hell; Casimir for an examination of "Dutchman" in light of the Proteus myth; Richards for a discussion of the images of women in "Dutchman"; Piggford for an examination of "Dutchman" in terms of the American Gothic, and in a later article, "Dutchman" and the psychology of race; Werner for a look at stereotyping; Lacey for a comparison of "Dutchman" to the biblical story of Joseph and his brothers; Weisgram for a reading of "Dutchman" in terms of interracial sexual violence; Levesque for a reading of "Dutchman" as allegory; Bergesen and Demastes for a discussion of how "Dutchman" demonstrates the limits of African American political realism; and Reck for a discussion of archetypes in "Dutchman."

7. For a discussion of *Plessy vs. Ferguson* as *the* turning point in black history see Olsen's *The Thin Disguise*. See also Litwack for a discussion of trains as contested space in the age of Jim Crow precisely because of their public nature (especially 105–8 and 217–56).

8. For example, see Flannery O'Connor's "The Artificial Nigger" and Thomas Wolfe's *You Can't Go Home Again*. In both of these texts, young white male characters come into contact with people of another race, and the experience serves to solidify their sense that identity is based on racial difference and of their solidarity or unity with other white men. Because they are not like the "artificial nigger," from the train, for example, they must be more like their own fathers and grandfathers.

9. See Hodes, *White Women, Black Men* in which she goes through the historical record, beginning with the 1681 marriage of Nell and Charles Butler up through Ida Wells's 1890s extended reporting on the agency of white women in pursuing liaisons with black men (19–124 and 190–208).

10. For an extended discussion of this topic, in addition to Hodes's text already mentioned, see Weigman's chapter on "white mythologies,"(149–79).

11. Everett LeRoy Jones married his first wife, Jewish poet Hettie Cohen, in 1958, changed the spelling of his name to LeRoi, and the two founded the influential Beat literary journal, *Yugen*. He and Cohen had two daughters together before they separated in 1964 (the year "Dutchman" was first produced) and divorced in 1965. In the late sixties, he converted to Kawaida, a hybridization of orthodox Islam and traditional African practices and changed his name from LeRoi ("the King") to Ameer Baraka ("blessed prince"). Promoted to the position of spiritual leader within the group, he added the title Imamu to his name and changed the spelling of Ameer to Amiri. He later dropped the title Imamu, finally settling on the name Amiri Baraka in 1970 when he married Sylvia Robinson (who changed her name to Amina Baraka). In the 1980s, Baraka moved away from a Black Nationalist platform and toward Marxism, and became a professor of African Studies. For a quick synopsis of Baraka's life see Nina Baym's introduction to Baraka in *The Norton Anthology of American Literature*, 5th ed. (2124–26) or Henry Lacey's entry on Baraka, in *The Oxford Companion to African American Literature*, edited by William Andrews, Frances Smith Foster, and Trudier Harris (49–51).
12. According to Michel Foucault's *The History of Sexuality*, sex is, of course, "the explanation for everything, our master key." For a critique of Foucault's work and his decision to "place sex at the center of [his] analysis while striving to demystify its cultural significance" see D. Stanton's "The Subject of Sexuality," in *Discourses of Sexuality* (1–46).
13. What constitutes excessive violence is, of course, open to debate. As anyone who has ever taught "Dutchman" in a class knows, some readers instantly conclude as did one student, that "any man who hits a woman is not a man," while others will feel as did another student, "that she was kind of asking for it, and he was just defending himself." In an article on the sexual violence in "Dutchman," D. Weisgram suggests that the real focal point of discussion should be over whether the "real" violence is what happens "inside or outside" (224). She also points out that Clay's more explosive and abusive threats, "I'll rip your lousy breasts off" are not ones he acts upon, and "he does not really hurt Lula at all" (225). Instead, he resorts to words. Lula, however, will hurt him. According to Weisgram, Baraka's message here is that "oral aggression in expressive language will not defend the black people so long as real destructive power is in the hands of whites" (226).
14. See Weisgram for a discussion of Lula as a mother figure in which the murder of Clay is interpreted as a birthing scene; Richards essay on the images of women in Baraka's work; and O'Sullivan's essay about Lula as a Lilith figure.
15. See Pastalidis's discussion of the play in terms of Foucault's theories; Piggford's essay on the psychology of race in which he argues that white dominance is the villain of the play that the audience must defeat via "race revolution and murder" (82); and Craig Werner's essay, which argues that Ba-

raka's play teaches that "the black everyman must kill the white devils in the name of life" (38).
16. Instead of a giant melting pot, Keto imagines America as a train. He suggests that before boarding "Train America," African American riders of the train must, in order "to be true to their fellow travelers, to themselves, and to what they have learned from their own history, they have a duty to raise questions about the final destination of Train America. That is their right as Americans and their privilege as human beings" (47).
17. E. U. Essien-Udom makes a similar point in his preface to *Black Nationalism: A Search for an Identity in America* when he states, "the tragedy of the Negro in America is that he has rejected his origins—the essentially human meaning implicit in the heritage of slavery, prolonged suffering, and social rejection . . . he thus denies himself the creative possibilities inherent in it . . . . This dilemma is fundamental; it severely limits his ability to evolve a new identity of a meaningful synthesis, capable of endowing his life with meaning and purpose" (vii).
18. There is a wonderful picture by Roland Freeman on the front cover of Baker's 1980 edition of *The Journey Back* which shows a young black girl, resting on the arm of a porch swing, as she examines what appears to be the inside front cover of an old family Bible, and an old, thin, frail man wearing two shirts, points to a place on what is presumably a recording of the family tree.

Chapter Six: Around the Corner and Down the Track

1. A great deal has been written about "the legacy of slavery." Swedish social economist Gunnar Myrdal's classic study of American racism with its use of the term *pathology* in conjunction with black life angered a variety of African American writers. According to Glenn Loury, early liberal twentieth-century social scientists believed that the "pathological behavior" of black Americans, defined as their "purported criminality, sexual profligacy, and intellectual inadequacy," was due to the legacy of slavery. In the 1990s, Loury says, sociologists looks at life-span, crime rates, pregnancy statistics, and the disparity in test scores between black and white children and try to find other reasons to explain away their findings as referring to the "legacy of slavery" is no longer fashionable with middle-class blacks and whites who prefer to view the cause of such disparity as one rooted in economics, not race. Loury maintains that the causes are "rooted in history" and that "the legacy of slavery lingers in our cities' ghettos" despite conservative rationalizations about the declining significance of race (38–42). See also Daniel Black's *Dismantling Black Manhood: A Historical and Literary Analysis of the Legacy of Slavery* and Venetria Patton's *Women in Chains: The Legacy of Slavery in Black Women's Fiction*.
2. See Preiswerk's *The Slant of the Pen: Racism in Children's Books* for an explanation of how adult values are subtly transmitted in children's literature. The

thrust of this collection of essays is the subtle way negative racial stereotypes are "taught" in children's books; the theory of how direct and indirect values are transmitted in children's literature is still relevant.

3. In an unflattering essay about Murray based on an interview with Murray in 1996, Joe Woods condemns Murray's *Train Whistle Guitar* for its "unintentional absurdity" saying that the novel is flawed precisely because Murray won't "face the truth" about race in America, and thus in the novel there is "no pessimism, no ambiguity, no ambivalence about America the beautiful" (107–8). According to Woods, Scooter's growth into healthy manhood is an unbelievable fiction and the character never, Woods says, "gets a chance to breath our air" (107–8). Because Scooter's coming of age is not riddled with black-white conflict, for Woods the book is a testimony to "the old man's [Murray's] failure" to accurately represent a black man's coming of age (108).

4. For a short story in which guns, trains, and manhood are linked see Richard Wright's posthumous 1961 *Eight Men*.

5. For more on the connection between manhood and the blues see Gene Seymour's "Talking with Albert Murray: A Hero and the Blues"; Wolfgang Karrer's "The Novel as Blues: Albert Murray's *Train Whistle Guitar*"; Murray's own *The Omni-Americans,* and *Stomping the Blues*.

6. For more on the subject of Northern migrations and the necessity of mobility see Arna Bontemps and Jack Conroy's *Anyplace But Here*, 158–215.

7. For additional biographical information not contained in the Gates biographical sketch of Murray, see Elizabeth Schultz's entry on Albert Murray in the *DLB*, vol. 38, *African American Writers after 1955*, ed. Thadious Davis and Trudier Harris (214–24).

8. For Murray's characters death means a complete loss of identity, and this so terrifies the boys that they immediately abandon all plans to be pirates or bootleggers. Kawash suggests that when "black and white bodies drown indifferently," they are "collected into a community of the dead to which race cannot apply" (203). Put simply, death is the great equalizer in that black or white, death reduces a man to anonymity.

9. See Preiswerk's introduction to *The Slant of the Pen: Racism in Children's Books* for a theoretical discussion of the patterns of racism in textbooks ranging from subtle to openly racist. Also included in the appendix is the World Council of Churches criteria for the evaluation of racism in textbooks and children's literature.

10. Toni Morrison, "Intimate Things in Place: A Conversation with Toni Morrison," by Robert Stepto, May 19, 1976: 391–92.

✟ WORKS CITED

Abrahams, Roger. *Talking Black*. Rowley, MA: Newbury House Publishers, 1976.
Allen, Harry. "Hip-Hop Hi-Tech." In *Step into a World: A Global Anthology of the New Black Literature*. Ed. Kevin Powell. New York: John Wiley & Sons Publishers, 2000. 91.
Allison, Ginna. "Steel Drivin'Man." *All Things Considered*. National Public Radio. November 25, 1995. Transcript.
Anderson, L. T. "Don't Turn John Henry into a Railroad Man." *The Charleston Gazette* July 22, 1979. Vertical Newspaper Clipping Files, West Virginia State Archives Library (Xerox copy Sept. 2003).
Andrews, William L., Frances Smith Foster, and Trudier Harris. *The Oxford Companion to African American Literature*. New York: Oxford UP, 1997.
Andrews, William L., and Henry Louis Gates Jr. *The Civitas Anthology of African American Slave Narratives*. Washington, DC: Civitas/Counterpoint, 1999.
Ashwill, Gary. "Henry Box Brown." In *The Oxford Companion to African American Literature*. Ed. William L Andrews, Frances Smith Foster, and Trudier Harris. New York: Oxford UP, 1997. 102.
Ayers, Edward L. *Southern Crossing: A History of the American South, 1877–1906*. New York: Oxford UP, 1995.
Baker, Houston A. Jr. *The Journey Back*. Chicago: U of Chicago P, 1980.
_____. "To Move without Moving: An Analysis of Creativity and Commerce in Ralph Ellison's Trueblood Episode." *PMLA* 5 (1983): 828–45.
Baker, Lee. *From Savage to Negro: Anthropology and the Construction of Race, 1896–1954*. Berkeley: U of California P, 1998.
Baldwin, James. *Giovanni's Room*. New York: Dell, Publishing, 1956.
_____. *Notes of a Native Son*. 1955. Boston: Beacon Press, 1990.
_____. *Tell Me How Long the Train's Been Gone*. New York: Doubleday, 1968.
Baraka, Amiri. "Dutchman." In *The Norton Anthology of American Literature*. 5th ed. Ed. Nina Baym. New York: Norton, 1998. 2126–39.
_____. "Revolutionary Theatre." In *Home: Social Essays*. 1961. Hopewell, NJ: The Ecco Press, 1998.
Baym, Nina. "Amiri Baraka." In *The Norton Anthology of American Literature*. 5thed. Ed. Nina Baym et al. New York: W. W. Norton, 1998. 2124–26.
BBC News Special Report. "Musical Trip: Take the A Train." April 27, 1999. Transcript available at http: //news.bbc.co.uk/1/hi/special_report/ 1999/04/ 99/duke_ellington/325798.stm.
Beam, Joe. "Making Ourselves from Scratch." *Brother to Brother: New Writings by Black Gay Men*. Ed. E. Hemphill. Boston: Alyson Publishers, 1991, 261–62.
Beavers, Herman. "Autobiography of an Ex-Coloured Man." In *The Oxford Companion to African American Literature*. Ed. William L. Andrews, Frances Smith Foster, and Trudier Harris. New York: Oxford UP, 1997. 39–40.

Beckson, Karl, and Arthur Ganz. *Literary Terms*. 3rd ed. New York: Noonday P, 1996.
Beebe, Lucius. *High Iron: A Book of Trains*. New York: D. Appleton-Century, 1938.
Bell, Kurt. "Tears, Trains and Triumphs: The Historical Legacy of African-Americans and Pennsylvania's Railroads." *Milepost,* September 1998: 10–15.
Belton, Don. *(Speak My Name) Black Men on Masculinity and the AmericanDream*. Boston: Beacon, 1995.
Bergesen, Eric, and William Demastes. "The Limits of African-American PoliticalRealism: Baraka's *Dutchman* and Wilson's *Ma Rainey's Black Bottom*." In *Realism and the American Dramatic Tradition*. Ed. William Demastes. Tuscaloosa: U of Alabama P, 1996.
Black, Daniel. *Dismantling Black Manhood: A Historical and LiteraryAnalysis of the Legacy of Slavery*. New York: Garland, 1997.
Blount, Marcellus, and George P. Cunningham. *Representing Black Men*. New York: Routledge, 1996.
Bogumil, Mary. *Understanding August Wilson*. Columbia: South Carolina University Press, 1999.
Bolden, Tonya. *And Not Afraid to Die: The Stories of Ten African-American Women*. New York: Scholastic, 1998.
Bontemps, Arna, and Jack Conroy. *Anyplace But Here*. Columbia: U of Missouri, 1966. Rpt. of *They Seek a City,* 1945.
Bradford, Roark. *John Henry*. New York: The Literary Guild, 1931.
Bradford, Sarah. *Harriet: The Moses of Her People*. New York: J. J. Little & Co., 1886.
Brown, Henry. *Narrative of the Life of Henry Box Brown Written by Himself*. Ed. Richard Newman. Foreward by Henry Louise Gates Jr. New York: Oxford UP, 2002.
Brown, Sterling. *The Collected Poems of Sterling A. Brown*. Ed. Michael S.Harper. Evanston, IL: Northwestern UP, 1980.
_____. "The Odyssey of Big Boy." In *The Collected Poems of Sterling A. Brown*. Ed. Michael S. Harper. Evanston, IL: Northwestern UP, 1980. 20-21.
_____. "Strange Legacies." In *The Collected Poems of Sterling A. Brown*. Ed. Michael S. Harper. Evanston, IL: Northwestern UP, 1980. 96–97.
Bruck, Peter. "Returning to One's Roots: The Motif of Searching and Flying in Toni Morrison's *Song of Solomon*." In *The Afro-American Novel Since 1960*. Ed. Peter Bruck and Wolfgang Karrer. Amsterdam: B. R. Gruner, 1982. 289–305.
Bryant, Jerry. *Victims and Heroes: Racial Violence in the African American Novel*. Amherst: U of Massachusetts P, 1997.
Cameron, Dan. "Living History: Faith Ringgold's Rendezvous with the Twentieth Century." *Dancing at the Louvre*. Ed. Dan Cameron, Faith Ringgold, and the Staff of the New Museum of Contemporary Art, New York. Berkeley: U of California P, 1998.
Campbell, Jane. *Mythic Black Fiction: The Transformation of History* .Knoxville: U of Tennessee P, 1986.
Carby, Hazel V. *Race Men*. Cambridge: Harvard UP, 1998.
Casimir, Louis Jr. "*Dutchman*: The Price of Culture Is a Lie." In *The Binding of Proteus: Perspectives on Myth and the Literary Process*. Ed. Marjorie McCune, Tucker Orbison, and Philip Withim. Lewisburg: Bucknell UP, 1980.

Cawelti, John G. *Leon Forrest: Introductions and Interpretations.* Bowling Green, OH: Bowling Green State U Popular P, 1997.

Chagnon, Greg. "A Heroic Treatment of the John Henry Legend." *The Atlanta Journal Constitution.* July 26, 2002. Available through LexisNexis online database. Friends University, Wichita, KS. Accessed December 10, 2003. http://www.friends.edu.

Chandler, Karen. "Folk Culture and Masculine Identity in Charles Burnett's *To Sleep with Anger.*" *African American Review* 3.32 (1999): 299–311.

Childress, Alice. "Florence." 1950. *Wines in the Wilderness: Plays by African American Women from the Harlem Renaissance to the Present.* Ed. Elizabeth Brown-Guillory. New York: Praeger, 1990. 110–21.

Ciuba, Gary. "The Worm Against the Word: The Hermeneutical Challenge in Hurston's *Jonah's Gourd Vine.*" *African American Review* 34. 1 (2000): 119–37.

Cottman, Gwendolyn. *The Historical Presence of African-Americans in the Atlantic Coast Line Railroad.* Wilmington, DE: Wilmington Railroad Museum and *Wilmington Journal,* 1998.

Delancey, Dayle B. "Motherlove Is a Killer: *Sula, Beloved,* and the Deadly Trinity of Motherlove." *SAGE* 7.2 (1990): 15–18.

Dickerson, Ernest, dir. *Bones.* New Line Cinema, Los Angeles, CA, 2001.

Dogma. Dir. Kevin Smith. Lion's Gate Films, Santa Monica, CA, 1999.

Dove, Rita. Foreword. *Jonah's Gourd Vine.* By Zora Neale Hurston. New York: Harper and Row, 1990. pp. vi-xv.

Du Bois, W. E. B. *Black Reconstruction in America.* 1935. New York: Russell and Russell, 1962.

_____. *The Souls of Black Folk.* 1903. New York: Penguin, 1969.

_____."Of the Coming of John." In *The Souls of Black Folk.* 1903. New York: Penguin, 1969. 245–63.

Eby, Clare. "Slouching Toward Beastliness: Richard Wright's Anatomy of Thomas Dixon." *African American Review* 35.5 3 (2001)..439–459.

Edwards, Louis. "Albert Murray on Stage: An Interview." In *(Speak My Name) Black Men on Masculinity and the American Dream.* Boston: Beacon, 1995. 42–58.

Elder, Arlene. "*MELUS* Interview with Nikki Giovanni." *Multi-Ethnic Literature of the United States Journal.* 9.3 (1982).

Ellison, Ralph. "Boy on a Train." In *Flying Home and Other Stories.* 1937–1954. New York: Vintage, 1996, 12–21.

_____. *The Collected Essays of Ralph Ellison.* Ed. John Callahan. New York: Random House, 1995.

_____. *Flying Home and Other Stories.* (1937–1954). New York: Vintage, 1996.

_____. "A Hard Time Keeping Up." In *Flying Home and Other Stories.* 1937–1954. New York: Vintage, 1996. 101–110.

_____. "Hymie's Bull." In *Flying Home and Other Stories.* 1937–1954. New York: Vintage, 1996. 82–88.

———. "I Did Not Learn Their Names." In *Flying Home and Other Stories*. 1937–1954. New York: Vintage, 1996. 89–96.

———. "The Little Man at Chehaw Station." In *The Collected Essays of Ralph Ellison*. Ed. John Callahan. New York: Random House, 1995. 489–519.

———. "A Very Stern Discipline." In *The Collected Essays of Ralph Ellison*. Ed. John Callahan. New York: Random House, 1995. 726–754.

———. "What America Would Be Like Without Blacks." In *The Collected Essays of Ralph Ellison*. Ed. John Callahan. New York: Random House, 1995. 577–584.

Epps, Jeff, and Darcy Zabel. "He Said/She Said: Baraka's *Dutchman* in Black and White." April 1, 2003. Unpublished article.

Essien-Udom, E.U. *Black Nationalism: A Search for an Identity in America*. Chicago: Chicago UP, 1962.

Faulkner, William. *The Unvanquished*. 1934. New York: Vintage Books, 1990.

Feeney, Mark. "The Unsquarest Person Duke Ellington Ever Met." In *Conversations with Albert Murray*. Ed. Roberta S. Maguire. Jackson: UP of Mississippi, 1997. 70–77.

Fetrow, Fred. "Portraits and Personae: Characterization in the Poetry of Robert Hayden." In *Black American Poets Between Worlds, 1940–1960*. Ed. R. Baxter Miller. Knoxville: U of Tennessee P, 1986. 43–76.

Fishwick, Marshall. "Uncle Remus vs. John Henry: Folk Tension," *Western Folklore*, v. 20, 1961: 77-85.

"Flying Dutchman (Myth)." *Encarta Online Encyclopedia* 2000. MSN Encarta Plus Service. June 17,2000.Keyword:FlyingDutchman. http://encarata.msn.com/encyclopedia.

Foley, Barbara. "Reading Redness: Politics and Audience in Ralph Ellison's Early Short Fiction." *Journal of Narrative Theory* 29.3 (1999): 323–39.

Foner, Philip S., and Ronald L. Lewis. *The Black Worker During the Era of the American Federation of Labor and the Railroad Brotherhoods*. Vol. 4 of *The Black Worker: A Documentary History from Colonial Times to the Present*. Philadelphia: Temple UP, 1979.

Forrest, Leon. *There Is a Tree More Ancient Than Eden*. 1973. Chicago: Another Chicago P, 1988.

Foucault, Michel. *The History of Sexuality*. New York: Penguin, 1981.

Franklin, John Hope, and Alfred Moss, Jr. *From Slavery to Freedom*. 7th ed. New York: McGraw Hill, 1994.

Franklin, V. P. *Black Self-Determination: A Cultural History of African-American Resistance*. Brooklyn: Lawrence Hill Books, 1984.

Fredrickson, George M. *The Black Image in the White Mind: The Debate on Afro-American Character and Destiny, 1817–1914*. New York: Harper andRow, 1971.

Freedman, Florence. *Two Tickets to Freedom: The True Story of Ellen and William Craft, Fugitive Slaves*. New York: Simon and Schuster, 1971.

Freeman, Gerene L. "What about My 40 Acres and a Mule?" *Yale New Haven Teachers Institute*.September23,2003http:www.yale.eduynhti/curriculum/units/1994/4/94.04.01.x.html.

WORKS CITED 221

Gara, Larry. *The Liberty Line: The Legend of the Underground Railroad*. Lexington: U of Kentucky P, 1996.

Gates Henry Louis Jr. "'The Blackness of Blackness': A Critique of the Sign and the Signifying Monkey." *Black Literature and Literary Theory*. Ed. Henry Louis Gates Jr. New York: Routledge, 1990. 285–317.

———. "Criticism in the Jungle." *Black Literature and Literary Theory*. Ed. Henry Louis Gates Jr. New York: Routledge, 1990. 1–24.

———. "King of Cats." *The New Yorker*, April 8, 1996: 70–76, 78–81.

———. *The Signifying Monkey: A Theory of Afro-American Literature*. New York: Oxford UP, 1988.

Gelfand, Marvin. "Taking a Leaf: A Talk with Albert Murray." In *Conversationswith Albert Murray*. Ed. Roberta S. Maguire. Jackson: Mississippi UP, 1997. 8–11.

Georgoudaki, Ekaterini. *Class, Race, and Gender Consciousness in Gwendolyn Brook's and Nikki Giovanni's Poems for Children*. Thessaloniki, Greece: Aristotle U of Thessaloniki, 1990.

Gibson, Donald B. *The Politics of Literary Expression*. Westport, CT: Greenwood, 1981.

Giovanni, Nikki. "One More Boxcar." In *Blues for All the Changes*. New York: Morrow, 1999. 24–25.

Glenn, Joshua. Interview with Henry Louis Gates "Read the Right Thing." *Sunday Boston Globe*, February 2, 2003: D4. Available through LexisNexis online database. Friends University, Wichita, KS.Accessed December 10, 2003. http://www.friends.edu.

Goellnicht, Donald. "Passing as Autobiography: James Weldon Johnson's *The Autobiography of an Ex-Coloured Man*." *African American Review* 30.1(1996): 17–33.

Goldwebber, David. "Home at Last: The Pilgrimage of Claude McKay." *Commonweal* 126.15 (1999): 11–13.

Gordon, Sarah H. *Passage to Union: How the Railroads Transformed American Life, 1829–1929*. Chicago: Ivan R. Dee, 1998.

Gould, Dale. *Blackie's Railroad Handbook: All You Ever Wanted to Know aboutRailroad Slang, Signs, Signals, and Definitions, But Didn't Know Who to Ask*. Yorba Linda: Railroad Lingo, 1976.

Grissom, Mary Allen. *The Negro Sings a New Heaven*. New York: Dover, 1969.

Hamilton, Virginia. *The People Could Fly*. New York: Alfred A. Knopf, 1985.

Hawthorne, Nathaniel. *The Celestial Railroad and Other Stories*. New York: NewAmerican Library, 1963.

Hayden, Robert. "Runagate Runagate." In *The Black Poets*. Ed. Dudley Randall.New York: Bantam Books, 1971. 128–30.

Heble, Ajah. "The Poetics of Jazz: From Symbolic to Semiotic." *Textual Practice* 2.1 (1988): 51–68.

Hemingway, Ernest. "Soldiers Home." In *The Complete Short Stories of Ernest Hemingway*. New York: Scribner, 1987. 111–116.

———. *The Sun Also Rises*. 1926. New York: Scribner, 1996.

———. *In Our Time*. 1925. New York: Scribner, 1996.

Hempel, Carlene, Deb Procopio, Dan Shaver, and Beth Novak. "The Man, Facts, Fiction, and Themes." In *The John Henry Steel Driving Man Project*. U of North Carolina at Chapel Hill Graduate Student Project. September 20, 2003, from http://www.ibiblio.org/john_henry/index.html.

Henderson, Mae G. "A Response to Houston A. Baker, Jr.'s There Is No More Beautiful Way: Theory and the Poetics of Afro-American Women's Writing." In *Afro-American Literary Study in the 1990s* Ed. Houston A. Baker Jr. and Patricia Redmond. Chicago: Chicago UP, 1992. 155–63.

Hodes, Martha. *White Women, Black Men*. 1971. New Haven, CT: Yale UP, 1997.

House, Elizabeth. "*Sula*: Imagery, Figurative Language, and Symbols." In *Approaches to Teaching the Novels of Toni Morrison*. New York:MLA, 1997. 99–105.

Houston, Charles. H. "Outline of Some Railway Labor Problems Affecting Negro Train, Engine, and Yard Service Employees." Special Collections, Oklahoma State Library, 1949.

Hughes, Langston. "That Boy, LeRoi." In *Anthology of the American Negro in the Theatre: A Critical Approach*. Ed. Lindsay Patterson. New York: The Association for the Study of Negro Life and History, 1967. 205–6.

Hughes, Langston, and Arna Bontemps. *The Book of Negro Folklore*. New York: Dodd, Mead, and Company, 1965.

Hughes, Langston, and Zora Neal Hurston. *Mule Bone*. 1931. Ed. George Houston Bass and Henry Louis Gates Jr. New York: Harper Perennial, 1991.

Humez, Jean. *Harriet Tubman*. Madison: Wisconsin University Press, 2003.

Hurston, Zora Neale. *Jonah's Gourd Vine*. 1934. New York: Harper and Row, 1990.

———. *Mules and Men*. New York: Negro University Press, 1969.

———. *Tell My Horse*. Philadelphia: J.B. Lippincott Company, 1938.

Iser, Wolfgang. *The Fictive and the Imaginary: Charting Literary Anthropology*. Baltimore: Johns Hopkins UP, 1993.

Jackson, Gale Patricia. "If He Ask Was I Running You Tell Him I Was Flying,If He Asks You Was I Laughing You Tell Him I Was Crying: Reading John Henry as American History." In *Racing & (E)racing Language: Living with the Color of Our Words*. Syracuse, NY: Syracuse UP, 2001. 57–76.

James, Stanlie M. "Mothering: A Possible Black Feminist Link to Social Transformation." *Theorizing Black Feminisms*. Ed. Stanlie M. Jamesand Abena P.A. Busia. New York: Routledge, 1993. 44–54.

Jenkins, Kenneth L. *The True Story of How a Christian Preacher Embraced Islam: The True Story of Abdullah Muhammad al-Faruque*. September 7, 2003, from http://www.themodernreligion.com.

Johnson, James Weldon. *Along This Way*. New York: Viking, 1933.

———. *The Autobiography of an Ex-Coloured Man*. 1912. Ed. by Carl Van Vechten. New York: Alfred A. Knopf, 1927.

Johnson, James Weldon, and J. Rosamond Johnson. *The Books of Negro Spirituals Including the Book of American Negro Spirituals and the Second Book of Negro Spirituals*. New York: Viking, 1947.

Johnson, Paul. *A History of the American People*. New York: Harper Collins, 1997.

Jones, Gayl. *Eva's Man*. Boston: Beacon, 1976.

Jones, Le Roi [Amiri Baraka]. *Home: Social Essays*. 1961. Hopewell, NJ:Ecco Press, 1998.
Jordan, Winthrop, Miriam Greenblatt, and John Bowes. *The Americans: A History*. Evanston, IL: Houghton Mifflin, 1996.
Josephson, Judith Pinkerton. *Nikki Giovanni: Poet of the People*. Berkeley Heights, CA: Enslow Publishers, 2000.
Joyce, James. *A Portrait of the Artist as a Young Man*. New York: Viking Press, 1964.
Kaplan, Cora. "'A Cavern Opened in My Mind': The Poetics of Homosexuality and the Politics of Masculinity in James Baldwin." In *Representing Black Men*. Ed. Marcellous Blount and George Cunningham. New York:Routledge, 1996. 27–54.
Karrer, Wolfgang. "The Novel as Blues: Albert Murray's *Train Whistle Guitar*." *The Afro-American Novel Since 1960*. Ed. Peter Bruck and Wolfgang Karrer. Amsterdam: B. R. Gruner, 1982. 237–62.
Kawash, Samira. *Dislocating the Color Line*. Stanford, CA: Stanford UP, 1997.
Keats, Ezra Jack. *John Henry: An American Legend*. New York: Pantheon, 1965.
Keto, Tsehloane C. *An Introduction to the Africa-Centered Perspective of History*. Laurel Springs, NJ: K. A. Publishers, 1991.
Killens, John Oliver. *Black Man's Burden*. New York: Simon and Schuster, 1970.
———. *A Man Ain't Nothing But a Man*. Boston: Little, Brown, 1975.
KRS ONE. "Ah-Yeah." *KRS ONE*. New York: Zomba Recording Corporation, 1995.
Lacey, Henry. "Amiri Baraka." *The Oxford Companion to African American Literature*. Ed. William Andrews, Frances Smith Foster, and Trudier Harris. NewYork: Oxford UP, 1997. 49–51.
———. *To Raise, Destroy and Create: The Poetry, Drama, and Fiction of Immamu Amiri Baraka*. Troy, NY: Whiston Publishing, 1981.
Lahr, John. "Been Here and Gone: How August Wilson Brought a Century of Black American Culture to the Stage." *The New Yorker*. April 16, 2001: 50–65.
Larsen, Nella. *Quicksand and Passing*. 1928. New Brunswick, NJ: Rutgers UP, 1995.
Lester, Julius. *John Henry*. New York: Dial, 1994.
Levesque, George. "LeRoi Jones' *Dutchman*: Myth and Allegory." *Obsidian* 5.3 (1979): 33–40.
Levine, Lawrence. *Black Culture and Black Consciousness*. New York: Oxford UP, 1977.
Lhamon, W. T. Jr. *Raising Cain: Blackface Performance from Jim Crow to Hip Hop*. Cambridge: Harvard UP, 1998.
Litwack, Leon F. *Been in the Storm So Long: The Aftermath of Slavery*. New York: Knopf, 1979.
———. *Trouble in Mind: Black Southerners in the Age of Jim Crow*. New York: Knopf, 1998.
Lott, Eric. "After Identity Politics: The Return of Universalism." *New Literary History* 31.4 (2000): 665–80.
———. *Love and Theft: Blackface Minstrelsy and the American Working Class*. New York: Oxford UP, 1993.
———. "Love and Theft: The Racial Unconscious of Blackface Minstrelsy." *Representations* 39 (1992): 23–50.

Loury, Glenn. "An American Tragedy: The Legacy of Slavery Lingers in Our Cities' Ghettos." *Brookings Review* 16.2 (1998): 38–42.

Love, Nat. *The Life and Adventures of Nat Love*. 1908. New York: Arno Press, 1968.

Lueth, Elmer. "The Scope of Black Life in Claude McKay's *Home to Harlem*." *Obsidian II*. 5.3 (1990): 43–52.

Lund, J. Herbert. *Herb's Hot Box of Railroad Slang Plus Heroes of American Railroading*. Chicago: Jay Herbert Publishing, 1975.

Maguire, Roberta S. *Conversations with Albert Murray*. Jackson: UP of Mississippi, 1997.

Marable, Manning. "Toward Black American Empowerment," In *Brotherman: The Odyssey of Black Men in America*. Ed. Herb Boyd. New York: Ballantine Books, 1995. 799–808.

Marx, Leo. *The Machine in the Garden*. New York: Oxford UP, 1964.

———. "The Railroad in the Landscape: An Iconological Reading of a Theme in American Art." In *The Railroad in American Art*. Ed. Leo Marx and Susan Danly. Cambridge: MIT Press, 1988. 183–208.

Mason, Theodore Jr. "Signifying." In *The Oxford Companion to African American Literature*. Ed. William L. Andrews, Frances Smith Foster, and Trudier Harris. New York: Oxford UP, 1997. 665–666.

McCready, Albert L., and Lawrence W. Sagle. *Railroads in the Days of Steam*. New York: American Heritage, 1960.

McKay, Claude. *Home to Harlem*. 1928. Boston: Northeastern UP, 1987.

McKee, Patricia. "Spacing and Placing Experience in Toni Morrison's *Sula*." *Modern Fiction Studies* 42.1 (1996): 1–30.

McMichael, George. "Richard Wright." In *Instructor's Guide: Anthology of American Literature*. Upper Saddle River, NJ: Prentice Hall, 2000.248.

McPherson, James Alan, and Miller Williams. *Railroad: Trains and Train People in American Culture*. New York: Random House, 1976.

———. "A Solo Song For Doc." In *New Black Voices*. New York: Penguin, 1972. 151–73.

Miller, David C. *American Iconology*. New Haven, CT: Yale UP, 1993.

Mitchell, W. J. T. *Picture Theory*. Chicago: U of Chicago P, 1994.

Mitchell-Kernan, Claudia. "Language Behavior in a Black Urban Community." Diss. University of California at Berkeley, 1975.

Moon, Michael. "Whose History? The Case of Oklahoma." In *A Queer World: The Center for Lesbian and Gay Studies Reader*. Ed. Martin Duberman. New York: New York 1997. 24–34.

Mootry, Maria K. "'If He Changed My Name': An Interview with Leon Forrest." *Chant of Saints: A Gathering of Afro-American LiteratureArt, and Scholarship*. Ed. Michael S. Harper and Robert B. Stepto. Urbana: U of Illinois P, 1979. 146–57.

Morrison, Toni. *Beloved*. 1987. New York: Penguin Books, 1988.

———. *Song of Solomon*. 1977. New York: Penguin Books, 1987.

———. *Sula*. 1973. New York: Penguin Books, 1982.

Mosley, Walter. "The Black Man: Hero." In *(Speak My Name) Black Men on Masculinity and the American Dream*. Boston: Beacon, 1995. 234–40.

WORKS CITED

Murray, Albert. *The Omni-Americans*. New York: Dutton, 1970.
_____. *Stomping the Blues*. New York: McGraw-Hill, 1976.
_____. *Train Whistle Guitar*. 1974. Boston: Northeastern UP, 1989.
Myrdal, Gunnar. *An American Dilemma: The Negro Problem and Modern Democracy*. New York: Harper, 1944.
Nasaw, David. *The Course of United States History, Volume 2*. Chicago: Dorsey Press, 1987.
Nies, Judith. Introduction. *Seven Women: Portraits from the American Radical Tradition*. Ed. Judith Nies. New York: Viking, 1977.
Nikola-Lisa, W. "John Henry: Then and Now." *African American Review* 32.1 (1998): 51–56.
Nikolajeva, Maria. "Children's Literature as Cultural Code: A Semiotic Approach to History." In *Aspects and Issues in the History of Children's Literature*. Ed. Maria Nikolajeva. Westport, CT: Greenwood, 1995.
Nock, O. S. *Railways Then and Now*. New York: Crown Publishers, 1975.
Nurse, Donna Bailey. "Putting the John Henry Tale Right: The Great Male Hope of African-American Writing Fizzles Out." *Edmonton Journal* June 17, 2003: E12. Available through LexisNexis online database. Friends University, Wichita, KS. Accessed December 10, 2003. http://www.friends.edu.
O'Connor, Flannery. "The Artificial Nigger." In *Flannery O'Connor: The Complete Stories*. New York: Noonday Press, 1996. 249–70.
_____. "The Train." In *Flannery O'Connor: The Complete Stories*. New York: Noonday Press, 1996. 54–62.
Ogunyemi, Chikwenye Okonjo. "Iconoclasts Both: Wole Soyinka and LeRoi Jones." In *African Literature Today: Africa, America & the Caribbean*. Ed. Eldred Durosimi Jones. London: Heinemann, 1978. 25–38.
Olsen, Otto. *The Thin Disguise: Plessy vs. Ferguson*. New York: American Institute for Marxist Studies, 1967.
Osborne, Mary Pope. *American Tall Tales*. New York: Knopf Books for Young Readers, 1991.
Ostendorf, Bernhard. "Ralph Ellison's *Flying Home*: From Folk Tale to Short Story." *Journal of the Folklore Institute* 13 (1976): 185–99.
O'Sullivan, Maurice. "*Dutchman*'s Demons: Lula and Lilith." *Notes on Modern American Literature* 10.1 (1986): 4–6.
Patsalidis, Savas. "Discipline and Punish: The Case of Baraka's *Dutchman*."*The North Dakota Quarterly* 60.3 (1992): 101–13.
Patterson, Raymond. "Autobiography of a Black Man." In *Step into a World: A Global Anthology of the New Black Literature*. Ed. Kevin Powell. New York: John Wiley & Sons, 2000. 350–51.
Patton, Venetria. *Women in Chains: The Legacy of Slavery in Black Women's Fiction*. Albany: State U of New York P, 1996.
Petry, Ann L. *Harriet Tubman: Conductor on the Underground Railroad*. New York: Crowell, 1995.

Pfeiffer, Kathleen. "Individualism, Success and American Identity in *The Autobiography of an Ex-Coloured Man*." *African American Review* 30.1(1996): 403–19.

Piggford, George. "Looking into Black Skulls: American Gothic, the Revolutionary Theatre, and Amiri Baraka's *Dutchman*." In *American Gothic: New Interventions in a National Narrative*. Iowa City: Iowa UP, 1998. 143–60.

―――. "Looking into Black Skulls: Amiri Baraka's *Dutchman* and the Psychology of Race." *Modern Drama* 40 (1997): 74–85.

Pinsker, Sanford. "The Bluesteel, Rawhide, Patent-Leather Implications of Fairy Tales: A Conversation with Albert Murray." *The Georgia Review* 51.2 (1997): 205–21.

Piper, Watty. *The Little Engine That Could*. 1930. New York: Platt and Munk Publishers, 1987.

Prahlad, Sw. Anand. "Guess Who's Coming to Dinner: Folklore, Folkloristics, and African American Literary Criticism." *African American Review* 33.4 (1999): 565–75.

Preiswerk, Roy. *The Slant of the Pen: Racism in Children's Books*. Geneva: World Council of Churches, 1980.

Reck, Tom. "Archetypes in LeRoi Jones' *Dutchman*." *Studies in Black Literature* 1.1 (1970): 66–68.

Reid, Calvin. "James Alan McPherson: A Theater of Memory." *Publishers Weekly* 244.51 (1997): 36–37.

Reid-Pharr, Robert. "Tearing the Goat's Flesh: Homosexuality, Abjection, and The Production of a Late-Twentieth-Century Black Masculinity." In*Novel Gazing: Queer Readings in Fiction*. Ed. Eve Kosofsky Sedwick. Durham, NC: Duke UP, 1997. 353–76.

Reyes, Angelita. "Using History as Artifact." *Approaches to Teaching the Novels of Toni Morrison*. New York: MLA, 1997. 77-85.

Richards, Sandra. "Negative Forces and Positive Non-Entities: Images of Women in the Dramas of Amiri Baraka." *Theatre Journal* 34.2 (1982): 233–40.

Ringgold, Faith. "any1canfly." http://www.faithringgold.com.

―――. *Aunt Harriet's Underground Railroad in the Sky*. New York: Crown, 1992.

―――. "Gifts of Speech: You Were Too Young to Remember What We Must Never Forget." http:www.gos.sbc.edu/ringgold.html.

Risher, Howard W., Jr. "The Negro in the Railroad Industry." Report no. 16. *The Racial Policies of American Industry*. Philadelphia, PA: Industrial Research Unit, Department of Industry, 1971.

Ruggles, Jeffrey. *The Unboxing of Henry Brown*. Richmond: Library of Virginia Board and Sheridan Books, 2003.

Sale, Maggie. "Historical Novel." In *The Oxford Companion Guide to African American Literature*. Ed. William L. Andrews, Frances Smith Foster, and Trudier Harris. New York: Oxford UP, 1997. 358–59.

Sale, Maggie Montesinos. *The Slumbering Volcano: American Slave Ship Revolts and the Production of Rebellious Masculinity*. Durham, NC: Duke UP, 1997.

Sanders, Mark. "Runagate Runagate." *The Oxford Companion to African American Literature*. Ed. William Andrews, Frances Smith Foster, and Trudier Harris. New York: Oxford UP, 1997. 638–39.

Schultz, Elizabeth. "Albert L. Murray." *Dictionary of Literary Biography*. Vol. 38. *Afro-American Writers After 1955: Dramatists and Prose Writers*. Ed. Thadious Davis and Trudier Harris. Detroit: Gale Research Company, 1985. 214–24.

Scruggs, Otey. "The Meaning of Harriet Tubman." In *"Remember the Ladies": New Perspectives on Women in American History*. Ed. Carol V. R. George. Syracuse, NY: Syracuse UP, 1975. 110–22.

Seidel, Kathryn Lee. "The Lilith Figure in Toni Morrison's *Sula* and Alice Walker's *The Color Purple*." *Weber Studies* 10.2 (1993): 85–94.

Seltzer, Mark. *Bodies and Machines*. New York: Routledge, 1992.

———. "Statistical Persons." *Diacritics* 17.3 (1987): 82–98.

Seymour, Gene. "Talking with Albert Murray: A Hero and the Blues." In *Conversations with Albert Murray*. Ed. Roberta S. Maguire. Jackson:UP of Mississippi, 1997. 54–56.

Shaw, Stephanie J. "Mothering under Slavery in the Antebellum South." *Mothering: Ideology, Experience, and Agency*. Eds. Evelyn Nakano Glenn, Grace Change, and Linda Rennie Forcey. New York: Routledge, 1994. 237–58.

Siebert, Wilbur H. *The Underground Railroad*. New York: Arno Press, 1968.

Small, Terry. *The Legend of John Henry*. New York: Doubleday, 1994.

Smith, D. J. "The American Railroad Novel." *The Markham Review* (1973): 85–93.

Smith, Valerie. "Literary History: Late Twentieth Century." In *The Oxford CompanionGuide to African American Literature*. Ed. William L. Andrews, Frances Smith Foster, and Trudier Harris. New York: Oxford UP, 1997. 456–59.

Smithsonian National Postal Museum. "David LaFleur Folk Heroes: John Henry." August 31, 2003. http://www.postalmuseum.si.edu/artofthestamp.

Snead, James. "Repetition as a Figure of Black Culture." In *Black Literature & Literary Theory*. Ed. Henry Louis Gates Jr. New York: Routledge, 1990. 59–79.

Sollors, Werner. "*Dutchman*, and *The Slave*." In *Amiri Baraka/LeRoi Jones: The Quest for a "Populist Modernism*." New York: Columbia UP, 1978. 117–38.

Sollors, Werner, and Maria Diedrich. *The Black Columbiad*. Cambridge: Harvard UP, 1994.

Spillers, Hortense. "'All the Things You Could Be by Now, If Sigmund Freud's Wife Was Your Mother': Psychoanalysis and Race." *Boundary* 23.2 (1996): 75–141.

Stack, Carol B., and Linda M. Burton. "Kinscripts: Reflections on Family, Generation, and Culture." In *Mothering: Ideology, Experience, and Agency*. Ed. Evelyn Nakano Glenn, Grace Change, and Linda Rennie Forcey. New York: Routledge, 1994. 33–44.

Stanton, Domna. *Discourses of Sexuality*. Ann Arbor: Michigan UP, 1992.

Stephenson, Brent. Letter to the author. 18 June 2003.

Stepto, Robert. "Afro-American Literature." In *Columbia Literary History*. Ed. Emory Elliott et al. New York: Columbia UP, 1988. 785–99.

_____. "Intimate Things in Place: A Conversation with Toni Morrison." In *Critical Perspectives Past and Present*. Ed. Henry Louis Gates Jr. and K. A. Appiah. New York: Amistad, 1993. 378–95.
Sterling, Dorothy. *Black Foremothers*. Old Westbury, NY: The Feminist Press, 1979.
_____. *Freedom Train: The Story of Harriet Tubman*. Garden City, NY: Doubleday, 1954.
Stover, John F. *American Railroads*. Chicago: U of Chicago P, 1961.
Stowe, Harriet Beecher. *Uncle Tom's Cabin*. 1852. New York: Dodd, Mead, 1952.
Strickland, William. "The Future of Black Men." In *Brotherman: The Odyssey of Black Men in America*. Ed. Herb Boyd and Robert Allen. New York: Ballantine Books, 1995. 351–58.
Sundquist, Eric J. *To Wake the Nations: Race in the Making of American Literature*. Cambridge: Harvard UP, 1993.
Taylor, M. W. *Harriet Tubman: Anti-Slavery Activist*. New York: Chelsea House, 1991.
Thayer, Ernest. *Casey at the Bat*. 1888. Brooklyn: Handprint Books, 2000.
Thomas, H. Nigel. *From Folklore to Fiction: A Study of Folk Heroes and Rituals in the Black American Novel*. Westport, CT: Greenwood, 1988.
Thompson, Carlyle Van. "The "White" to Pass: Miscegenation, Mimicry, and Masquerade in Chesnutt, Johnson, Larsen, and Faulkner." Diss. Columbia University, 1997.
_____. Letter to D. Zabel. August 19, 2003.
Tobin, Jacqueline L., and Raymond G. Dobard. *Hidden in Plain View: A Secret Story of Quilts and the Underground Railroad*. New York: Doubleday, 1999.
Turner, George Edgar. *Victory Rode the Rails*. Westport, CT: Greenwood, 1953.
Uma, Alladi. "Collapsing Walls: The Individual and the Community in Claude McKay's *A Long Way from Home*." *Indian Journal of American Studies* 27.2 (1997): 25–26.
Updike, John. "Tote That Ephemera: *John Henry Days*." *The New Yorker* May 7, 2001: 87–89.
Van DeBurg, William L. *Black Camelot: African–American Culture Heroes in Their Times*. Chicago, IL: Chicago University Press, 1997.
Ward, Jerry. "The System of Dante's Hell: Underworlds of Art and Liberation." *Griot* 6.2 (1987): 58–64.
Warren, Kenneth W. "Thinking beyond Catastrophe: Leon Forrest's *There Is a Tree More Ancient Than Eden*." *Callaloo* 16.2 (1993): 409–18.
Washington, Mary Helen. "'Taming All That Anger Down': Rage and Silence in Gwendolyn Brooks's *Maud Martha*." In *Black Literature and Literary Theory*. Ed. Henry Louis Gates Jr. New York: Routledge, 1990. 249–62.
Weich, Dave. Interview. *Post Office to Unveil Colson Whitehead Stamp*. June 28, 2003 http://www.powells.com.
Weisgram, Dianne. "LeRoi Jones' *Dutchman*: Inter-racial Ritual of Sexual Violence." *American Imago: A Psychoanalytic Journal for Culture, Science, and the Arts* 29 (1972): 215–32.
Werner, Craig. "Brer Rabbit Meets the Underground Man: Simplification of Consciousness in Baraka's *Dutchman* and *Slave Ship*." *Obsidian* 5.1–2 (1980): 35–40.

White, Hayden. *The Content of the Form: Narrative Discourse and Historical Representation*. Baltimore: Johns Hopkins UP, 1987.
Whitehead, Colson. "I Worked at an Ill-Conceived Start-Up and All I Got Was This Lousy Idea for a Novel." http://www.randomhouse.com/whitehead /essay.html.
_____. *John Henry Days: A Novel*. New York: Doubleday, 2001.
Whitman, Walt. "To a Locomotive in Winter." In *The Norton Anthology of American Literature*. 4th ed. Ed. Nina Baym et al. 1876. New York: W. W. Norton, 1994.
Wiegman, Robyn. *American Anatomies: Theorizing Race and Gender*. Durham, NC: Duke UP,   1995.
Wilde, Lisa. "Reclaiming the Past: Narrative and Memory in August Wilson's *Two Trains Running*." *Theater* 22.1 (1990): 73–74.
Wilentz, Gay. "If You Surrender to the Air: Folk Legends of Flight and Resistance in African American Literature." *MELUS* 16.1 (1989–90): 21–32.
Williamson, Joel. *After Slavery*. New York: W. W. Norton, 1965.
_____. *The Crucible of Race: Black-White Relations in the American South Since Emancipation*. New York: Oxford UP, 1984.
Wilson, August. *Two Trains Running*. New York: Plume, 1993.
Wolfe, Thomas. *You Can't Go Home Again*. 1934. New York: Harper Perennial, 1998.
Wood, James. "Virtual Prose: A Review of *John Henry Days* by Colson Whitehead." *Review-A-Day* August 16, 2001. June 21, 2003. http://www.powells.com.
Woods, Joe. "The Soloist: Albert Murray's Blues People." In *Conversations with Albert Murray*. Ed. Roberta S. Maguire. 1996. Jackson: Mississippi UP, 1997. 94–109.
Woodward, C. Vann. *The Strange Career of Jim Crow*. New York: Oxford, 2001.
Work, John W. *American Negro Songs and Spirituals*. New York: Bonanza Books, 1940.
Wright, Richard. *Black Boy*. New York: Harper Perennial Classics, 2003.
_____. *Eight Men*. New York: Thunder's Mouth Press, 1987.
_____. *The Ethics of Living Jim Crow: An Autobiographical Sketch*. New York: Viking Press, 1937.
_____. "The Man Who Was Almost a Man." In *The Concise Anthology of American Literature*. 5th ed. Ed. George McMichael et al. Upper Saddle River, NJ: Prentice Hall, 2001. 1908–16.
_____. *Native Son*. New York: Harper Perennial Classics, 1987.
X-Files. "Kaddish." FOX TV, February 16, 1997. DVD Available for purchase at http://www2.foxstore.com/listing.html.
Yannicopoulou, Angela. *Fables and Children: Form and Function*. Liverpool: Manutius Press, 1993.
Zabel, Darcy. "'Two Trains Running': The Train as Symbol in Twentieth–Century African American Literature." Diss. University of Connecticut. 2001.
Zucker, Joseph. "Exodus Via Overground Railroad: Illinois Central's Role in the Great Migration." *RailNews* 421 December 1998: 50–51.

# AFRICAN AMERICAN LITERATURE AND CULTURE

EXPANDING AND EXPLODING THE BOUNDARIES

General Editor
Carlyle V. Thompson

The purpose of this series is to present innovative, in-depth, and provocatively critical literary and cultural investigations of critical issues in African American literature and life. We welcome critiques of fiction, poetry, drama, film, sports, and popular culture. Of particular interest are literary and cultural analyses that involve contemporary psychoanalytical criticism, new historicism, deconstructionism, critical race theory, critical legal theory, and critical gender theory.

For additional information about this series or for the submission of manuscripts, please contact:

> Peter Lang Publishing, Inc.
> Acquisitions Department
> 275 Seventh Avenue, 28th floor
> New York, New York 10001

To order other books in this series, please contact our Customer Service Department:

> (800) 770-LANG (within the U.S.)
> (212) 647-7706 (outside the U.S.)
> (212) 647-7707 FAX

Or browse online by series:

> www.peterlangusa.com